S0-EQE-845

Design Research: The Store That Brought Modern Living to American Homes

by Jane Thompson
and Alexandra Lange

Foreword by Rob Forbes
Afterword by Paul Goldberger

Concept Development by
Sheila McCullough
Creative Direction by Pentagram
Edited by Ruth A. Peltason

CHRONICLE BOOKS
SAN FRANCISCO

2

Experiencing the Store: Brattle Street, 1953–69
34

Foreword
By Rob Forbes
7

Prologue
By Jane Thompson and Alexandra Lange
11

Why This Book?
14

4

Expansion Without Imitation, 1959–65
96

1

Ben: The Man Behind D/R
16

3

A "Uniform for Intellectuals": Marimekko Arrives
70

5
A General Store of Good Design
116

6
D/R's Glass Bazaar: New Headquarters, 1969
144

7
The D/R Legacy
172

Afterword
By Paul Goldberger
183

Ben Thompson Chronology
186

D/R Stores
187

The Backstory
187

Contributors
188

About the Authors
190

Acknowledgments
190

Credits
191

Rob Forbes "I loved the name the first time I heard it. I grasped the notion that design was not about superficial styling but about a process and a passion."

Foreword
Who's Your Daddy?

By Rob Forbes
Founder, Design Within Reach

In 2000, a year after launching Design Within Reach, I undertook a national market survey of our clients, asking which stores they thought of when it came to good design. I was assessing the competition to see if there were any design shops I did not know about. Design Research got more mentions than any other operation, and it had been closed for nearly twenty-five years.

The lasting influence of D/R has been astounding, not unlike appreciation for the larger role that modern design itself played in the 1950s and 1960s. Our design community was establishing a foundation, and D/R was at the heart of it. It was a period of great optimism. Conversely, the 1980s and 1990s were a low point in modern design. Only one store was mentioned as being influential for design during this postmodern period: Esprit, the youthful apparel company. I would wager that Doug and Susie Tompkins, Esprit's founders, had been influenced by D/R as well.

Without question, D/R was the most influential force in twentieth-century America in creating an awareness and appreciation for modern design in the consumer world. D/R had actually been my model for Design Within Reach; at one point I had even looked into trying to revive the D/R name and identity. My last image of the store was in San Francisco's Ghirardelli Square in the late 1970s. The post-Thompson D/R had moved to the arcade and no longer animated the Clock Tower, but its spirit was alive and well both in my mind and in the collective memory of the design and retail communities. Design Within Reach managed to tap into the fertile ground that Ben Thompson had seeded fifty years earlier.

Moreover, it's not just Design Within Reach that owes its existence to D/R. If you study their origins, many independent design stores and showrooms can probably be traced back to D/R, the Conran Shop in London among them. Just as much of postwar modern design in the United States traces its roots to George Nelson and the Eames Office, modern lifestyle retailing has its roots in Ben Thompson's D/R. Consider contemporary visual merchandising: Crate & Barrel set the standard in the

1980s and 1990s. Yet Gordon Segal, the man behind the Crate, was directly inspired by the Cambridge D/R and was an early customer, buying wholesale items like Marimekko fabric. (Segal later took over the D/R headquarters building, designed by Thompson, where it remained the Crate in Cambridge until 2008.)

In the 1960s, department stores took lessons from the casual, vivid, chock-full interior presentation of D/R stores. Stanley Marcus, president of the luxurious and internationally famous Neiman Marcus, would come regularly from Dallas with his merchandising staff to "observe" the Cambridge store. There are other curious connections: the clever high-end tchotchke catalogue, The Horchow Collection, is also a D/R scion. For a short while in 1970, S. Roger Horchow ran D/R when it was under new management. During this past decade, the modern design market has flourished, driven largely by the younger generation. If I did a survey today asking which name has the greatest influence on design, the majority would respond quickly and definitively: Apple. Other names might include Target, DWR, IKEA, and Prada. A New Yorker might name Moss. But most of the younger generation would not know the name D/R. This book is the opportunity to correct that gap—to turn postwar myth back into a living legend.

Design Research. I loved the name the first time I heard it. I grasped the notion that design was not about superficial styling but rather about a process, an investigation, a try-out, and a passion based in curiosity and discovery. How radical that was back in the 1950s. In leading industries, a modern design "look" was applied to surfaces as dynamic symbols of speed and power — appliances with aerodynamic trim, auto grilles with great big tin teeth. Names familiar abroad and to the cognoscenti, like the Bauhaus, Mies, Gropius, Aalto, were yet to be translated into new forms, new products, and finally new design meanings for the masses.

In fact, the notion that design is more about research than styling still runs counter to much design thought today. We have designer hotels, designer jeans, designer wine labels—in fact, a whole range of slick branding passed off as "design." But Design Research was a fresh and authentic store. It was unsullied by the designer mannerisms, clichés, and revolving commercial styles that have trivialized the humane foundation of modern design as I first came to know it. D/R was genuine, like the original VW Bug compared to the later revived models.

This postwar golden era for design also had glaring cultural contradictions and contrasts. It was the greatest period of modern residential architecture in history. Modern jazz as an art form reached its zenith. American cars were well built and handsome. But this was simultaneously a period of extreme social conformity and conservatism. The U.S. military-industrial complex was flourishing and expanding internationally as if to dominate the world. IBM and GM reigned supreme. Suburban America was drawing people away from cities and creating urban ghettos. The civil rights movement was simmering, ready to burst. Women wore pointed brassieres. Guys had crew cuts. We ate TV dinners watching *Leave it to Beaver* and *Mr. Ed* interspersed with ads featuring the Marlboro man.

At this apex of midcentury American life, Design Research opened, and offered, a liberated vision of the home and family. It showed good form as an expression of quality, asking customers to think differently, to be bold, and to live differently.

I believe that D/R occupied the same benchmark—originality, innovation, education, being social yet cool—that Apple does today. I write this having just spent an hour at the new Apple store in Manhattan at 11 PM. The experience felt like a community center for people with shared aesthetic values; it was certainly more than just a store. Five decades before, D/R was similarly used as a gathering place, a mixing space for town and gown, young and old, in a setting with high standards

Long before "design research" was an academic discipline, Ben Thompson used his store to pursue knowledge of how things were made, how they could best be used, and how they looked together.

for both its product and its social agendas. Each D/R store became a destination in its city where new ideas were originated, shown, and tried out.

By bringing the best available modern goods from a much more hip European marketplace, and by making them available for the first time in a comprehensive retail store, D/R woke Americans up to a modern lifestyle. That effort was revolutionary. And it was done with unprecedented finesse and flair: its products were selected and displayed with a sensory appeal that made it an irresistible place to see and to shop and to hang out. That too was revolutionary. And behind it was an ethic, a responsibility attached to delivery of good design at any price level. Like the best in midcentury architecture, it may not be replicable. But it can be remarkably influential.

Modern Design 1.0 has now been released and fulfilled. By this I mean that modern design is widely recognized and broadly distributed, an e-mail click away for millions. The dreams of the Bauhaus have largely been realized: the union of shape and purpose in the tools we use, beautiful and useful products within the economic reach of nearly everyone. Few of us who appreciate good design lack a comfortable chair, a balanced knife, or a simple shirt to wear. Contemporary design exists at IKEA and at exclusive designer shops like Moss. Efficient markets exist as at no other time.

If you hear the words "modern lifestyle" and don't connect the dots to Design Research, then you are probably too old with a fading memory or too young to know who's your daddy.

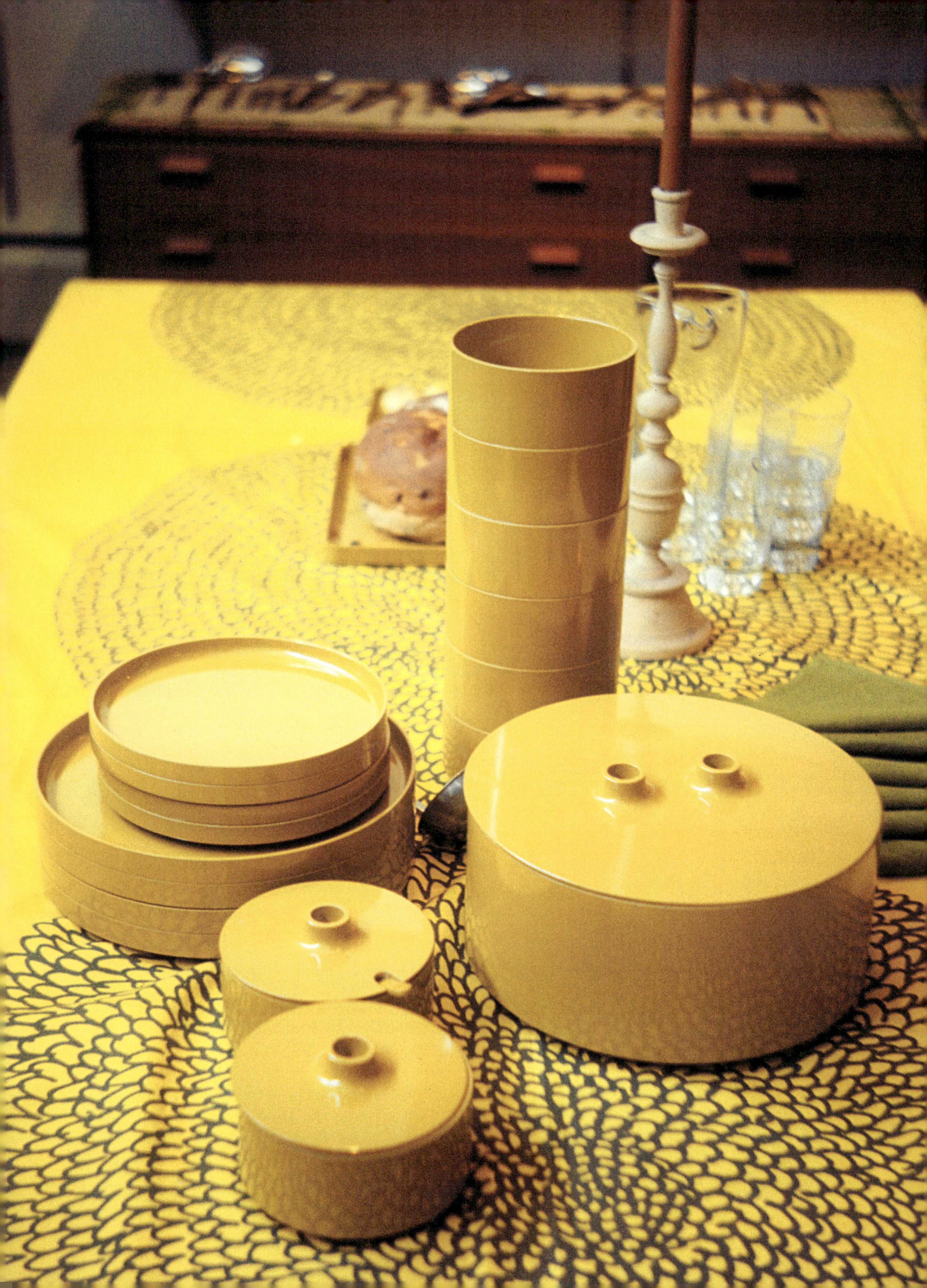

Prologue

**By Jane Thompson
and Alexandra Lange**

OPPOSITE: Never afraid of color, D/R introduced Massimo Vignelli's stackable melamine Max I dinnerware in 1969, shown here on a matching Marimekko cloth.

Before *lifestyle* was a buzzword, architect Benjamin Thompson (1918–2002) sold it—his version of the most up-to-date way to live—from a clapboard house on Brattle Street in Harvard Square. His store, founded in 1953, was called Design Research, and what it sold was a warm, eclectic, colorful, and international version of modernism, one that mixed folk art and Mies van der Rohe, Noguchi and no-name Bolivian sweaters, offering newlyweds and Nobel Prize winners one-stop shopping for tools to eat, sleep, dress, even to party in a beautiful way.

After World War II, returning servicemen in need of homes provoked a radical restructuring of the American domestic landscape. William Levitt and Sons outside New York and Martin Cerel outside Boston dropped Cape Cods like seeds that hatched into new towns, multiplying little boxes essential to house the imminent baby boom. These nascent suburbs aped earlier architectural styles, but their rapid construction exploited new technologies. A few American architects, several trained by the first generation of European émigrés, thought they could do better, combining the latest building technology with a new residential form.

In 1948, Benjamin Thompson and his seven partners in The Architects Collaborative (TAC) established a pioneering planned neighborhood with a common modern aesthetic called Six Moon Hill in Lexington, Massachusetts. TAC ultimately built approximately two dozen modern homes for themselves and their clients, creating the first American development whose architecture furthered prewar European modernism: celebrating materials in their natural state, blurring the relationship between interior and exterior, and opening an interior landscape of spaces rather than rooms. Like the Los Angeles–area Case Study houses, built at the same time, Six Moon Hill (and its successor, Five Fields) was intended as a corrective to the cheap historicism of many new developments. Its designers and clients thought they could spread the seeds of modernism if they simply lived this modern life.

The owners of the country's first glass houses served as publicists for two extremes of the style. In his 1949 Glass House in New Canaan, Connecticut, Philip

In 1948, The Architects Collaborative established Six Moon Hill, a pioneering residential development in Lexington, Massachusetts. The Martin House was one of 29 homes eventually built on the 20-acre site, all of which share a common language of open plans, natural materials, and glass walls for indoor-outdoor connections.

Johnson juxtaposed the purity of Mies van der Rohe furniture with his seventeenth-century Poussin painting, exiling his bedroom to a bunker out of sight. In his 1950 Case Study house in Pacific Palisades, California, Charles Eames used prefab panels and struts, and he and wife, Ray, filled its modules with a seeming paradox of handmade toys, brilliant fabrics, antique china, and their own pioneering fiberglass furniture—just the sort of mixture of cheap and expensive, folk and high-tech that Thompson would promote. (When D/R opened in Beverly Hills, Ray Eames was, naturally, a customer.) In the RKO film of 1948, *Mr. Blandings Builds His Dream House,* even Cary Grant as Mr. Blandings, who embodies the fantasy of a perfect life in a perfect home, was savvy enough to envision a streamlined interior in his neo-Colonial dream house.

Throughout the country, select outlets began to sell the furniture for these open spaces. The Museum of Modern Art began its Good Design program in 1950, showing the public that most common household objects could be works of art, and providing a list of where to buy the best. The Frank Brothers furnished the Case Study houses from their Southern California store. In Chicago, Baldwin Kingrey (est. 1947) was the first American outlet for imported European functionalist furniture and upstart American brands Herman Miller and Knoll. New York offered

Northern European wares: Swedish modern at Bonniers (after 1949), Danish modern at Georg Jensen, and Norwegian design at Form and Function. And Boston had architect Ralph Rapson's eponymous store, which opened in 1950.

But each of these stores tended toward oversimplified or monochrome modern. Thompson thought he had a better solution, a solution tested in his own Six Moon Hill home: a store that would sell all the elements necessary for contemporary life under one roof. A department store without departments but with the best machine- and handmade products from around the world (and even, in the example of the Chemex coffeemaker, from nearby Pittsfield, Massachusetts). Its name was Design Research, long before that was a discipline, and it sold Danish furniture and Finnish china, Swiss glassware and French rustic pottery, poppy-print fabric and butcher-block sofas, all of it then new to most American eyes. Unlike some of his colleagues, Thompson didn't think modernism meant minimalism. More could be more, as long as it was chosen with a careful, eclectic eye, one which saw the whole house as a palette for personal expression and the most humble household object as a potential masterpiece. Thompson believed that people should be encouraged to imagine for themselves what their lives would be like inside a clean-lined shell. They did not need an architect or decorator to lead them from one trade-only showroom to another. All they needed was a forum in which to pick props for living from the best available national and international goods.

To make his point clear, Thompson sold the objects from a series of buildings that aped the domestic setting: first, a clapboard row house in Cambridge in 1953, then a limestone townhouse in New York in 1963, and finally a loftlike former factory in San Francisco in 1965. Only when he had a chance to design a new home for D/R did he finally make a glass house for his growing collection of imports and exclusives, an award-winning building that opened in 1969. His first and second careers (as architect and shop owner) combined in his third act: After losing control of D/R in 1970, he went on to revitalize downtowns, turning old factories into vibrant marketplaces at Faneuil Hall in Boston and Harborplace in Baltimore, among many others, before his retirement in 1994 and death in 2002. Along the way, he also opened four restaurants, including the pioneering Harvest just behind D/R's Harvard Square headquarters.

In the pages that follow, those that experienced the stores tell the story of Design Research—about Ben, about the buildings, and about the people and products that populated the spaces. Think of it, as Thompson always did, as a window onto a world that could be your own, for one dollar or a thousand, if you were looking for a brighter, lighter, more delicious, and more beautiful life.

Why This Book?

Sheila McCullough I knew I wanted this book to become a reality on September 20, 2001, when my mother, Jane Thompson, was scheduled to give a talk about Design Research at MIT. Under the circumstances, we had considered postponing the talk, but in the end she decided to go ahead. As we walked into the auditorium I could feel the kind of stunned quiet that was palpable during those first days after 9/11. But as she progressed through the slide show, images of the store and the period seemed surprisingly immediate and full of hope, and the feeling in the room seemed to thaw a little. What came across was the sense of optimism that Ben Thompson demonstrated in most everything he did as a designer and as a person. He knew like no one else how to create a joyful environment.

I had the good fortune to have Ben as my stepfather. I loved Ben; growing up with him had a huge effect on my life and how I see the world around me. Creating this book with my mother was a way for me to share this gift.

Jane Thompson After the positive response to my D/R presentation at MIT, I decided to attempt a permanent retelling of the D/R story. For nearly four decades I had been living the legacy of a bygone episode. But D/R was history; talk was about the future. I had to become an investigative journalist, searching for scattered fragments that might lead back to lost facts: Why did D/R—which joyfully occupied a quarter century of our dedicated effort—matter? After fifty years, why should it still matter? Indeed, why does design matter?

In the 1980s and 1990s, D/R would occasionally come up. I found people eager to describe a favorite chair or Marimekko pattern. Once this book project began in 2005, numerous acquaintances not connected to the store surprised me by saying they knew all about D/R and, as happy customers, were eager to revisit those moments. Witnesses came out of the woodwork.

Alexandra Lange I wrote my dissertation on American corporate architecture and design of the 1950s and 1960s, and one of my discoveries was the amount of color and texture in the work of designers like Florence Knoll and Eero Saarinen. The black-and-white photos we typically see of their work leave that out, as do many of the history books. Caring about interiors began to seem like a subversive interest for an architectural historian, yet it turns out it was a subversive interest for architects such as Ben Thompson. The domestic interior was long the realm of women—cooking, cleaning, decorating—so women were often the ones choosing the furniture and hanging the curtains. But in the 1960s many aspects of domestic life were starting to shift, walls were opening up, the food revolution brought men into the kitchen, and D/R was ready to serve the new lifestyle.

Sheila McCullough **"Ben Thompson knew like no one else how to create a joyful environment. Creating this book with my mother was a way for me to share this gift."**

Jane Thompson "This is literally an 'autobiography' of the store told by those who lived it, worked it, added to it, and—as Ben would have it—made it their own."

Jane Thompson As I investigated, I realized D/R had been a thematic thread in my own design career. As founding editor of *I.D.* magazine, I had published the first articles about D/R's pioneering exhibitions on design in Denmark, Japan, and Finland. In the early 1960s, I shopped in the D/R Cambridge store and began work on a commission to write about Walter Gropius's Bauhaus. In 1962, I was on the board interviewing architects for a regional school in Vermont, and we selected Ben Thompson of TAC. Thus we met, eventually became partners in business and, with completion of the school in 1967, in life.

Sheila McCullough In 1968, my mother and brother and I moved from a rural town in Vermont to Harvard Square to live with Ben. The store and all its contents were mesmerizing to me: I remember vividly the rhythmic clacking of the marbles on the marble slide, the vinegary smell of the handmade wooden toys, the polka-dot dress with a ridiculous number of pockets. I would climb the bunk beds, swivel in the office chairs, stack translucent plastic rings on my fingers, wrap my head in colorful scarves.

To me D/R often seemed like another world. One particularly dreary weekend I returned from Vermont in a heavy snowstorm. As we came down Brattle Street, I saw D/R's display window: bright yellow-and-white umbrellas floated upside down with blue and orange dresses hanging beneath. At that moment it seemed to me that all the light and color on Earth radiated from that window. It was the most un-lonely place I had ever seen.

Alexandra Lange My grandmother and mother both shopped at D/R, first on special trips from Hanover, New Hampshire, and later when my family lived in Cambridge in the 1970s. As I began to look through the photos of D/R, I recognized many objects and fabrics I grew up with: Japanese paper globes, rainbow Heller plates, the Finel bowl with mushrooms. I never knew where these things came from, but I had already started rebuying them for my own house on eBay and at rummage sales.

I suspect other children of the 1970s will have the same experience. We usually see icons like Eames chairs in a vacuum: in expensive catalogues against a white background, or in minimalist apartments with white walls and oak floors. As museum pieces they seem like a cliché. But the D/R way of combining modernism and folk and crazy fabrics and fruit and flowers was much richer, more interesting, and more personal than that, as I hope this book shows. Ben Thompson was trying to overcome staid, matchy-matchy formalism; today we need to overcome matchy-matchy modernism.

Jane Thompson By 2000, as Ben dictated his memoirs near the end of his life, he knew but a few living D/R alumni. In 2006, we collaborators began to search for them. In more than seventy interviews, and dozens more telephone contacts to research facts, names, and special memories, we have succeeded in locating a lost but living tribe—the D/R alumni association—with members from Maine to California to England and Switzerland. So this is literally an "autobiography" of the store told by those who lived it, worked it, added to it, and—as Ben would have it—made it their own.

I found for myself what Ben Thompson knew all along: the chorus of voices—participants, customers, and observers—told us all the reasons that design mattered and still matters. The story of D/R contains the kernel of meaning of the postwar 1950s and 60s: It was upbeat, expansive, open to new tastes and colors and forms. D/R expressed a kind of reinvention of life in America.

Ben
The Man Behind D/R

By Jane Thompson

1

He was Ben to one and all. Students, partners, clients, housekeepers, and doormen were all on first-name terms with the guy who asked, the minute he met you, where you were from — "Boulder, really?" — and invariably knew someone or something that made your hometown special.

Ben exuded a natural informality, which he wore first with rumpled professorial tweeds, later with shaggy alpaca sweaters and an old camel-hair coat or with striped Finn Farmer shirts, preferably green, and a necktie only when required. It was not an affect, but an essential quality — "unpretentious" is an understatement. Whatever he did was convincing, not because he relied necessarily on what you thought, but because he was thoroughly convinced of being himself, and that self always left room for you too.

Ben's journey in design was an everyday statement of his philosophy of life: comfort for the body, beauty for the senses, and power for the imagination. Though Ben spent years as a graduate-school educator, department chairman, and businessman, he knew that seeing, smelling, and hearing would teach more than books or words.

Ben had his D/R office on the third floor of 57 Brattle Street, where he surrounded himself with the things he liked—vernacular director's chairs, butcher-block tables of his own design, stackable TC 100 china from Thomas. One long shelf was reserved for newly discovered products awaiting judgment by Ben and the design selection group at periodic lunches.

Ben's aesthetic was not a form or a theory, but an observation of how to live well in a healthy environment, preferably in good, clean, open air. In buildings and in objects, he was deeply responsive to evidence of the human hand. He developed Design Research's modern aesthetic while also honoring the imperfection that extends craftsmanship in a life of machine-made goods. He sought out crafts, both simple and polished, to balance the desirable perfection and simplicity of industrial production. By setting up a dialogue between contrasting material qualities—rough and smooth, new and old, handmade and machine-made—Ben illustrated intuitively the Japanese philosophy of *wabi-sabi,* a concept unfamiliar to Americans in the 1950s, but which has become meaningful in recent decades: slight imperfection validates perfection.

Although raised with high propriety on Summit Avenue in St. Paul, Ben was a true child of the southern Minnesota farms and duck passes where he camped out in summer. A son of the plains, a scion of Minnesota's egalitarian Scandinavian ethic, he was a born naturalist-as-conservationist, living imaginatively as close to the earth, seasons, the arc of the sun, birds, wildlife, and all growing things as a Johnny Appleseed or any Native American.

Ben's early life was hard in many ways; his response was to find and create positive balance, to seek out the beautiful, the joyful, and the enriching in whatever he might be doing. He had a knack for seeing *it*—the positive experience, the exciting juxtaposition—and wanted to share the idea that you should enjoy it too.

Design Research was his opportunity to spread these satisfactions in physical form. A sofa filled with goose down to sink into, silky alpaca blankets to wrap up in, a silky sealskin hat to pull down, and fresh daisies, bearing the scent of new-mown fields, to inhale. At home in Lexington, Massachusetts, and later in Cambridge, Ben's gesture of welcome was to hand you a drink. He did not ask what you wanted. He knew you wanted a Bloody Mary with a flagstaff of celery, and here it is. Natural, no fuss. No formal pretense. Ben's idea for the store was the same. It was there to increase your pleasure in life, and to provide all the things he could imagine in your life. Please just look around. Please touch the furniture and test its comfort. At Christmastime, have a glass of Swedish glugg to assist your imagination.

His hospitality found its natural counterpart on Cape Cod. In 1959 Ben discovered an unwinterized hunting camp on a bluff overlooking Barnstable Harbor and the dunes of Sandy Neck. He bought it after his first visit, swept away by the 250-degree view of sky, sand, marsh, and waterbirds, and the changing light over the moving tides. It was a natural ensemble for hourly and seasonal dramas, which were a reference for each landscape that Ben designed, often working with native grasses. Summers there expanded his vocabulary of pleasure in nature.

Our trips to Finland inspired him to build a wood-burning sauna, a center of both health and ongoing sociability. Instead of a pool plunge, we, and often overheated clients, would run down the grassy path to plunge into the harbor's bracing water. Other than a Baltic sauna, nothing was better.

As an extended family, we had picnics on the dunes, sunset dinners at a long Marimekko-covered table on the bluff. We cooked everything on a wood-fired rotisserie: eggplants, clams, and just-plucked *alouettes* (named in French so the children would not mourn the doves he sometimes shot). We gardened vigorously—organic well ahead of our time—and brought the superabundance to table, serving innumerable children, guests, and patrons in our restaurants in Cambridge and Boston.

But don't be fooled. This easygoing, huggable, teddy-bear of a man was not infrequently misjudged as a right-brained soft thinker, dismissed pejoratively as an *artist* in the male business lexicon. His casual, playful demeanor led even his devoted employees to believe he was short on discipline. Au contraire. Ben had

TOP: Ben, nine years old, leading a team of Percheron horses on the Thompson family farm in southern Minnesota, where he spent his childhood summers close to nature.

BOTTOM: Ben in 1941, just after completing his naval training. He later served as a captain in the navy for four years during World War II.

Ben's summer office on the bluff at his Cape Cod home was a place where living and working were always intertwined. His Marimekko shirt and glass, and wire grid chair, designed by Heinz Wirth, were all D/R products.

both of his brains fully linked and interoperational. With his eye always on a distant mountain, he could be as directive and incisive as any moment might require.

As a U.S Naval Officer in the North Atlantic, 1943, he took command of the Corvair crew in the confusion following a collision with the underwater base of an iceberg and directed the ship's slow, delicate retreat as the towering 30-story-high iceberg swayed, dangerously close to toppling on them. As a natural seaman and a leader, he summoned his objective brain. But Ben was happiest using his creative brain, which was heuristic and holistic. He experienced and analyzed not in a simple straight line but by encircling a problem or place to see things as a whole. His patterns of thought, informed by well-honed intuition, were circular and inclusive and at the same time moved forward in directions based on a broad grasp of observed conditions. Thus ideas and outcomes were always shaped—as was his architecture and design— from the inside out, from the need and function that offered and found expression in visible form. Then the discovered entity—a plate on a dinner table or a school within a city—was considered further for its harmonious role in its much larger context.

Design Research was Ben's response to a historic moment-in-time of national human and social need for homemaking, which also opened a unique business opportunity in his area of expertise. His business calculations combined insight, intuition, and careful customer testing. Preexpansion testing of store locations, for instance, was carried out by launching small exploratory shops in Hyannis, Massachusetts, and New York City.

As an attitude to life, Design Research could be carried out on the bluff or in European cities, over dinner, or with a three-carousel slide presentation simulating in images some memorable scenes of Helsinki's market or the piazzas of Venice.

As a store, Design Research displayed Ben Thompson's latest, greatest finds, and gave the customer the opportunity to see them, touch them, try them out, and make direct personal life choices. Many times, they turned out to be life-altering choices as well.

Voices

Ristomatti Ratia **"He drew from the experience of his senses, not from rules and orthodoxies."**

Gordon Segal, cofounder, Crate & Barrel Ben Thompson was one of those very inspirational, very unusual men who brought a new point of view to the way Americans should look at products, the way they should look at architecture, and the way they should live. He was a remarkably innovative human being. Like any good educator—and he was a good educator and a good architect—he was an inspirational retailer, if not financially a highly successful retailer.

When he had time in that old clapboard house he would give talks to his staff. He had some fabulous people at that time, and he created this environment of constant learning, of developing relationships. It was a way of running a retail operation like one big interactive family.

Catherine Milton **"D/R considers itself the avant-garde's answer to *Good Housekeeping*'s seal of approval."**

OPPOSITE: Ben's off-hours time on the Cape was dedicated to wildlife, wildflowers, and exploring the marshes on Cape Cod Bay.

Ben and Jane were photographed for *Food & Wine* magazine while entertaining Julia and Paul Child in the 1980s. The Thompsons owned and designed four innovative restaurants in Cambridge and Boston from 1975 to 2000.

Kathy Keating, D/R staff, 1962–65 Often at night when the shop closes we sit at his feet on the floor of the attic, the office area, of the old shop on Brattle Street. Our boyfriends and husbands are overworked in each's graduate endeavor and we, the "little girls and boss ladies," do not hustle home to families. We sit, drink Aquavit or Lillet Blanc, and listen to Ben.

They are never planned, these sessions. Perhaps Ben picks up on something that happens that day in the shop. Perhaps someone asks a question, or we plan a party for Armi Ratia, or Ben talks about an architectural project he is involved with.

We sit at Ben's feet and he talks to us about life and about beauty. There is always music. There are always flowers and candles. Now that I know more than I did then, these evenings remind me of Persian poetry. To work there is a lesson in light. To know Ben is a lesson in grace.

Ristomatti Ratia, founder, Décembre Oy, 1970–74; Marimekko creative director, 1974–85 Ben was my hero because, with a casual movement of his hand, he painted another world for us to see. He was like a big bear and spoke very much with his hands, drawing large creative circles in the air strengthening his words. To me, the casual elegance of Ben showed in everything—in his low-key speech, in his movement, the way he walked, the way he dressed, the unique slide shows he selected, and most importantly, the words he chose to go with the pictures. This all illuminated a new and unseen world to us. He was open to new ideas from different people.

Pauline Dora, D/R staff, 1968–77 I remember saying to him one time, "Ben, why are you doing this? You are a famous architect. Why are you running a store? This is so small time." He said, "Come with me." We went up to the front of the store. This was in the old building, and when you walked in the main part of the store was in front of you, with a long table where the register was. He walked around and found a big, beautiful ceramic bowl and put some oranges in it. Then he went someplace else and brought these wonderful pillar candles that were in different colors. He did an arrangement right there at the register. Two seconds later a customer came up and bought a candle. And he said, "Architecture takes five to ten years."

He liked that immediacy, that contact. You put it together and somebody responds. Immediate feedback, if it works, gives you confidence: that works; let's try something else. "Today we got some red fabric in and let's work around it." It just happened. It wasn't planned six months in advance because you didn't know what you were going to run into.

Robert Campbell, architecture critic, *Boston Globe* Rambling in speech, a bit shy in public, rumpled in appearance, Thompson was the opposite of the crisp, arrogant image of the architect made famous by Gary Cooper in the film *The Fountainhead*.

Catherine Milton, *Boston Sunday Globe*, 1966 If D/R is Cambridge's shrine to design, then Benjamin Thompson, an architect, is its high priest. President of D/R is not a title to Thompson. He oversees every detail in the operation from the girls who are hired ("he prefers Northern Europeans") to the background music ("this year it's Sonny and Cher") and, most important, the items that are sold.

Ben Thompson, Memoirs I was born in Minnesota where my family founded the First National Bank of St. Paul. After high school in St. Paul, in California, and in Connecticut, and a couple of years at the University of Virginia, I went to the Yale School of Art and Architecture, from which I graduated in 1941 just before the U.S. entered the war. Architecturally, it was a very exciting period. People in this country had just begun to think about modern architecture; anyone who did anything modern was a hero. Yale was a good school. It never did have a serious formulation of its purpose, but it exposed you to many influences, a few of them pretty advanced, which was fine.

Then it was the war, and I went into defense construction, helping to build a small-arms plant outside Minneapolis. After six months I came to New York and worked for the Corps of Engineers on camouflage of our sixteen-inch batteries at Montauk Point. Then I joined the navy, and served as a deck officer on a corvette destroyer escort for the rest of the war, four long years.

In the spring of 1944, my corvette, called the *Courage,* docked at Boston from long North Atlantic duty for overhaul. On a special Sunday leave, not knowing Walter Gropius at all, except through his books, I somehow managed to find my way from the Mystic River shipyards to his house in Lincoln. There I had the first impression of Gropius and Ise together, of a house surrounded by green, carefully cut grass, birds, and flawless gardens.

A year later, still in uniform and now assigned to special duty in Washington, D.C., I was making an effort to organize a new architectural office in collaboration with several associates from architectural school, including Norman and Jean Fletcher and Louis McMillen. Then Chip Harkness, visiting Washington, suggested that our group come to Cambridge to meet Gropius and talk about forming an architectural office. From that meeting — again on a Sunday in Lincoln — came the beginnings of The Architects Collaborative.

Robert Campbell In 1946, he and six other young architects joined with the much older Walter Gropius (who was also one day to win the [AIA] Gold Medal) to form a partnership in Cambridge called The Architects Collaborative, which grew over the years into one of the nation's largest firms.

Ben Thompson, "Talk of the Town," *The New Yorker,* 1963 We started out doing houses, mostly for middle-income families, and then we began doing schools and college buildings. We've designed thirty or forty public schools in Massachusetts, Rhode Island, Connecticut, and Vermont, and buildings at Andover, Harvard, Brandeis University, and Williams. Gropius is over eighty, but he's still active in the firm.

Ralph Caplan, design writer and author Ben always said that when he was at TAC they were designing modern houses and the clients wouldn't know what to put in them. From my experience with clients, this could easily be literally true: "Now what do I do?" Ben broke ground in figuring out something to do about getting them a total environment, with a place to eat and sleep.

Ben Thompson, *New York Times,* 1963 It was very difficult right after the war to find really good things to make a home interior work. I couldn't go out and design everything myself so I tried to find separate pieces that worked in a harmonious relationship to each other.

Lorraine De Wet Howes, D/R staff, 1957–60 After Ben started The Architects Collaborative, the biggest obstacle for the architects was finding good furniture. He thought, "Well, I know about good furniture, so I'll start a store right next to TAC, and we'll bring in the things we need." Scandinavian furniture designers probably were his ideal. It was done with the idea of architects being able to get everything they needed for the houses and apartments, and that's what happened. The architects and their clients got everything at D/R.

OPPOSITE TOP: TAC was a partnership between Walter Gropius, center, and seven younger architects launched in 1946; jobs included many schools, universities, and private homes.

OPPOSITE CENTER AND BOTTOM: In 1966 Ben launched his own practice, BTA, which expanded his work from architecture into planning urban centers and restoring waterfronts around the world.

Ben photographed sitting on an Albini chair outside his Six Moon Hill home for a picture story about Design Research in *Look* magazine, 1962.

Henriette Mladota **"Everything he did and wore was to get away from formality and rigid design. He wanted to escape the matched costume tradition in favor of the skillful combination of harmonious separates. That applied to his interior design attitude as well."**

Ben 23

Ben checking on the Christmas toy display at the new Cambridge store, days after its grand opening in 1969.

OPPOSITE: As chairman of architecture at Harvard's Graduate School of Design, Ben hosted a reception in 1964 for the Kennedy family during the selection of an architect for the Presidential Memorial in Boston. Guests included Jacqueline, Robert, Ted, and Eunice Kennedy, as well as world-renowned architects, including those on the selection committee: Alvar Aalto, Franco Albini, Sven Markelius, Sir Basil Spence, Kenzo Tange. I.M. Pei won the commission.

Sandra Sheeline, assistant, The Architects Collaborative, 1960–65 Ben might arrive in the morning dressed in his tweed pants and jacket and tie — I could see his long underwear poking out — and carrying a brace of ducks. He had been out on the river. He would hand them to me and I had to take them over to Sage's and get them dressed. I was from Wisconsin, so it didn't faze me. That was the beginning of the troubleshooting. Nobody could ever find him, yet they always wanted answers from him.

Mildred F. Schmertz, architecture writer I was surprised that he would be full-time partner at The Architects Collaborative and also have a shop. Then in 1964 he became chairman of the Department of Architecture at Harvard. Here's this guy: he runs this shop, he goes to Finland and imports all this stuff, he is running architecture at Harvard's Graduate School of Design. He is amazing.

Claud Bunyard, D/R staff, 1953–61 Ben had marvelous taste. As an architect, he'd start a project by enunciating the philosophy he wanted. Then he chose two or three guys to work on the idea. After watching for a time, he'd say, "Well, that one's the best," and concentrate on that direction.

Tom Green, partner, Benjamin Thompson & Associates, 1966–80, 1988–2001 The TAC partners' early work was totally residential. Then they started designing elementary schools, then college work, and then they went into grander buildings and master plans all over the world. Initially there would be a partners meeting once a week, when each partner would show preliminary work and other partners would comment. That's where the word "collaborative" came from. But for the most part the partners were doing their own things.

I think the other partners were annoyed by the amount of time he spent on D/R. But Ben was pretty close to Gropius, and Gropius encouraged him in the development of Design Research.

Robert Campbell At Andover and the Brandeis dormitories he did with TAC, Ben brought materiality back into what had been a white stucco kind of architecture. Ben was very much interested in materiality and texture and color. The buildings in retrospect look a little formal, a little monumental, but I think they had an influence then in bringing that aspect of architecture back. They're not as good as Colby, which had a much looser, more relaxed kind of attitude that came later.

Ben was a sensualist. He was always trying to make a cocoon for himself to protect himself from the violence of the world, which upset him. The cocoon could be flowers or beautiful girls or food or wine or architecture, but the cocoon was what drove him, I'm convinced. Or music, to make a kind of world that he could move in.

Ralph Caplan Ben's philosophy seemed to come down to the idea that you should have a nice life with nice things. Why can't everybody have such pleasure as this, or look as good as this? He had a view of the world as a more gracious and civil place than could ever be made by material improvements.

Rebecka Tarschys, *Mobilia,* **1966** Relaxed of manner and self-possessed, Thompson has the appearance of being able to work all through a busy day without ever being pressed for time, [and that] he always has the time for profound and meditative discussions about new ideas, new things. Playing simultaneously the role of three characters, he demonstrates his conception of the unity of the different aspects of design. "I have no hobbies, I wear only one hat. It has three sides."

Pauline Dora He liked entertaining. He liked easy. He didn't like formality. He liked things that could stand on their own, whether it was Marimekko, or a dinnerware line called TC 100, which was used at the Museum of Modern Art's café, or glass from Finland that was decorative but not over the top. It just was a certain idea about how design and living worked together. When he invited people to his home, everything was casual. He cooked while people stood around the kitchen chatting, participating. People just didn't do casual things at that particular time — everything was much more formal.

Ralph Caplan ## "Things he sold, he used himself."

Ralph Caplan Things he sold, he used himself. He was a master cook, and his cooking was like everything else he did. You didn't notice it. You would be having a very fragmented conversation with him that didn't seem to be going anywhere, and suddenly you'd notice that in front of your very eyes he seemed to have made an omelet. A proper omelet — an omelet with bay scallops.

Mildred F. Schmertz A tremendous amount of work was being done while he appeared to be relaxing. When I visited their place on Cape Cod for a weekend, the spirit of relaxation was almost total, but there were still things going on. A client was coming for dinner, the occasional phone call, cables to send. This was true on the Cape. This was true out at Aspen. Always a certain amount of background hard work in terms of business and the things they believed in. I don't mean pushing to get clients, I mean pushing the various things of value and interest to them, environmental concerns, breakthroughs in education, adaptive reuse of historic buildings.

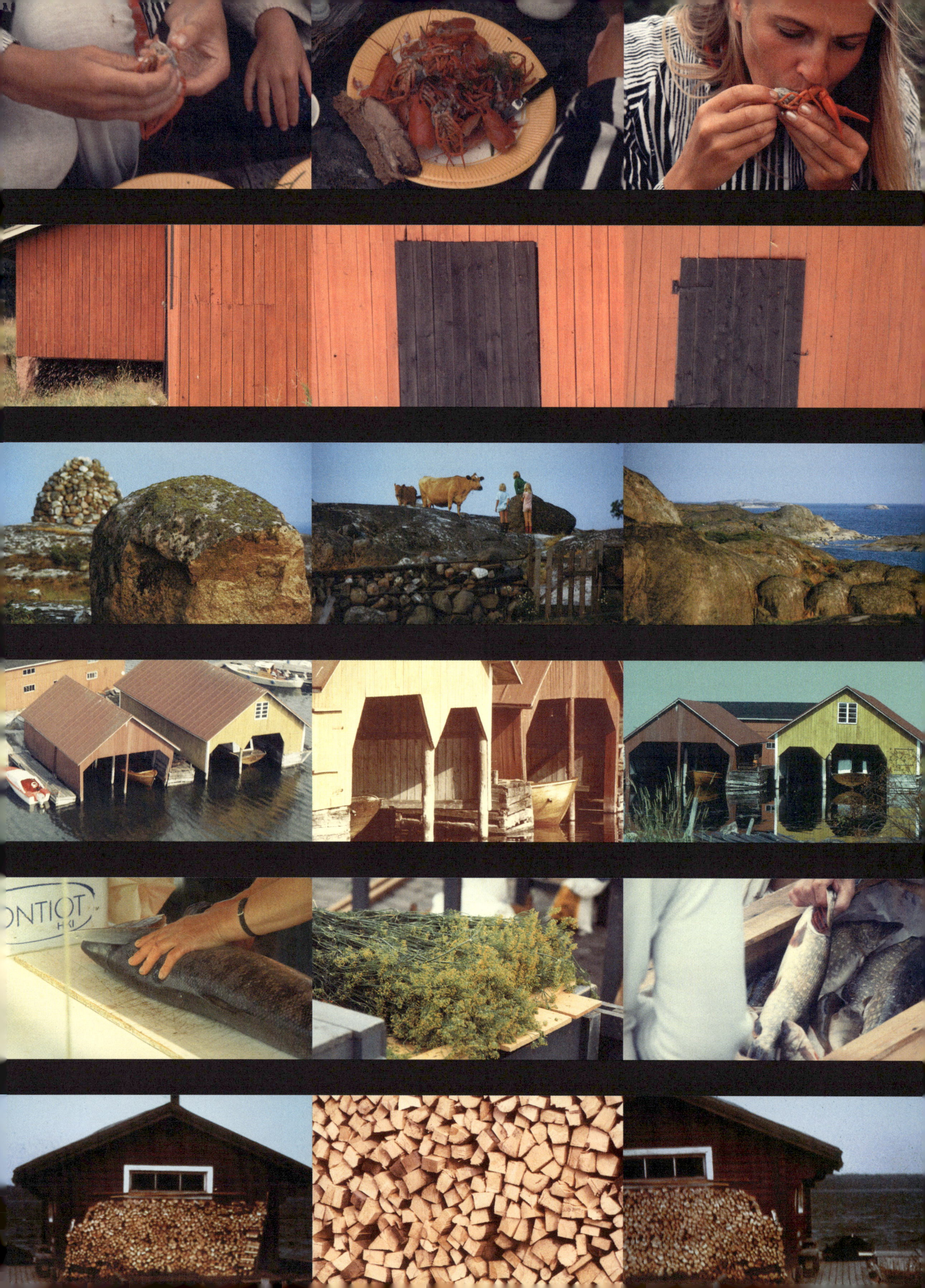
ONTIOT
HKI

Ben Thompson **"The architect's place on this planet is to create that special environment where life can be lived to its fullest—dedicated to the brilliance of this glowing orbiting world and its magic moments."**

Nancy Hemenway, D/R staff, 1968–76
What Ben really taught me was how to see things. Staff meetings would never be about sales, not even really about products. Nothing remotely businesslike. It was all about beauty, how to make things beautiful. He would do multi-image slide shows on a big screen with music, and he'd narrate. It was to get you feeling this love and enthusiasm. He incorporated nature images. Products and stores were in there, but there were different countries, what people wore, what people ate, great scenes of nature, great scenes of animals. And that would be our business meeting. I don't recall actual numbers ever coming up with Ben. For him, numbers followed ideas.

Paul R. Lawrence, professor emeritus, Harvard Business School I was a friend and neighbor, and Ben knew I had an interest in how he ran his firm. He suggested I turn up early at a staff meeting—this was probably in the late 1960s. So I arrived at Ben and Jane's third-floor BTA studio on Story Street at nine. People, mostly very young people, were milling around, and there was lots of lively talking. Ben found me a seat in a corner. He gently got the group to settle down, many sitting on the floor, to listen to his morning guidance.

He quietly began a rather rambling line of speculative questioning, centered on the Charles River and its role in the Boston/Cambridge community. He threw out one question after another to the group in no apparent order. One could observe on their faces signs of puzzlement, then a growing interest, then excitement. No one tried to answer Ben's questions out loud, but they were clearly thinking hard. Finally Ben handed out some rather vague assignments, really just suggestions, like "Joe, why don't you and Susan go down to the place on the lower Charles where the old canal comes in. Observe what is going on there now. How is the space being used? Take a camera. Bring back some shots or sketches and some ideas about possible future uses there." He sent off four or five such teams to different locales along the river. They were asked to report back mid-afternoon to the entire group.

It was all very simple. But those young people had stars in their eyes as they hurried out for their day's work. They were doing independent research, with new awareness of the much larger context.

OPPOSITE: Ben, who had a strong affinity for the unspoiled landscape and vernacular architecture of Finland, photographed hundreds of images of the countryside around Poorvu and the Baltic Islands for his multi-image slide shows.

When he traveled, Ben liked to sketch, often on 4-by-6 note cards. This view of the Provence landscape was made on a barge trip along the Canal du Midi.

"Report on the
 Brussels World's Fair,"
Industrial Design,
August 1958

Brussels

FINLAND'S FOREST GLADE

*The deep solitude of the forest sets the mood of Tapio Wirkkala's installation for Finland.
Echoing the linear masses of architect Reima Pietila's slatted building,
are many thin vertical strips of fabric as dividers to draw
the eye from low display tables up through lighted high overhead space, where
large photomurals of the Finnish countryside adds to the illusion that this is a
Scandinavian glade in the dim light of a summer night. Exhibits include lumber products, outdoor life, an impressive section on furnishings and decorative arts.*

28   Design Research

Ben 29

Design Research was the first American market application of the ideals of the German Bauhaus, founded by Walter Gropius. As TAC partners, Ben and Walter's relationship brought those ideals into the American postwar context, where the dissemination of modern design ("art in everyday life") coincided with a desire for simpler, more informal living.

Walter and Ben

By Jane Thompson

The development of D/R can and must be seen as the evolutionary outcome of the modern design philosophy launched in 1919 at the Bauhaus School in Weimar, Germany, under the leadership of Walter Gropius. Nearly thirty years later, Gropius became one of Ben Thompson's partners at The Architects Collaborative in Cambridge. The lineage is significant, but not as obvious as it might seem.

Gropius's search for post–World War I modernism in Germany was not a didactic one, and did not follow a straight line of formal thinking. He was asked to lead the *Kunstgewerbeschule* (Arts and Crafts School) in 1915, a time when, among leading young professionals in Europe, there was call for a radically different approach to architecture, as troubled times, in war and postwar, demanded new creative solutions to building and housing. But to reorient design attitude, Gropius decided to start with a new basic education, the *Vorkurs,* or foundation course, to rethink the properties and potential of materials.

In 1919, following the Armistice, Imperial Germany had collapsed, and the nation faced postwar devastation and inflation-driven poverty. Germany's traditional craft guilds organized their training around mastering materials — stone, glass, wood, metal — and the resulting skills were the economic basis of the construction industries. All guild workers were schooled as apprentices, then journeymen, and finally masters in a chosen workshop,

30 Design Research

learning traditional techniques from recognized practitioners — masters of craft — and passing qualifying exams.

Gropius evolved a curriculum to refocus centuries-old attitudes to building. He invented team teaching. He brought artisans from each craft to instruct students in collaboration with practicing artists, most of them painters. Lyonel Feininger, Johannes Itten, Oskar Schlemmer, Paul Klee, Wassily Kandinsky, and Joseph Albers, plus a sculptor and a potter, were all instructors. As a team they were supposed to integrate the knowledge of form and material skills that the "new architect" would need, both to pass the traditional exams and to respond to the multiplying needs of the new industrial age.

The *Vorkurs* was a way to approach the design of anything and everything in new ways, a synthesis intended to bridge state requirements and futurist visions. Gropius believed in the liberated imaginations and perceptions of fine artists and felt that, after mastering the Bauhaus's innovative workshop production, designers would be able to come together to grasp the complex requirements of the modern architecture waiting for articulation. Gropius's mantra was, *As future architects, we must prepare our skills and sensibilities in radical new ways. This synthetic multi-disciplinary training will prepare us for building design, the last and hardest task to achieve.*

Gropius attracted an innovative group of masters to lead hands-on workshop experiments with a diverse group of students gathered from Central Europe and Asia. Lázló Moholy-Nagy and Marcel Breuer came from Hungary. Other students were Czech, Swiss, Austrian, Russian, and Japanese. The school held together for thirteen turbulent years against the mounting reactionary forces in the Weimar Republic and later in Dessau, as Nazis took action against any independent expression — word, design, art, or belief — which the Bauhaus explicitly symbolized. Finally, militias marched against the school and closed its doors in 1933. Gropius, Ludwig Mies van der Rohe, Moholy-Nagy, Breuer, and many of their students found their way to the United States soon after.

Gropius and Breuer settled in Cambridge, where Gropius became Chairman of Architecture at Harvard's Graduate School of Design (GSD). Ben Thompson, a graduate of the Yale School of Architecture before entering the navy in 1941, had been familiar with Bauhaus publications on furniture, industrial arts, and the boldly modern architecture of the Dessau Bauhaus school and masters' houses. While docked in Boston in 1945, Thompson went ashore to look up Gropius and paid him a visit in Lincoln. The following year, at the war's end, Thompson gathered a group of architect friends to formally organize a practicing partnership with Walter Gropius. The Architects Collaborative, formally organized in 1946, included Chip Harkness, Norman Fletcher, Robert S. McMillan, and Louis A. McMillen, as well as Sarah Harkness and Jean Fletcher, who were architects and wives of partners. Gropius staffed his Harvard studios with his future partners, recent graduates of both Harvard and Yale.

From this international parentage evolved a notable family of GSD graduates, all practitioners of an evolving American modernism, from the mid-1940s to the present day. Among the first generation of graduates of the Gropius era were Paul Rudolph, Edward Larrabee Barnes, I. M. Pei, and Ulrich Franzen.

Thereafter Ben Thompson was one of Gropius's closest friends and collaborators. It would be easy to assume that he was cloned by the Master, by a straight transfer of ideas that the pioneering European was now exploring with his younger partners. Certainly, all of them were hoping to influence structure, form, and utility in American building. But Gropius was not a didact and Ben was not a follower; he already had a well-formed aesthetic philosophy to exchange with Gropius. He also had a holistic and intuitive mind that balanced well with the Berliner's rational nature. As partners they lunched several times a week over some twenty years, and in Ben's recollection, "We did not talk about form-follows-function, or dynamic asymmetry, but about politics, food, books, politics, ideas, and women." As families they adopted each other and shared holidays and celebrations as a three-generation unit.

Despite their different backgrounds, they shared many central convictions about the ethical and social responsibility of architects in a changing society — not only for building but for communities and societies in a war-free world. Their aesthetic judgments grew from resolution between complex inner problems and tough external conditions. "Designing from the *requirements*," Gropius often intoned, emphasizing that the old orthodoxy of external symmetry, formalism, and monumentality could no longer meet the challenges of people, nature, or human habitation.

Each espoused the belief in a continuum between art and design — indeed, design as applied art, better yet, industrial art. Art was for more than hanging on walls. Its qualities could be invested in products for use and pleasure. Talent and imagination, embracing truth to materials, could elevate the quality of production of textiles, metal, glass, ceramics, and all building, with the potential to enrich daily life for Everyman. Gropius's life work was to create objects and places of utility and beauty within the reach of the working man.

Thompson's particular interest in the quality of interiors and appointments in the houses TAC built grew from his days on Minnesota farms attuned to land, nature, and seasons. He deeply believed that one's immediate environment had direct impact on all the senses, on one's mood and well-being. At TAC he extended his talent to spheres inside the building shell itself, joining Gropius in a lasting commitment to mitigating the impact on humans of the depersonalized output of an industrial society.

In founding Design Research, Ben revitalized the Bauhaus goals of quality in every realm of design. Pushing the professional envelope beyond the roles previously defined for the architect into design practice and retail operations, he was often belittled by his colleagues for tangling with "commercialism." Ben found that his main TAC supporter was Walter Gropius. Thirty-five years after his own career redefinition, the elder professional deeply appreciated and supported Ben's continuing campaign to spread the message of useful art in the daily life of everybody.

Ati Gropius Johansen **"Walter always said, 'We had to wipe the slate clean. How could we get there using the technology of our time?'"**

Six Moon Hill, Lexington, Mass., 1947
Five Fields, Lexington, Mass., 1952
Howlett House, Belmont, Mass., 1947–48

Ben Thompson's early work with TAC was primarily residential. But the firm's Bauhaus roots forced the partners to think about how to make modern living affordable and flexible. As a result, the TAC partners, acting as entrepreneurs, launched two pioneering developments outside Boston. The first, Six Moon Hill, began in 1947 with the purchase of twenty acres in Lexington. Seven TAC families (including Ben's, which eventually included five children) drew straws for what would eventually become twenty-eight lots, with fields, a pool, and tennis courts open to all. TAC architects designed their own houses as well as their neighbors' with a common vocabulary of vertical redwood siding, flat roofs, multiple vistas through large windows, Plexiglas skylights, and easy movement from interior to exterior.

Five Fields, begun in 1952, was a far larger development initiative with eighty acres, sixty-five home sites, and the same parklike common facilities. A typical Five Fields house had an asymmetrical gable roof, a split-level plan, a combination living-dining room off a kitchen with pass-through, a feeling of open space, and amenities not offered in most postwar builders' homes.

While the TAC partners were executing these developments, individual clients also came to Ben. A June 1950 issue of *Architectural Forum* described the house he designed for Dr. Clarence Howlett and his wife, Jeannette, as having many of the same interior planning ideas:

> The unique feature of the house is the almost sleight-of-hand cleverness with which its three different levels face three different kinds of terrain with three different kinds of character, never losing the homogenous quality of the whole. To the nearby street the house presents a discreet cypress front with a low silhouette to blend with a conventional neighborhood. On the side away from the street the one-story top-floor living area turns an all-glass face to tree-covered, rolling ground. The two floors of the sleeping and playroom areas front on a smooth lawn at the lower level . . . From almost any viewpoint, the open plan of the house gives a sense of spaciousness, yet the split-level arrangement of the living and sleeping areas insures privacy where it is needed.

The Howlett House, like many of its contemporaries, was furnished by TAC Interiors, working out of a Cambridge house next door to the future Design Research. In its rooms one can see designs Ben selected that would later be sold with great success at D/R: the Saarinen Womb chair, webbed seats by Sweden's Bruno Mathsson, and a Breuer bentwood stool in a child's bedroom.

of TAC partner Robert McMillan, far left, and the interior of the Martin House, near left.

TOP LEFT: The Martin House exterior at Six Moon Hill.

TOP RIGHT: The Grossier House at Five Fields.

Belmont, Massachusetts, an early private home designed by Ben Thompson before founding D/R.

Experiencing the Store
Brattle Street, 1953-69

2

While traveling for TAC commissions in Greece, Scandinavia, Italy, and Switzerland, Ben Thompson saw the full range of international modern design—much of it with more color, more natural materials, and more textures than anything made and sold in America. With the newly built homes around Boston in mind, he began shipping furniture and textiles back to a Cambridge storeroom in a clapboard row house at 57 Brattle Street, close to the Common and bordering Radcliffe Yard.

That storeroom became a store in 1953, when Ben opened his inventory to the public. It originally occupied just one house and two stories. Customers walked up four wooden steps to the first level, which served as a showroom, while Ben and his loyal assistant, Nancy Gathercole, occupied the basement. Ben brought clients to browse, insisting that they select and compose their own interiors.

Over the next decade, those two floors expanded vertically and laterally, eventually colonizing all three houses in the row. A new store emerged, cutting all ties to the brown years of depression and war. The old walk-up's tired façade was reshaped with an all-glass bay window, giving pedestrians a clear view of the new domestic landscape. A staircase led to the second

From D/R's beginning, objects were displayed against glass and natural light, the better to emphasize their common, organic shapes. Every display was an opportunity for a fresh, inviting composition.

At D/R, tables were always set dramatizing the ways the store's colorful products worked together. Here, atop a Marimekko Sarafan tablecloth (a design by Maija Isola from 1960), Finnish traditional turned-wood candlesticks provide height in contrast to the low curves of Arabia Kilta dinnerware by Kaj Franck, 1952.

floor, filled with Marimekko dresses, which became the most popular department in the store. The walls between the houses came down, with only the old fireplaces serving as reminders of the original domestic scale. A glass-walled extension pushed into the garden, its backlit shelves carrying an iconic display of glassware from Scandinavia and Switzerland.

Thompson served as founder, buyer, underwriter, researcher, and merchant, and went about building a staff of exceptionally personable and worldly women (many of them current or future wives of architects) who knew their goods, their cuisine, their design, and their customers. As salespeople, they were in a class with the clientele, the younger "girls" selling dresses and accessories, the older "ladies" the costlier furniture.

The name "Design Research" was a simple statement of what Ben was up to in cities and countrysides abroad: he was gathering a global harvest from emerging modern craftsmen and designers, whom he often visited to fill his expanding collection. While it can't be said that D/R made all modern furnishings affordable, it made them accessible, and to that end D/R showed people what they could aspire to. Many lifelong customers first purchased just two Kaj Franck coffee cups, starting their new beautiful life at breakfast and building from there.

D/R tapped into an era of great change in ideas about living: *This is your life, not your grandmother's.* With place mats instead of damask tablecloths, ethnic stews instead of Sunday roasts, Marimekko smocks instead of tartan kilts, Thompson pioneered a new sort of retail mix in America, combining materials, nations, and eras—classic products like Japanese rice paper lamps or $1 Mexican drinking glasses with a handmade Hans Wegner chair and Mies coffee table. Ben did not separate fine art on the walls from functional objects on the table, or the table itself. A porcelain cup or a sculpted chair were not just objects but beautiful works of the human hand, whether individually crafted or mass-produced.

The store itself was something of a dream house, no bigger than customers' homes, and divided loosely into departments whose displays aped living room, dining room, and kitchen. Space, color, and light were enhanced by the store soundtrack, up-to-the-minute music of the era, from Joan Baez and Judy Collins to Django Reinhardt and José Feliciano. Special days would be celebrated with Sonny and Cher. And Thompson and his staff always treated you as a guest—nickels for the parking meter, a bowl of daisies or apples at the door, a warm drink on a cold day. It was a welcome home.

Experiencing the Store 37

Voices

Nancy Gathercole Riaz, TAC assistant, summer 1953; D/R staff, 1953–64
I worked at TAC one summer as a secretary. I bonded with Ben because the other partners would complain if I didn't put every comma where they wanted it. Ben was the only one who would accept a rewrite. He was always willing to see another side of something. A few months later, Ben called me on Thanksgiving Day and said, "Would you like to come to work for me this Monday?" I said I would come for a week, but no longer than that. It was 1953. It took me eleven years to leave.

Betsy Cushman Whitman, TAC Interiors, 1952–53; D/R staff, 1953–54, 1957–58
In the beginning, D/R had three of us. Claud Bunyard was the salesman, John Woodard was the commercial designer, and I was the interior designer. By the time I left in 1955, there was something like nine people in that little place on Brattle Street.

Ben Thompson, Memoirs I had always been more interested in interiors than my partners at TAC. As part of each job I was doing, I built up files with source information about materials, lighting fixtures, curtains, upholstery fabrics, furniture—the best we could find, at a time when products of a quality appropriate to our interior aspirations were hard to find. At my initiation, we soon had an interiors department and source library in the office, finishing the interiors of our houses and schools as a contract service to achieve what I thought of as "complete architecture," which was quite unusual for architecture firms in the early 1950s.

Jane Thompson The few suppliers of appropriate modern furnishings and accessories were all in to-the-trade showrooms, off limits to the ordinary shopper. To outfit their adventuresome new homes, TAC and its clients had to make trips to New York wholesale showrooms, primarily Knoll and Herman Miller.

Ben Thompson, Memoirs I started D/R with three other partners; we each invested a small amount to own a 25 percent interest. One was Spencer Field, who had a local furniture factory that produced our original designs, a business that increased with time. As we needed capital beyond our meager investments, Spencer arranged loans that became the working capital for growth and expansion that was otherwise in short supply. John Woodard was in contract furniture. The third partner was Art Trottenberg, a Harvard administrator who later went to New York with McGeorge Bundy as vice president for administration in the Ford Foundation.

Lorna Dawson Elkus, D/R staff, 1961–70
Spencer had brought into the business a furniture shop that he had inherited, a very fine Boston furniture building and refinishing business called Gilbert-Estabrook. They built the down sofas, tables, and quite a bit of TAC's contract furniture, including the butcher-block pieces.

Massimo Vignelli "Having arrived in the U.S. as a young architect from Italy in 1957, I was astonished to find D/R in Cambridge—a unique store with everything you needed for life. And I still believe that to be true today."

OPPOSITE: Three clapboard walk-ups were modified as D/R grew and added two projecting showcase windows on Brattle Street.

The store was an adapted residential space that grew to three levels, with a two-story annex for textiles and kitchenwares. The main display here shows a D/R-designed Quartic table surrounded by Hans Wegner chairs in the rear, and a TAC daybed and Saarinen womb chair, front.

OVERLEAF: D/R grew from one walk-up to three, cutting a very modern, oversized display window into the last house in the Brattle Street row.

Experiencing the Store 39

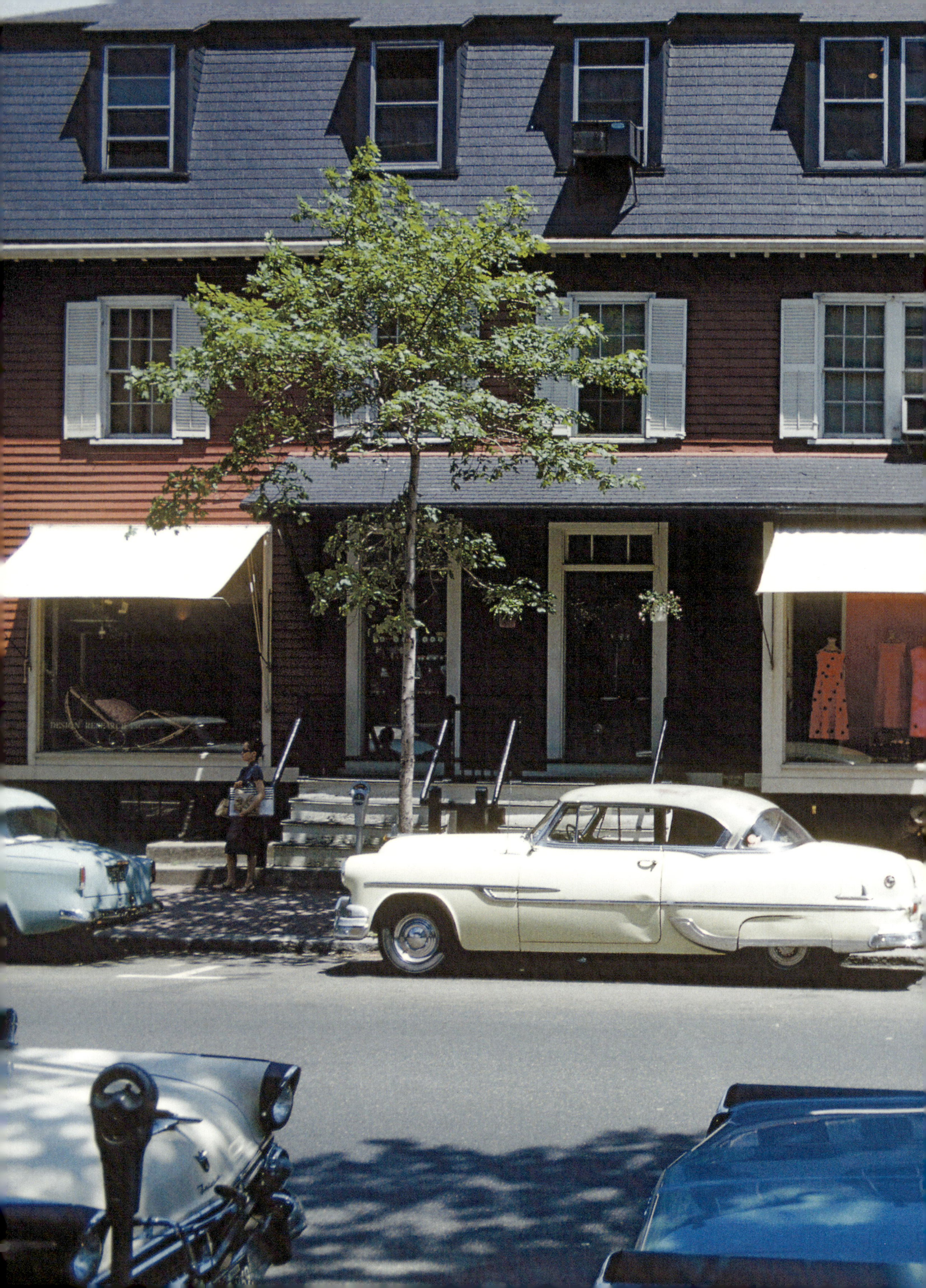

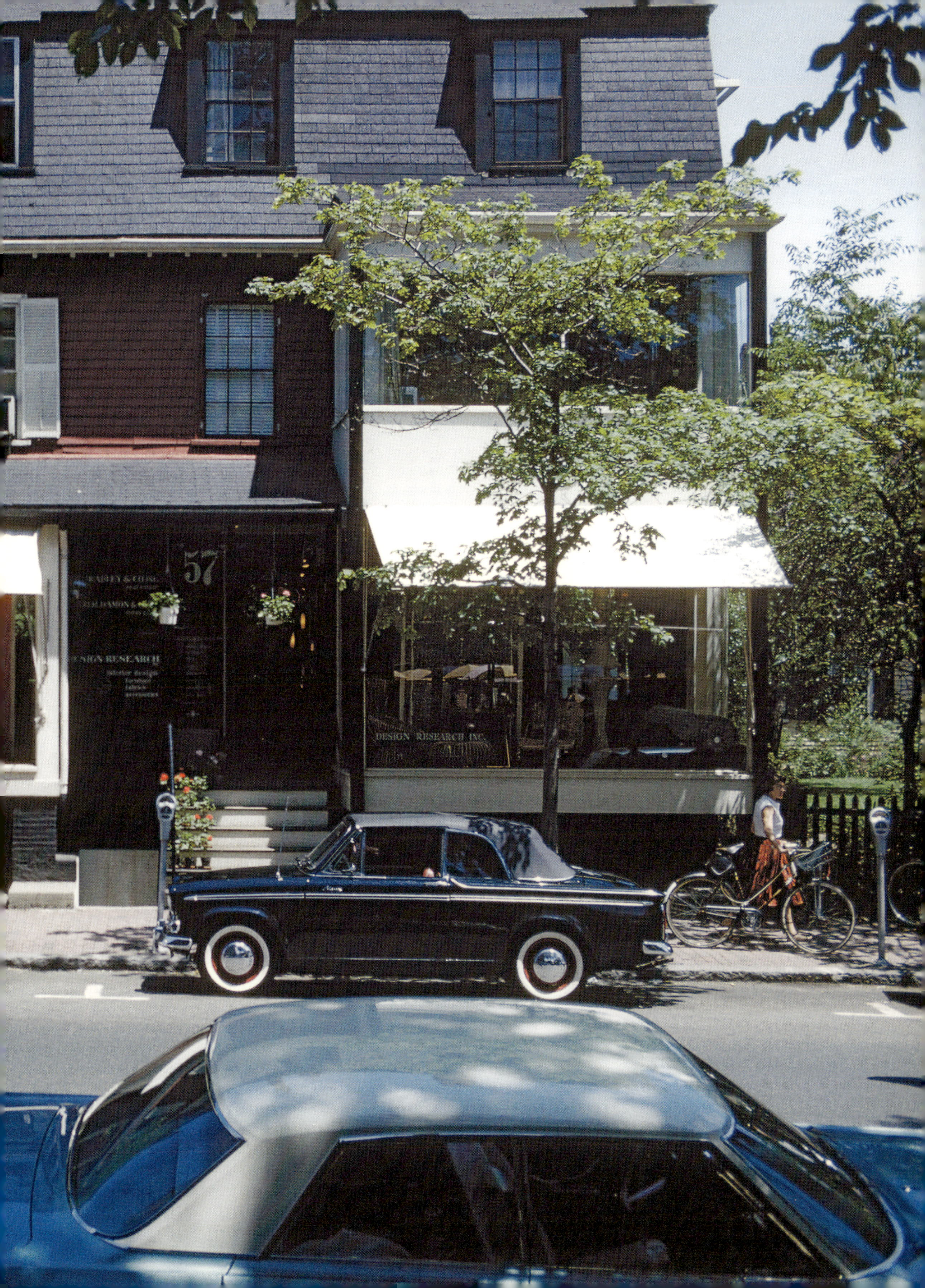
57
interior design
DESIGN RESEARCH INC.

Alan Heller **"Ben had the inventiveness of Girard and Eames, also the playfulness of Alexander Calder—that childlike sense of wonderment."**

Agnete Larsen Kalckar, D/R staff, 1953–70

When we started D/R, nobody had a job description. We just came together for purposes that were not quite known, only sensed, and went to work tackling whatever came along. It was experimental.

I came to the store after working with Ben as the architect advising on a house we bought, which was in terrible condition. Ben gave me drawings and ideas about what we should do. Probably because of my early life in a Danish home, I actually corrected them. He liked that and said, "Maybe you could come to the store and help get the Danish furniture I want." That's how it started.

I had a lot of architect connections in Denmark and my job was to connect with them part-time while my kids were in school. Most of my communications were telephone calls—in Danish! Finn Juhl was one. He was a very close friend of mine.

We didn't carry his furniture but he had good connections. He knew Johannes Hansen, who produced Hans Wegner's furniture.

I introduced Ben to people with new design ideas that he continued to work with. At D/R we would first get a single piece for a test. We would use it and sit on and feel it. If Ben liked it, he would order a lot. And he would assume that everybody else should like it too, although some items were never reordered.

Jane Thompson Ben and I ended up with a lot of furniture samples in our house. But that wasn't about making mistakes, that was just *testing*. It was the right way to do it: you *always* bought and tried the product before putting it out for customers to buy.

Betsy Cushman Whitman D/R had these ready markets—everybody was buying a new home, and everybody needed eight chairs because they were having big families—Peacock Farm, Five Fields. They ordered our Clore chairs, which were $8 each, and Wegner chairs, which cost $15.

Henriette Mladota, D/R staff, 1955–70
I had worked at Bonniers, a Swedish publishing company, on Madison Avenue. It was also wholesaling some modern products—glass items, the Noguchi lamp, and some furniture. Ben was buying a few items for the new D/R. When we moved to Boston, I thought I might like to work there. One summer afternoon in 1955, I walked into the D/R store and said, "I am looking for a job." Agnete asked where I'd been working, and I said, "I worked for Bonniers for four years." In the background I heard a lazy voice say, "Take her coat so she cannot get away." Ben hadn't even seen me.

I started that afternoon. I did purchase orders and handled merchandise matters. On staff then were Agnete Larsen, Betsy Cushman Whitman, Frances West, Claud Bunyard, and Phoebe Bruck. A recent graduate of the New Bauhaus in Chicago, Phoebe was doing the contract design of house interiors and sometimes display.

Ben Thompson, Memoirs Sometimes I would relate the idea behind D/R to cooking. When you cook you have a rather standard set of ingredients. We all go to the same markets to buy the vegetables, the fish, the meat, and we cook over the same stove. Yet what we produce can be rather different, ranging from great to poor, and diners of all kinds can sense the difference in the quality of the ensemble, the blends, with tools of judgment that are not logical and certainly not academic or verbal; they are built into the coordinated use of taste, smell, touch, vision, and color sense. The chef—the designer—makes a difference in the assemblage. I think these standards applied very much to D/R as they do to architecture as a whole.

Sandra Smith Griswold "D/R was a real hangout. Ben wanted to put in an espresso bar, saying 'Let's keep people longer. Let's give them some coffee and make them comfortable.' How prophetic was that?!"

Christa Marcelli, D/R staff, 1957–70
When I first came here from Germany in 1957, there were days when maybe two or three real customers came in. There were always people in the store looking, and some people even asked, "Is this a museum?" They didn't quite believe that things were for sale because it was all so gorgeous.

Tom Green, partner, Benjamin Thompson & Associates, 1966–80, 1988–2001
The original store had two big bay windows. Ben and staff probably changed the display in the windows at least once a week. They were frustrated by the fact that you couldn't see into the store. They wanted to bring this new stuff, their merchandise, out in the open as much as possible. In those days, Boston and even Cambridge was a fairly conservative place. They were trying to bring people in from the sidewalk. In working with Ben and the D/R staff on the new store in 1968–69, this became one of the main requirements: give us show windows as big as possible. When we broke the building into the two bumps along Brattle Street, we had one, two, three, four, five, six, seven outside corners. Every corner had a piece of merchandise in it.

Tizzie (Elizabeth) Lambert, D/R staff, 1962–64
I was a student at Wellesley and when I got really fed up with the gray February weather, I can remember going into Cambridge, plodding through this terrible slush, just to get the color that was at D/R. You could fill your eyes with color. It was like taking a vitamin pill.

A Marimekko window display on Brattle Street mixes geometric textiles, bright hats, and greenery.

OPPOSITE: Upstairs, the annex's high ceiling was good for hanging displays like the wire sculptures by featured artist Ruth Asawa, front and rear left. Also visible are Akari lamps by Isamu Noguchi, woven chairs by Bruno Mathsson, and D/R's luxurious Down Seating Group chairs in dark fabric.

Experiencing the Store 43

Agnete Larsen Kalckar In the store's different approach to everything, you have someone who wanted to inspire the whole act of living, the everyday possibilities for delight and pleasure. Ben's product choices were put together to show that they were harmonious and related. That's the main story: so many opportunities for art in everyday life.

Jack Lenor Larsen, textile designer
By the mid-1950s, small design stores were failing. Many had started after the war in the late 1940s; at one time there were 200 in America. They would be named Modern this or Contemporary that. Most of them were started by architects' wives or enthusiasts for modern design who had some aesthetic prowess but who knew very little about business, either finance or marketing. Early on in my small firm, as suppliers we learned that if a client had one of those buzzwords in its name we had better double- and triple-check their credit.

In the 1940s, when we hit a new city, our first move would be to check out their design store before seeking the museum or anything else. Design was something we believed in, and new retailers might have something we wanted to buy or at least look at. Pretty soon the economics weren't so good. Some shops were buying from the same sources. They all had Arzberg china and Danish flatware and teak furniture. Design Research was different. Hard times didn't bother them. To graduates from the universities who were going overseas for one reason or another—and a lot of them were—they would say, "If you see something good, let us know about it." So they were getting in new things that no one else had, and they weren't so price conscious. If it was a little difficult, or a little upmarket, that was fine.

"What is Design Research?" statement, 1950s Nothing has been selected simply because it will sell or is "what people want." To appear in the store at all, it must be weighed on a series of scales; if it does its job well, shows careful workmanship, if it serves a function that is needed in contemporary life and makes that life a little richer and more fun, and if Ben Thompson *likes it,* then it probably belongs in the store.

Agnete Larsen Kalckar He was a very unusual merchant because money didn't come first. To Ben it was about identifying good design and supporting those who made it. And that was an educational process.

"What is Design Research?" statement, 1950s Thompson makes frequent trips to Europe and on these trips takes full responsibility for merchandise buying. His choices have been highly selective and as directly as possible from the source. Thompson also tracks down products along other unbeaten paths—goods from Tunisia, Greece, Algiers, Malta, and Bolivia are to be found in his store and often nowhere else in the country. There may be important elements of his own design in commission-made products. The total effect is a harmonious collection of whatever is best.

Lorna Dawson Elkus He was more interested in the folk art than anything. That was the Mexican stuff, through Alexander Girard and also through our Mexican connection, architect Max Chetto. We also had a Bolivian connection, and Jim Thompson in Thailand, and such people scattered about. And then all the European pieces— the Maltese weavers and Niederer glass and Aubock brass.

Henriette Mladota After some months, I became Ben's assistant. I guided the staff in their attitudes. I told them, "Don't be too eager to sell something. Don't exaggerate or you may create disappointment. Lead the customer to like it. Don't show that you are impressed by what you are selling, as others may take its quality or price for granted." Most salesladies came from the same background as the clientele and could talk with customers easily.

Minkie West McKevitt, D/R staff, 1961–64, 1968 We were a big family and Ben was our father. He used to sit us down and tell us what we should be wearing and how we should talk. He didn't like us ever, ever to say, "Can I help you?" We had to get around that by just starting a conversation. When wearing our Marimekkos, we were told to be casual and not use petticoats or wear a lot of makeup.

OPPOSITE: Ben Thompson's belief in design for every aspect of daily life extended to the joys of children, and D/R found and featured colorful wooden toys designed for imaginative play, shown here on modular furniture by Pirkko Stenros.

A D/R Christmas card from the 1950s, designed by Ati Gropius Johansen, with a poem by Harvard's Art Trottenberg, one of the original D/R investors.

Experiencing the Store 45

Tizzie Lambert **"At D/R, you could fill your eyes with color. It was like taking a vitamin pill."**

A D/R window celebrating Walter Gropius's 80th birthday in 1963. The Marimekko-clad staff offering Gropius his cake includes Anne Solley, third from right.

OPPOSITE: Printex fabric (the original name for the textiles) was always displayed on open shelves. Many young women who admired the Marimekko imports from Finland worked as salesgirls at D/R.

Nancy Hemenway, D/R staff, 1968–76
Sometimes Ben would move things around. I learned that you can get to a great place by continuing to move things. Ben said, "If you don't touch a product it becomes dead. So there's no life to it anymore and people ignore it. It must be moved, as it is in life." I have found that to be so true. If you don't change a display, no matter how good it is the first day you make it, after a couple of days it starts to look flat. When a new product comes in and you are taking it out and putting it on the shelf is when people choose to buy it.

Christa Marcelli We would work all night to change the displays. I remember the first time Ben asked me to set a table and I did it sparsely. I thought it was beautiful. And he came along and said, "What is this here? Where are the glasses? Where are the ashtrays?" I said, "Well, we usually don't smoke at dinner!" So then we loaded it up with other things, and two days later he said, "This table looks terrible! We've got to change this!" He was always going from sparse — putting just a few things out — to massing it on the shelves. It was dynamic — always a total change from one to the other.

Tizzie (Elizabeth) Lambert To exaggerate the color (which was overwhelming when you walked in), there were often long panels of fabric hanging in the stairwell going down two levels, or at least hanging in the window. Anne Solley once did a whole window of orange and chartreuse, which nobody at that time would have thought of doing. Red and pink and orange and together, well, fine, that was almost old hat. But the orange and chartreuse was just such a wonderful new way of looking at color.

Henriette Mladota Our simple word is *happiness* (a guarantee of the Declaration of Independence that hasn't turned up in the curriculum of the Business School). Happiness in the early years was a bowl of nickels kept for parking meters. Happiness was a crate of apples at the door in the autumn, spiced wine bowls in winter, fresh jonquils in the spring. Happiness was "old Bill" and the ladies cleaning brick sidewalks and watering flowers at 8 AM. Happiness was evolving a design for work that reflected in the faces of the staff and made everyone feel a bit special.

Rebecka Tarschys, *Mobilia,* 1966 A smell of spices and home is coming from somewhere. Fresh flowers just everywhere. And music filling the house; something promising in the jazz notes adventuring away. Candles burning, a loaf of bread. Something does it — the light, happy colors, gay sensuality. This is a modern store.

Henriette Mladota "**Happiness in the early years was a bowl of nickels kept for parking meters.**"

Experiencing the Store

D/R Catalogue, 1960s D/R won't sell it unless it looks and lives beautifully. We don't care how much it costs. That's why, in this catalogue, you'll find designs that cost only 75 cents. You'll also find some that are close to $1,500.

Lorna Dawson Elkus The unique constant source of goods was really Henriette, who had moved with her husband to Switzerland. She had a high sense of quality, which Ben also had. Henriette, who was on a retainer as a scout and buyer throughout Europe, would send over her discoveries. Ben always made the final selections and would make suggestions for tweaking the final designs. They were "architect-ified" a bit, if possible. Which meant simplifying really, taking off all decoration. Henriette would negotiate a two-year exclusive if she could get a U.S. exclusive with the craftsperson.

Henriette Mladota I went to Roberto Niederer's workshop in Zurich. Even then he had a name as a glassmaker for his ornaments and table glassware. He had some pieces blown over wood which he called "wood-blown glasses." At home I still use the Niederer goblets with the short stems. I also went to Murano, in Italy. D/R had mostly practical glass but always displayed some great handblown items. I also found Jackie Aubock's shop in Vienna. It is amazing that both Aubock and Niederer are still going now, run by the sons who are very like them. And seem to have a full line of things going way back.

Ben avoided the middlemen-importers. We worked directly with producers, as sole importers to the United States, particularly from Denmark.

Barbara Plumb, design reporter, *New York Times*, 1963 The most copied piece of D/R furniture, a trim but supremely comfortable down sofa at $680, was designed by Mr. Thompson for a client and later incorporated into the line. This same thing happened to a love seat, easy chair, oval walnut dining table, and a series of butcher-board tables, which range in price from $115 to $205. Besides a sprinkling of Knoll, Herman Miller, and other furniture sold only through decorators, there are exclusive imports like an Italian rattan arm chair by Paolo Tilch at $115 and a beautiful white peeled willow bed from Germany that doubles as a sofa ($375).

Lorna Dawson Elkus There was a basic Design Research image, which was the TAC sofa, the down sofa, the butcher-block tables, which were part of the TAC line. D/R also made the Quartic oval table, which was a fine-dining table made by Gilbert-Estabrook. Then there was the Mies Barcelona table and the Disa lamp from Spain and the good Danish modern, the best of the line, Wegner and Mogensen. There were the Thonet Prague chairs, which had come through Stendig. There was the Stendig line, the Knoll line, the Herman Miller line. These pioneering American firms were represented by a few selected pieces that fit into the eclectic D/R family of furnishings.

Lorraine De Wet Howes, D/R staff, 1957–60 One of the biggest sellers at that time at D/R was the goose-down sofa and chairs, which was $1,000 in those days. We all thought, "A thousand dollars for a sofa!" It was covered in Maltese wool, later in heavenly Haitian cotton. Every architect had a Maltese wool sofa and a sisal rug. I made myself some clothes with that Maltese wool, and then I'd go out to architects' houses where they had the sofas, and I wouldn't want to sit down because I would disappear!

Lorraine De Wet Howes I arrived in Cambridge in 1957 after my husband, Gerry Howes, had been offered a job by Walter Gropius at TAC. We went to D/R the next weekend, where I met Ben, who asked me to work at D/R. In the beginning I worked in accessories, but soon I worked with Ben doing setups. Within a month or two I had made myself great new clothes using D/R fabrics: Thai silks, ticking, raw silk, and Maltese wool. Ben loved them and I suggested D/R should carry them. Claud Bunyard's wife, Frankie, helped with production. For instance, there was a dramatic waterproofed felt cape that came in brilliant colors. A highlight of my life occurred when Walter Gropius came in to get a birthday present for his wife and chose one of my capes!

Claud Bunyard, D/R staff, 1953–61 If a customer wanted something D/R didn't carry, I would sketch it and have it made up by Gilbert-Estabrook. I would try to sneak it onto the floor before delivery, to get the customer's reaction and Ben's.

OPPOSITE, TOP TO BOTTOM: A mobile by architect Bill Wainwright; a room setting with a D/R butcher-block sofa and tables against a Marimekko Joonas pattern backdrop; and table setting with Vico Magistretti chairs and Finel enamel pots.

A page from D/R's 1967 Christmas catalogue.

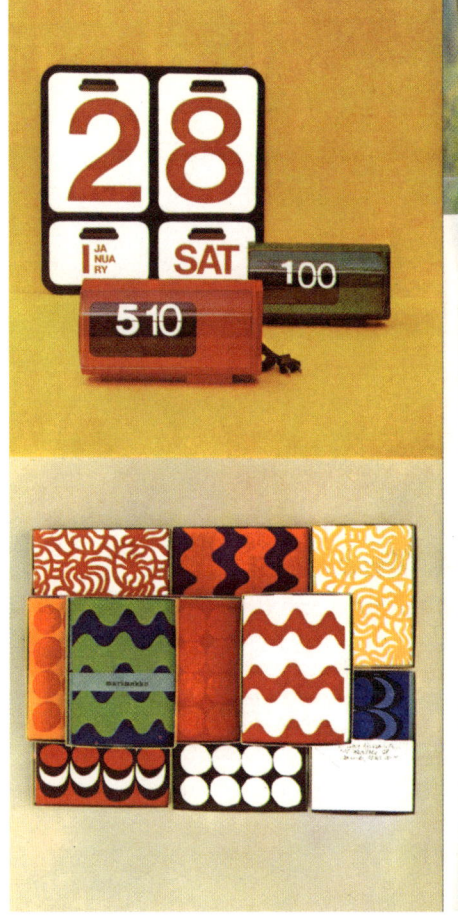

48. DOUBLE DECANTER
Styled for cocktails with scotch and drambuie, or for dinner with wine and liqueur, designer Kaj Franck coordinates the occasion with the shapely double decanter. Equally elegant in two separate pieces. Smoke grey tints the quart base, burnt almond the stopper. $27.50

49. VASES
Swiss vases of thick hand-blown glass display your holiday nuts and fruit, or individually show off HIS bouquet of flowers. Designed by Roberto Niederer. ((49A) Double-handled "Bernerhumpfen" 9½" high $30.00; (49B) Goblet shaped "Pokal" 13" high $25.00; (49C) Cylinder shape 12" high $10.00; (49D) Cylinder shape 16" high $15.00.

45. DIGITAL CLOCK
With the past and future out of sight, the flip of a white number on black card announces the minute for living. Designed by Massimo Vignelli, the light weight synchronous motor-operation of the futuristic Solari digital clock is enclosed in an unbreakable melamine cylinder case of white, red, blue or green. 3¾" x 7". $40.00

46. PERPETUAL CALENDAR
Striking interplay of color, texture and graphics create a timeless design for a wall calendar that is never outdated by New Year's Eve. Red or black numerals on white plastic cards hang on a black or white brushed aluminum square to be flipped forever by the day and month. $14.00

47. STATIONERY
Fresh graphics will stimulate the creative writer of notes, invitations and thank-yous. Each 6" x 8" sheet folds into personal cards for Christmas, New Year's and everyday thoughtfulness. Circles in yellow/orange, pink/red, black/white; waves in blue/green, red/white, purple/orange; half moons in purples, black/red/white, spider web in yellow/white, red/white. $2.00

Experiencing the Store

Swiss glassblower Roberto Niederer created hanging glass teardrops that could be turned into seasonal ornaments by adding colored water.

BELOW: The poster for D/R's Finland design exhibition in 1959.

OPPOSITE: Scenes from two international exhibitions at the store—designs from Japan, 1956, and "From Finland with Love" in New York, 1967, which included a Finnish lake boat in the front window.

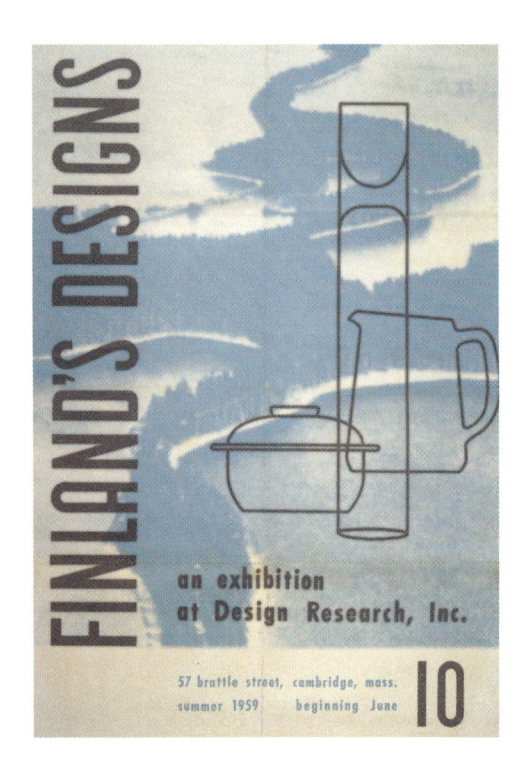

Nancy Gathercole Riaz Roberto Niederer was glass—I remember the *butzen,* a round disk like a CD. The *butzen* were different colors and they were hung up against the front window of Design Research where the daylight poured in. And then there were Christmas ornaments that were teardrop in shape and they were filled with different colored liquids. They too were hung up against the windows.

Tizzie (Elizabeth) Lambert At that time color Polaroid film was being developed, and men from Polaroid would come in to test the film by photographing those glass objects in the back window with the light shining through them so beautifully. They wanted to test for strong, clear color and they found it in our glass window.

"What is Design Research?" statement, 1950s There were three major national exhibitions during the store's first decade: products from Japan, Finland, and Denmark. Each time an intensive search was made for the best material available in each country and the articles were located, imported, and the entire store was turned over to displaying these designs in an imaginative way.

It was in the course of the Finnish exhibit in 1959 that D/R launched one of its most unexpected and far-reaching influences on women's fashion. The unusual Finnish Marimekko dresses were first shown in the USA at that exhibition. But what was a home-furnishings shop to do with dresses? Just what it had long done with its other products—single them out for their simplicity, utility, personality; treat them as another design element in the environment and let the customers take care of the rest.

Industrial Design, **1956** Last month Design Research, Inc., a design office and shop for carefully selected home accessories and furniture in Cambridge, Massachusetts, devoted most of its space to Japanese household objects and fabrics. Chosen "by leading Japanese architects and designers," the products were complemented by nine pieces of wire mesh sculpture by American-born Ruth Asawa. . . . Toys, teacups, and yard goods in abstract geometric patterns gave intimate reflection of everyday life in Japan, while the installations carried out the scale and open spaces of the Japanese house, with *ikebana* arrangements of tree-trunk slices, twigs, leaves, and stones. Just as screens, porcelain, straw, and paper products from Japanese interiors have been adapted to Western interiors, some Japanese are adding Western rooms in their houses for an exotic touch, and a home market has been created for chairs and other products alien to a floor-oriented décor.

Lorraine De Wet Howes Another successful fabric in the accessories department was Thai silk. Jim Thompson had started this business in Thailand. You could scratch off a letter and say, "We would like greens and blues," and he would send samples. It turns out he was in the CIA. He organized these fabulous silks and got them out to the West single-handedly while he was stationed in Thailand.

Nancy Hemenway Now it is so different because every little store has things from all over the world, but Ben was the first one to do that of any store, anywhere in America. We had the very modern with the furniture, but we also brought in goods from France — from Vallauris, the village where Picasso worked. These were rustic stoneware pots that you could cook in. There was one thing, the Arthur Hocking goblet. It was huge, on a stem. Unbreakable. We sold these for soups, for desserts, as wineglasses. Each one held about half a bottle of wine. They were so inexpensive when the store was considered pricey. Under one dollar each.

Henriette Mladota In Switzerland, as in Finland, there were wonderful wood toys. Many were handmade, each beautiful in its own right. Ben loved toys. They spoke to his idea of joy, color, and fantasy. I remember finding Rudolf Steiner toys in Basel and some in Zurich. Great toys came from Jussila in Finland.

Ralph Caplan, design writer and author Ben didn't make foolish distinctions. The criterion was quality rather than modernism or postmodernism or newness. If it was good it was good. I think this was true for the best designers. In the Eames studio you could find anything from anywhere. And in the Eames house, as at D/R, a lot was new but some things were old and better.

Experiencing the Store

"U.S. Retailer Looks at Foreign Design," *Industrial Design,* September 1957. This was the first magazine article about D/R.

The Design Research building stands just across the street from Longfellow's spreading chestnut tree on Brattle Street in Cambridge, Massachusetts. Specializing in foreign goods, they import about 80 per cent of their accessories, 40 per cent of their furniture, 50 per cent of their lighting fixtures and 70 per cent of their rugs. The shop's director, Benjamin Thompson, is an avid buyer who collects much of his merchandise from out-of-the-way points, and has assembled a handsome interior as well as a popular store.

DESIGN RESEARCH INC.

U.S. retailer looks at foreign design

At a time when the popularity of imports is reaching a new high, a retailer discusses why he seeks out foreign merchandise—and why it sells in the U. S. A.

Benjamin Thompson, director of Design Research, Inc. of Cambridge, Massachusetts, a shop specializing in a complete range of interior furnishings, launched the store six years ago to fill a need he had felt personally. An architect by training, and a partner in The Architects Collaborative, which designs both commercial and residential buildings, he was aware of the difficulty of assembling from countless foreign and American sources ingredients that would make distinctively appointed interiors. What was needed, he concluded, was an international selection of furnishings, fabrics, and other contemporary accessories available from a single source.

To make Design Research the kind of store he envisioned, Thompson became an indefatigible shopper, uncovering little known sources and seeking out manufacturers and designers abroad who could supply products that met his standards of esthetic and practical excellence. The store, which began in 1951 as a two-room shop with a two-man staff, has enjoyed several major expansions into new wings as his stock has grown to include tableware, glassware, painting and sculpture, and jewelry, much of which is hard to find even in big city specialty shops. It now has a staff of twenty.

Imports currently account for a major portion of Design Research's stocks; that this has meant a continuing upswing in business may hold some lessons for American designers and manufacturers. What is particularly interesting is the question of why the imports are growing more popular with consumers here. Some of their appeal may lie in factors beyond the control of designer or manufacturer—the availability of craftsmanship or labor, for instance; but Americans like them by and large because of the way designers have made them look and work. At least so Ben Thompson believes on the basis of his retailing experience, and we have asked him to elaborate on this viewpoint in the following interview.

What do Americans especially want from abroad?

"There is a demand for unusual things, whether they come from Italy or Albany. It is hard to intellectualize on the value of being exotic—try it with poetry or good food; the necessity is doubtful to one who hasn't been touched. But there is a value in both a certain specialness and simple, useful common articles. Yet as a retailer you must know what you're looking for. It is combinations of things —whether colors, herbs or interior paraphernalia—that produce personality. In the U. S., we are heavily industrialized, while Europe retains some handcraft traditions.

86

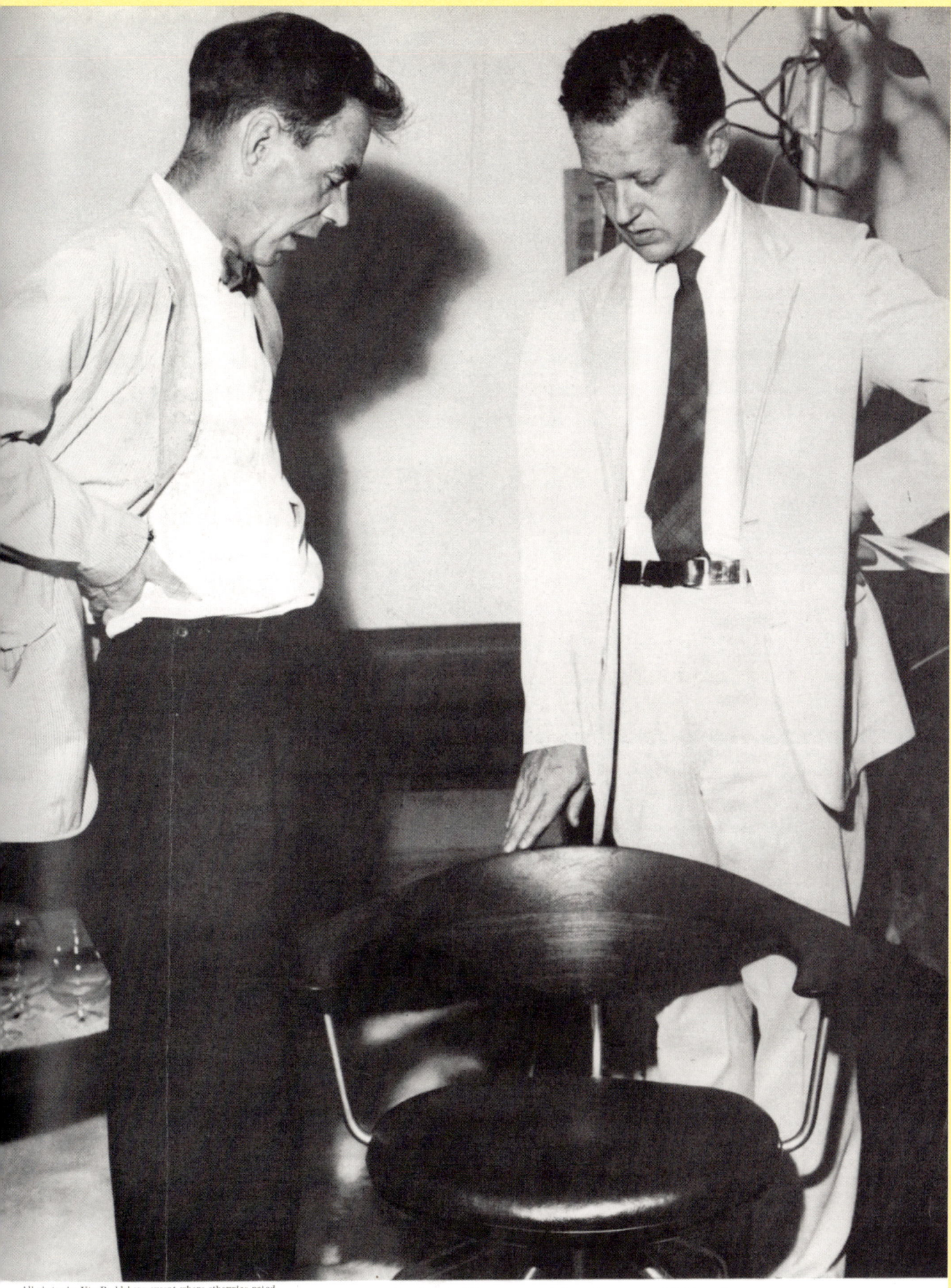

All photos by Uta Buddeberg except where otherwise noted

Benjamin Thompson (right) discusses with his sales manager, Claud Bunyard, a newly imported Hans Wegner desk chair.

Experiencing the Store 53

U. S. Retailer

which sometimes result in 'one-of-a-kind' products. As time passes and the world develops fewer artisans, certain handcraft items will take on even greater value. The link with the past is appreciated, particularly those things which have retained a folk-way shape, material and use for thousands of years.

"In the U.S. concern with style-change and the seeming economic necessity of 'keeping up with the market' has resulted in confusion of design direction. We have a Japanese phase with oriental-type furniture which a percentage of manufacturers produce that year. Then some magazines develop the 'latest' colors, all furniture is lowered six inches, and you have a new 'trend.' If you have a bad back and can't raise yourself from a low chair, you don't furnish your house that year. (I have even noticed copying by Scandinavians of flamboyant Italian ideas and then recopying by the Italians of the Scandinavian foolishness.) But the European designers have a less self-conscious approach. I guess they've been around longer. When the Scandinavian designs a high desk for a small room to hold small objects, he may be influenced by the roll-top desk design. But he's trying to solve a simple problem in an obvious way. He usually isn't influenced by 'the trend.' When the roll-top desk arrives in the U.S. it suddenly becomes a great invention—nobody thought of it until now, apparently. The trouble is that American designers have often overlooked pedestrian problems of space, of function, of use in the search for some extravagant expression, such as a pear-shaped coffee table of impossible finish and built-in native cactus. The result is that at Design Research we often buy Scandinavian goods since those designers have

↑ *Design Research, Inc. carries unique goods which often do not appear even in large foreign specialty shops.*

Top *"For thousands of years people have been working on the problem of designing implements with which to eat. Here are the latest patterns sold by Design Research, illustrating the shape and form of stainless steel forks and spoons."*

→ *"Seven variations on enclosing, directing, transmitting light from a simple bulb on a cord. The materials are metal, paper and glass. Eliminating base, stem, and stand, the hanging lamp is simplest solution."*

88

54 Design Research

"Arzberg porcelain cups: the lines are simple, unaffected and relatively timeless. Mixed in are cups from the Finnish firm, Arabia. They have been producing the sort of unaffected designs for which Americans will pay a premium."

Experiencing the Store 55

U. S. Retailer

a more relaxed attitude toward designing for the daily routines of living."

What are the problems of importing from Europe?

"Obviously, direct importing involves some technical rigmarole that implies an efficient internal organization. Finding important products at the right price is always a puzzle. This does not necessarily mean that we look for inexpensive things. We don't, but we try to find products which fill the elementary furnishing vocabulary. However, many European things become too expensive when imported to the U.S.A. through a complex chain; unfortunately they become luxury items to the customer. Competition in finding the new and the unusual is great; essentially we all work with the same parts and often it's a matter of combinations rather than uniqueness. Difficulties are encountered dealing with small foreign manufacturers, few of whom can afford even travel to the U.S. to discover the intricacies of national distribution, and usually do not realize the scale of this country. We have often thought that the best distribution system for 'good design' products would be this: a series of regional agents (quality design stores) located in eight or ten principal areas of the country — Boston, New York, Washington, Atlanta, Chicago, Dallas, Los Angeles, San Francisco, Miami — group advertising and pooled orders but direct purchasing by each member store."

What kinds of products are easiest to sell?

"Furniture is perhaps easiest to sell once it arrives in this country. Obviously, it is the most difficult to handle, ship, protect, etc. Textiles are the easiest to import. Since textiles must be bought in large quantities from manufacturers, a small store generally does better through a wholesaler who buys in quantity.

"Lighting fixtures are an enigma for us. New lighting designs in this country are constantly copied and downgraded. For some reason the better, simpler lamps are expensive. Lamps by the thousands have yet to be designed while there is an endless procession of style change with little concern for really good design in lighting."

What are the major differences in the designers' overall situation here and abroad?

"Historically the European designer is not as commercialized, though we hear the picture is changing. At the same time, observations from Scandinavia, Austria and Italy suggest that certain designers are closer to the shops which produce their articles than are those in the United States. Because of the abundance in these three countries of small shops, it may be easier and more stimulating for designers to have their own articles produced for direct sales, like Auboeck in Austria and Bojesen in Denmark, who have a multitude of special designs produced in small separate workshops around Vienna and Copenhagen.

"One interesting example is Augusto Morello of La Rinascente. Initially trained at Olivetti, this designer-engineer develops ideas for the largest department store in Milan (and Italy). He prods other designers and manufacturers to develop ideas which can be produced at home in Italy. From his office several floors above the buying public, he watches the response to these ideas. His relationship to both the department store and the public is much closer than that of the more specialized U. S. designer."

↑ *"One of the oldest pliable natural materials, wood has a character impossible to imitate. Why try? Variations on a slice of a tree by a skilled craftsman bring admiration not only of the materal but also of the 'art' employed to obtain the result."*

Below: cups and containers in varying colors by Kay Franck.

Bottom: "A container to hold and from which to pour hot liquids. The top should stay on, the handle support the hand."

90

56 Design Research

Foreign designs, such as the toys shown above and the Danish rocking horse and bed at left, are a constant source of interest and stimulation to designers in this country. Taking their place beside American merchandise, they are becoming by far the most popular sellers in some areas. Mr. Thompson says: "Our buying public has been most intelligent, and we don't talk down to them. They seem to both trust us and enjoy the sense of participation. This is half the fun of running our kind of business."

Experiencing the Store 57

"Designs from Abroad: Finland's Designs," *Industrial Design*, September 1959. The article introduced the hand-printed Printex fabric and Marimekko dresses, as well as three-dimensional works by leading Finnish artists in ceramic, metal, and glass.

DESIGNS FROM ABROAD

Design Research gives Americans long-needed review of Finnish design

Above and below: Pietinen   2   3   Studio Wendt

98

58   Design Research

As the first major exhibition of Finnish design to be seen in this country in recent years, the show which opened at Cambridge's Design Research, Inc. this summer has received an enthusiastic welcome. A cross-section of objects for the Finnish home, it includes Finland's industrial design as well as her arts and crafts, and ranges from mass-produced chairs to textiles, ceramics, rugs, furniture, sculpture, toys and women's fashions.

Finland's high standards were evident at the eleventh Triennale in Milan (ID, July, 1957) where six of the 28 first prizes, including the Grand Prix, went to Finnish products. These high standards, which were established long before the last Triennale, are impressively maintained in the present exhibition. But Finland has embarked in several new directions since the Triennale. Although her designers continue to emphasize the natural qualities of the materials with which they work, some of them are developing increasingly elaborate forms. Kaj Franck, for instance, who has long been familiar for his elegantly simple, natural lines, has moved to quite baroque forms in his onion-shaped decanters (ID, October, 1958) in the current show. And even the blown-glass vase (right) is a more formally elaborate object than one would have expected from him a few years ago. Surprisingly embellished

1. *Bowls in earth brown chamotte by Kyllikki Salmenhaara.*
2. *Glass bowls. Timo Sarpaneva.*
3. *Tobacco jug of Britannia metal by Bertel Yardberg.*
4. *Blown-glass vase with bird stopper by Kaj Franck.*

Experiencing the Store 59

Marimekko was the uniform for all D/R staff, female and male, both on the floor and behind the scenes, creating a whirl of moving color throughout the store's many levels. Mary Brewster Kennedy, left, and an associate confer on a Willow sofa, a vernacular classic that also served as a spacious daybed.

OPPOSITE, NEAR RIGHT:
Sales staff Heinke Brendler on the phone.

TOP, FAR RIGHT:
Each staff member brought her individual style to the dresses she selected.

BOTTOM, FAR RIGHT:
Frances Gitter, head of the Marimekko department, in Kivet black and white dots.

Anne Flynt Amory Solley "**In some ways D/R was used as a house — *our* house.**"

Lorna Dawson Elkus Ann Holmes was the ultimate store floor manager. She embodied the concept that Ben had, which was based on hospitality. Ann was a big, blond, loud Swedish girl with a huge laugh and fantastic legs. She wore these very short Marimekkos in bright colors. And she was running everything. She had come from the hotel business so she was really a very practical kind of person.

Christa Marcelli In 1957, I was just here from Germany. My dream was to live in New York for a year, and I tried everything and I couldn't seem to get someone to sponsor me. Because my father had studied at the Bauhaus, I wrote to Ise Gropius, not really expecting an answer, but within three days she invited me and said, "This friend of mine just opened a store, and I don't know if they're looking for anyone," but she gave me the train schedule and said, "Come up and we can meet in Ben's office about five, and then we'll meet you and you can come stay with us."

My mother had given me this little fur-covered seal from Iceland as a going-away present. I walked to the store, and there were all these little seals lined up identical to mine! And I thought "this is it! I have to work there." The next morning Ben interviewed me for two hours. He kept saying, "There are no jobs," and how bad he felt about that. I had worked for a similar store in Germany that had a lot of the same goods, and I was familiar with the merchandise, so I kept pointing out that I knew the designers. At the end, I was halfway out the door and he said, "Can you start on Monday?"

60   Design Research

Mary Brewster Kennedy, D/R staff, 1957–69
I came to work there because I liked looking in the window! My husband was an architect, and I was very much interested in what we used to call "modern architecture." From living with him I knew something about it, but I never had much to *do* with it. When my daughter got old enough to take care of herself by going to school, I thought, "Well, why don't I find something I really like to do?" So I went to D/R, knocked on the door, and Claud Bunyard was there. All I did was to tell him that I liked what he had and that I'd like to work there. And he said, "Well, I'll think it over," and I went off, wondering. Then he called me up and told me to come in, which I did. And it was very useful for my education as I was kind of rotated to different departments.

Anne Flynt Amory Solley, D/R staff, 1960–67
In the summer of 1959 I was shopping at D/R and Claud Bunyard came up to me and asked if I wanted to model at a party to introduce Marimekko to the United States. It was a nice party with Finnish food, and they used all the things from the accessories department. It was the opening of the Marimekko department at D/R, September 1959. Armi Ratia was there. I met Armi and she made nice remarks about how I looked in one of the dresses. Of course I wanted the dress but I couldn't afford it.

Nancy Hemenway Ben liked personable young women as his staff, and he liked you to be educated. He liked it if you spoke a language or two and had traveled. That seemed to be the criteria more than any specific skill. I don't recall that retail experience ever came up. The reason he hired me was my sheer enthusiasm because I had never seen anything like Marimekko. I am from Arkansas, but when I saw that store something just clicked. I thought, "This is it!"

Experiencing the Store 61

Nancy Hemenway "**We always wanted to do an ad showing how many Nobel Prize winners wore Finn Farmer shirts. That was our idea of who wore the shirts, the best and the brightest of men. We could count them.**"

Bold Marimekko designs were scaled to work with architecture, large enough to read across the room as a wall covering or space divider, a quality D/R demonstrated in every store. Here, intimate furniture display spaces are created by hanging lengths of an overscaled flower pattern.

Florence Seiders, *Retailing Daily,* 1954
In this college town, Design Research draws a heavy transient trade, mostly visiting alumni, which has led to a steadily growing business in china, glassware, and accessories—and also to furniture sales.

Clients for the firm's interior decorating services are described by Mr. Bunyard as "largely young married couples, most of them university graduates, and also a number of middle-aged couples who are doing over their homes after their children have married." These customers, for the most part, come from a "solid wedge" from Waltham around to Lexington, where many faculty members from Harvard and the Massachusetts Institute of Technology live. This is also an area where many modern homes have been built in recent years.

"With so many young married couples moving into new homes, our summer business has been very good," Mr. Bunyard stated. He noted that the firm does a big business in dining tables and chairs. "We seem to have become specialists in those items. We more than broke even during our first six months' operation, and we look forward to even better business when we can carry out our expansion plans," said Mr. Bunyard.

Anne Flynt Amory Solley Everybody bought wedding presents at D/R. Bowls were always good. Toward the end people could actually register there. We had some beautiful Mexican glasses with a blue rim that were handblown. The other really popular thing was the different-size carafes for wine or salad dressing. They were big handblown carafes by Kaj Franck for Iittala. They came in three pieces and the stopper was shaped like a bird. I still have a small one with the bird. There were candles and Finnish candlesticks turned out of natural wood. Also Iittala glassware that was very plain and went with everything. And then of course the Arabia china. People would buy patterned things as accent pieces.

Nancy Gathercole Riaz Speaking of who shopped at the store, there was James Watson. He and an Englishman by the name of Francis Crick got the Nobel Prize for their discovery of the DNA double helix. He was a constant customer. I think he came in because there were so many attractive ladies—as well as to buy a teacup.

Christa Marcelli For a while we offered a 20 percent discount for architects. All of a sudden, everybody in Cambridge was an architect. I know there are a lot of architects, but...

The first summer that I went to Denmark and Copenhagen, I saw half the customers that I knew from Design Research buying their own products!

From *The New Yorker*
December 28, 1963

Talk of the Town: New Store
By Geoffrey Hellman

One of the newest and most unusual stores in town is D/R International, which opened a couple of weeks ago, in a five-story house on East Fifty-seventh Street, with a party that lasted until three in the morning. Its intention, it announced in a press release, is to select "from all parts of the world the best in contemporary furniture" and to display, "under one roof, complementary lines of fabrics, rugs, lamps, tables, and kitchenware—in short, everything necessary to furnish a house, an apartment, or a series of business offices." Owned by Design Research, a mother emporium of similar scope in Cambridge, Massachusetts, it has an unusual president—Benjamin Thompson, an architect and the chairman of the Department of Architecture at Harvard. Dropping in at the store the day after the party, we found Mr. Thompson—a blond, curly-haired man in his middle forties, wearing a blond polo coat—wandering about among his wares. "I keep this on because otherwise people ask me to wait on them," he said. "Have an apple."

We selected one from a large Finnish bowl on a nearby table, and solicited Mr. Thompson's curriculum vitae.

"I was born in Minnesota," he said. "My family founded the First National Bank of St. Paul. After school in Minnesota, in California, and in Connecticut, and a couple of years at the University of Virginia, I went to the Yale School of Art and Architecture, from which I graduated in 1941. Architecturally, it was a very exciting period. People in this country had just begun to think about modern architecture; anyone who did anything modern was a hero. Yale was a good school. It never did have a serious formulation of its purpose, but it exposed you to many influences, which was fine."

We asked Mr. Thompson what happened after New Haven.

"Well, it was the war, and I went into construction; I helped build a small-arms plant outside Minneapolis," he said. "After six months, I came to New York and worked for the Corps of Engineers on the camouflage of our sixteen-inch batteries at Montauk Point. Then I joined the Navy, and served as a deck officer on a corvette for the rest of the war."

In 1946, following a postwar stint with the Office of Strategic Services, Mr. Thompson joined some New Haven architectural friends and, with them and Walter Gropius, who was then chairman of Harvard's Department of Architecture, formed the Architects' Collaborative. "We started out doing houses, mostly for middle-income groups, and then we began doing schools and college buildings," he said. "We've designed thirty or forty public schools in Massachusetts, Rhode Island, Connecticut, and Vermont, and buildings at Andover, Harvard, Brandeis University, and Williams. Gropius is over eighty, but he's still active in the firm. I opened the Cambridge store in 1953."

"Why?" we asked.

"I believe the furnishing of the interior is part of architecture," Mr. Thompson said. "You can't draw a line between the two things. Once you put up a building, it's very difficult to get it properly furnished. Very often, you finish a building and the damn thing is ruined by its occupancy. By—call it environment, if you will, I wanted to show people the next step. Even things like dresses should be attacked not as a style problem but as an architectural problem, arising from the function of the activity the wearer is involved in. We simply don't recognize *fashion*. I think that for art to be part of our life we must live with it, not just go to museums. In a way, things like museums and Lincoln Center kill art and music. Art is *not* for particular people but should be in everything you do—cooking and, God knows, in the bread on the table, in the way everything is *done*. In Cambridge, I think we've served a little as a museum and a little as a store, and we hope to do the same here."

After remarking that he lives in a new house of his own design in Lexington, Massachusetts, with his wife and five children, Mr. T. took us on a five-story tour of environmental objects culled from fifteen countries; we were struck by their cohesive presentation—in living room, dining room, kitchen, children's room, and bedroom areas furnished for use—and by the number of attractive young women engaged in selling them. "I don't want professional salesladies," their employer told us. "I want girls with freshness, vitality, and enthusiasm. You have to get the right feeling in the store, and you get it through the salesladies. I want the store to be a place where wives can come and bring their husbands, and bring their children. In Cambridge, and now here, I have chosen to work with girls. Not a difficult choice."

He smiled, and, as we left, pressed another apple on us.

D/R Collaborates with Julia

After twenty years in France studying, cooking, recipe testing, and struggling with American publishers, Julia Child achieved publication of *Mastering the Art of French Cooking* in 1961. The book was a radical departure in cookbook concept and format, developed with her French coauthors Simone Beck and Louisette Bertholle.

That same year Julia returned from a long European diplomatic tour with her husband, Paul Child, and settled in Cambridge, Massachusetts. They soon joined friends, neighbors, Harvard faculty, and students as customers of Design Research. It happened that Paul Child had been Ben's teacher in prep school; reconnections were made. Thus, a year later, Julia had no hesitation in ambling over to Ben's office and declaring in her ebullient voice, "I have contracted with public television to show Americans how to cook the French way. I am going to be 'The French Chef' every week, starting with three pilot shows, and I need my *batterie de cuisine!*" Impressed by the parallels in their modern lifestyle missions, Ben invited Julia to present her list of equipment and decor needs to his senior staff. D/R was eager to collaborate in a public demonstration of new informal traditions in cooking-dining-living, which depended on well-designed cookware that would go handsomely from stove to table.

Only a few knowledgeable friends and supporters believed that French cooking could pull in an American audience. But Ben's deal was struck: Julia submitted her weekly menus, and the *batterie* requests were delivered to the studio every Tuesday by D/R staff that dressed the set and later took it away. The audience saw a parade of colorful and professional-quality kitchen products from France and Finland, even a backdrop of lamps and Marimekko panels hanging behind the dinner table.

Formally launched in 1963, *The French Chef* had a record-breaking run through 1976. During that time, D/R created the mise-en-scène for all of the shows from 1963 to 1967. By then, the show was a success; the producers budgeted the purchase of a permanent *batterie* with which, in her successive long-running programs, Julia kept on cooking until 2002.

OPPOSITE: Kitted out by D/R—Julia wears a Marimekko apron and the lighting is D/R's signature wooden Disa lamp from Spain. D/R provided custom settings for each week's episode of *The French Chef*.

ABOVE: Julia visiting the Thompsons in 1980.

BELOW: Ben and Jane cook for Julia and Paul, far left, in their Cambridge home, as photographed for a *Food & Wine* magazine story on the Thompsons as restaurateurs.

Experiencing the Store 65

Russell Morash

"We had to simulate atmosphere and style. Voilà! Those handsome D/R ladies arrived in stunning dresses, bearing tables, chairs, candles, tableware, a few flowers. They put us in business, or rather, into looking that way."

Russell Morash, director-producer of *The French Chef* (1963–73), WGBH

Filming a three-show pilot was impossible to imagine in 1962, when WGBH didn't have two twigs to rub. We had to scrounge for everything. We had had a terrible fire that burned our studios down, so we had to set up a fake kitchen in an auditorium owned by the Boston Gas Company in downtown Boston. There was gas for a stove, but running water was not to be had.

As a young producer with little culinary background, I knew we had to simulate atmosphere and style. Julia's transition from creating recipes in a bare-bones kitchen to putting ready dishes on a well-styled table would demand some gorgeous props. Voilà! Those handsome D/R ladies arrived in stunning dresses bearing tables, chairs, candles, tableware, runners, a few flowers, plates, and platters in combinations that could mix into a different look for each show. They put us in business, or rather, into *looking* that way.

As the three pilots were deemed a success, in early 1963 we filmed a thirteen-week series in a really primitive "kitchen" with a fake curtained window and a tub-style washer-dryer in the corner, generously provided by Cambridge Gas and Electric. We built a cooking island and wild walls faking the dining room, and filmed two complete programs in one day. Each time, Julia was live on camera for twenty-eight minutes without a break or a prompt. It was virtuoso cooking, and making it look easy took a lot of preparation.

Tizzie (Elizabeth) Lambert Sometimes Ruth Lockwood, Julia's assistant, would come in with a clipboard and list. She would know what Julia was planning to cook. There were two sets in the studio, the kitchen where she cooked and the dining room, which was meant to be next door. She would always outline what Julia planned to serve at the dining table and what kind of platters she needed, and how many place settings and place mats she wanted at the table. Flowers were a budgetary no-no, but we managed to round them up.

Julia had much of her own cookware, but there would be other things, like a fish poacher needed to prepare her entrée, a large Finel pot for boiling, a colorful enamel casserole, and of course the Vallauris clay pots for baked dishes. She was showing off our innovative wares—bright cheerful cookware, sauté pans, earthy dinnerware, and even Cuisinart choppers—as if they were the norm for any American household. Which they soon became.

Each week I would organize all the goods and go off to the studio to set up the

Anne Flynt Amory Solley In 1962 Julia went to Ben about needing sets, kitchen equipment, and dining room setups for the weekly show, starting with the filming of a pilot series. Thereafter she came to the accessories department each week to pick out equipment she wanted. Ben had us assemble the *batterie de cuisine* and carry it over to the TV station for each show.

There were furniture, pots and pans, table settings, serving pieces, even lamps and dishcloths. The new idea of stove-to-table cookware was prominent in our selections. And it was usefully interactive— Julia would tell us about then-unknown quality tools and equipment we should carry in Accessories. D/R staff covered Julia's show equipment and set needs for sixty-six shows, from 1963 through 1966.

66 Design Research

dining room, which looked ready for a nice dinner party. We often used Marimekko fabrics and those wonderful Arabia china platters that were either oval or rectangular to show off the food being served. Paul Child was a good painter and his paintings were on the walls of the set.

Russell Morash *The French Chef* stayed at Cambridge Gas and Electric's primitive kitchen set until WBGH's new studio space was ready. Almost five years later *The French Chef* won its own studio space — and an Emmy, for Julia, in 1966.

Julia's sets introduced many prized products procured by D/R at her suggestion, which became D/R staples, such as the Peugeot pepper mill (her favorite), a superior wine cork pull, a garlic press, French sauté pans — all inaccessible to the American home chef until this program pulled ideas from across the Atlantic.

Henriette Mladota Julia did for cooking in America what Design Research did for living. Before Julia, kitchen stuff stayed in the kitchen behind closed doors, often with servants. Now Julia showed a beautiful casserole acting as a cooker and a serving dish — people could *see* that a casserole did not need to stay in the kitchen. Good-looking things could go to the table and the living room. Indeed, everybody could gather and work in the kitchen, then wash up after the meal — an idea unheard of a decade earlier.

Julia was determined to have the best tools for her craft. She was resolutely unstylish in this. Julia believed with Ben that something really practical is beautiful too. This means there was an integration of purpose and design — she had her pot lids hanging in graded sizes on the kitchen wall, looking useful and decorative and easy to find. She pointed out that a stainless knife would not hold its sharpness; it required real carbon steel, so we bought the best knives from her Parisian knife supplier, Dehillerin. Julia made it clear, on air and off, that "No gadget can replace a sharp knife."

Sara Moulton, executive chef, *Gourmet* magazine Julia really got people back in the kitchen for several reasons. First, she showed you how to cook. She was teaching French cuisine, but she was teaching good technique, period. Second, she made mistakes and didn't seem flustered by it. Later I think she went out of her way to make mistakes so she could show you how to fix them. The viewer thought, "If she isn't all worried about it being perfect on TV, why should I worry about it in my home?"

The last thing was that she was having so much fun. When we would do dinner parties out of her house, we would be in the middle of everything and she would turn around and say, "Oh, aren't we having so much fun?" It was contagious. She led the charge back into the kitchen.

Julia was also the first one to really encourage consumers to go into supermarkets and say, "I want a leek, I want a shallot." We didn't have access to the ingredients we do now, so chefs had to scramble. There was a boutique produce company that could get us then-unusual ingredients like fiddleheads in season or sorrel. Or fresh herbs, which were still a novelty. I would design a whole dish around a fresh herb, like Chicken with Fresh Thyme. Today, that is just one of a zillion ingredients.

OPPOSITE: A line of French copper pans—here used by Julia to demonstrate proper flipping technique—was custom-made in France and labeled Design Research.

Finel cooking pots, bowls, and coffeepot in bright blue were used regularly on *The French Chef*, where Julia showed colorful cookware going from stovetop to dining table.

Experiencing the Store

Burke House, Oyster Bay, N.Y., 1952-54

The Burke House was designed for Japanese art collector Mary Griggs Burke (a St. Paul neighbor of the Thompson family) and husband, Jackson Burke, a printer and book designer. The house's three floors are stacked rather than stepped in order to take advantage of the site's views of Long Island Sound, but the overall planning principles remain the same as in Ben's smaller, earlier projects: separating the functions of family life by levels, opening up the walls with huge windows in the public spaces, and sequestering the bedrooms.

The living room, raised high enough to have a view only of nature through its wall of glass, shows Ben's mixing ability at work: the only art is an Edo-period Japanese screen, which offers an alternative view of the clouds, and the furniture includes Hans Wegner caned chairs, Noguchi Akari lamps, and the first iteration of what came to be known as the D/R down sofa. Ben wrote: "It wasn't meant to have a pristine shape to be treated as a sculptural object. It was simply something comfortable to sit on and to look good."

More Wegner chairs turn up in the dining room, where they circle a table centered under a round, glowing skylight that brings natural light over the dining table deep into the house. The view from this lower level is of the house's Japanese-style garden, with pebbled beds and frothy trees. Across the garden, the later pool house (1961-62) is Ben's take on the glass box.

At Mary Griggs Burke's luxurious Long Island home, Ben created open-plan interiors with outdoor views on several levels, choosing D/R and Hans Wegner furniture to coordinate with Burke's Japanese art collection. He created the iconic Down Sofa Group for her living room, top left, and another pair of built-in sofas for the intimate study and den, bottom left.

BELOW: A view of one of the outdoor decks with Bahamian wicker chairs.

OPPOSITE: The living room facing Long Island Sound, seen from above.

A "Uniform for Intellectuals"
Marimekko Arrives

3

In the minds of many customers, Design Research and Marimekko were and are synonymous. When D/R introduced the loose shifts and brilliant prints to consumers in 1959, they were the exclusive American representative of Marimekko; this was just a year after the cotton fabrics were shown to the international design world at the 1958 World's Fair in Brussels. The striped shirt your father wore on Saturdays, the flower-covered comforter on your childhood bed, and the big dotted fabric you tacked to your dorm room wall were all there thanks to D/R. The store, then six years old, had been selling furniture and home accessories successfully, but the addition of Marimekko boosted its profile and paved the way for national expansion. Ben Thompson and Marimekko founder Armi Ratia were immediate and lifelong friends, bonding over their common ideas about the good life with good design, and cementing their friendship with visits to their mutual country retreats—his in Barnstable, Massachusetts, hers in Bokars, Finland. The Marimekko dress seemed to sum up the D/R aesthetic perfectly: it was bold, colorful, elegant, and ungirdled. When Jacqueline Kennedy, the glamorous future First Lady, appeared on the cover of *Sports Illustrated* in a red-and-pink shift, the success of the partnership was sealed.

A stack of Finn Farmer shirts, made by Marimekko after 1956 in the striped Piccolo fabric, designed by Vuokko Nurmesniemi. The tin buttons became a signature of both men's and women's clothes, and Nurmesniemi eventually created more than 200 Piccolo colorways.

Boldly patterned, with hand-screened overlapping colors and dense figures, Marimekko fabrics were used both architecturally and sartorially. A view of the San Francisco store in 1965 shows the textiles as hanging screens, in bolts, and on the racks.

72   Design Research

The 1958 World's Fair was the first international expo since before World War II. Once-warring nations like the Soviet Union and Italy, and once-occupied allies like the Netherlands, France, Poland, and Finland, were all participating. Edward Durell Stone designed an exhibition pavilion for the United States that showcased the nation's open spirit, displaying everything interesting to be found here, from futurist automotive dreams to exquisite carved decoys to a towering slice of a giant redwood— an eclectic sampling of the American experience. American designers and architects returned to Europe, some for the first time in twenty years, in anticipation of discovery. It was their first chance to see new work by the world's best. There were to be national pavilions by France's Le Corbusier, Italy's rising Peressutti & Rogers, Finland's Reima Pietilä, and Japan's Kunio Mayekawa.

Ben traveled to Brussels as a buyer, his eyes open for the work of fellow architects and for the products of designers and craftsmen closeted during the war years. He sought out the Finnish Pavilion, remembering Alvar Aalto's version at the 1938 fair, which had captured the essence of Finland's island forests of tall pine trees, their trunks reaching for the sky. In Brussels, the same arboreal solitude was evoked by Pietilä's slatted pavilion, with an installation by designer Tapio Wirkkala.

Ben studied the selvedge on a panel: *Printex Kivet Maija Isola.* He wrote it down. Coincidentally, a former TAC employee named Robert Eskridge would return from a Fulbright in Finland, where he and his wife, Peggy, who also worked for TAC, had befriended Armi Ratia. Once all were back in Cambridge, Thompson asked Eskridge to contact Ratia, and Marimekko was added to his D/R exhibition of the latest Finnish design planned for June 1959. Armi Ratia arrived with a staff of one, designer Vuokko Eskolin (later Nurmesniemi), following a large shipment of bright textiles. The exhibition, which also included the work of Kaj Franck, Antti Nurmesniemi, Timo Sarpeneva, and Oiva Toikka, filled the ground floor of the small shop on Brattle Street and wowed the Cambridge community.

Marimekko products rounded out the inventory of Design Research with additions to the collection in accessories, upholstery, and, most of all, fashion. Marimekko was then a small Finnish craft business, but Armi Ratia was ready to take on the new world. The easy comfort of her untraditional styles gave women of every age and shape permission to move freely and assuredly, at just the moment when American women began to seek an equal place in society. The *New York Times* labeled the dresses the "Uniform for Intellectuals"; soon the dresses, and the fabrics, bags, boots, and housewares also sold in the striped, floral, and abstract prints, spread beyond the narrow confines of Cambridge society. They worked equally well as an antidote to French designer fashions in New York, or as an addition to the supergraphics of the Bay Area architects in San Francisco. Marimekko traveled, and so did the women wearing it.

Voices

Ben Thompson

"Marimekko clothes have grown to meet different hours, situations, and climates of daily life. An important idea being that everybody of all sizes should be able to dress happily."

TOP: Armi Ratia in 1964, against a Lokki fabric background.

BOTTOM: Ben introduces Armi Ratia to Faneuil Hall, Boston, 1977.

OPPOSITE: Marimekko in motion in Harvard Square. The scallop pattern and dress were designed by Annika Rimala.

Ben Thompson, Memoirs Marimekko really means "a dress for little Mary"—a kind of house dress—but since the gay and fresh Finnish dresses came to us in America, it simply has become a way of dressing, saving time, and adding a lot of inspiration to this part of life.

Colorful, simple, and comfortable, Marimekko arrived as the alternative to the tired informality of "just staying home." Why not do it in fresh happy cottons? The Marimekko clothes have grown to meet different hours, situations, and climates of daily life. An important idea being that everybody of all sizes should be able to dress happily. Color can do it for you, and certainly this is new thinking about "ideal" models. There is a Marimekko way of thinking both in terms of classics and extra kicks... Is it just a new way of using stripes, or a cotton boot with flowers up to your knee? Or a triangular scarf to end a knitted total look?

Roberta Smith, art critic, *New York Times*, 2003 The company's founder and presiding spirit was Armi Ratia (1912–1979), who took over Printex, a small producer of hand-printed oilcloth that her husband had purchased in 1949. Applying her Bauhaus-inspired vision of total, coherent design, Ratia stepped into the public eye with a fashion show, called Marimekko-projekti, staged in a restaurant in Helsinki in 1951.

Ratia had a strong design sense, a good nose for talent, and, judging by the diversity of the designs here, a healthy tolerance for those whose sensibility differed from hers. Ratia's first two designers were Maija Isola, who began her career specializing in deft, Dufyesque glosses on peasant motifs, and Vuokko Nurmesniemi, who favored the casual geometric patterns that became a Marimekko signature. Ms. Nurmesniemi was responsible for the familiar Piccolo fabric (1953) whose narrow stripes became synonymous with the unisex shirts named Jokapoika (Everyboy). While some patterns are printed with stripes of a single color on white fabric, the most interesting alternate two colors that overlap slightly to form a third.

Jack Lenor Larsen, textile designer In 1957 I met Armi Ratia and Vuokko Nurmesniemi, then her designer, at their first show outside of Helsinki, which was at Artek in Stockholm. Printex was founded because the Finns absolutely could not afford to import anything. They had been in the war six years longer than anybody else and they owed Russia huge reparations. They weren't going to be importing clothes or any consumer goods. Armi's husband owned the Printex fabric company and Vuokko knew how to make patterns and dresses and shirts, and in supplying the Finns they soon had something the world wanted.

After the war modern fabrics were slubby and trying to be something a little more interesting than canvas. Armi was using the simplest cotton weaves. Those of us who were printing made every attempt to disguise where repeats occurred. Vuokko made a feature of it.

Ristomatti Ratia, founder Décembre Oy, 1970–74; Marimekko creative director, 1974–85 We used a normal hand-screening technique, but the total screen size and area was bigger so as to allow the large, bold, painterly images; and they left large distances to the repeats. Overprinting was both the charm and the obstacle. Some people think it is charming and others that there is a mistake.

Every design was hand-printed, and the ladies went over the table-length fabric say four to five times to give the fabric a deep penetration of color on the heated silkscreen table. After printing, the lengths of fabric were lifted above the tables to dry. Then they were rolled up and placed in a steamer especially designed for setting the color. Those prints are famous for their ability to last forever. Ben wore green, the same favorite-color shirts all his life.

Hedvig Hedqvist and Rebecka Tarschys, *Marimekko: Fabrics Fashion Architecture,* 2003 Printed textiles with distinctive patterns were already present in the home furnishings market at the time. In the 1950s the furniture company Herman Miller introduced geometrical and stylized patterns in strong colors by architect Alexander Girard. The fabrics were used for furniture designs by Charles and Ray Eames. Girard had traveled with the Eameses to Mexico, and in 1959 he designed the interior of La Fonda del Sol, a restaurant in the Time-Life Building, New York. Its checkerboard-square tables, tablecloths and napkins, and striped porcelain chinaware, all in bright folkloric colors, must have been an inspiration for Marimekko. Knoll International, another progressive American design firm, also used Swedish textile prints, including the geometrical Pythagoras pattern by architect Sven Markelius, which hangs in the United Nations headquarters.

Anna Sui, fashion designer Marimekko was right for the sixties moment and ushered in the whole mod look. You can see the same influences in Knoll prints and in the work of Alexander Girard, which also uses a combination of Mexican colors. Both Girard and Marimekko were inspired by folk art.

Jack Lenor Larsen **"Marimekko was a furnishings aesthetic in clothes for the first time."**

A "Uniform for Intellectuals" 75

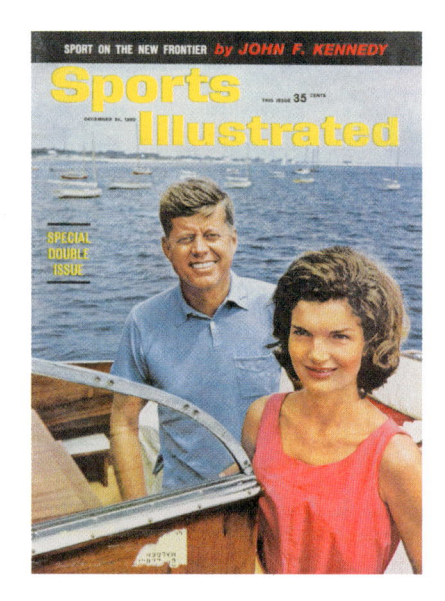

TOP: When a new shipment of Marimekko dresses came, Ben would dispatch D/R salesgirls to parade around Harvard Square displaying the "Just Arrived" styles.

ABOVE: Jackie Kennedy's appearance on the December 1960 cover of *Sports Illustrated* wearing Marimekko set off a nationwide buying frenzy.

Robert Eskridge, The Architects Collaborative, 1958–63 In 1957, while I was an architecture student at MIT, my wife, Peggy, and I were working for TAC in Cambridge. I then received a Fulbright Grant for study in Finland in 1957 and 1958. Near the end of our year, after traveling in Europe, we became good friends in Helsinki with Armi Ratia, who had a silk-screen production factory and was thinking about an overseas market for her colorful fabrics and unique dresses.

Ben Thompson, Memoirs By the late 1950s I was in contact with and presenting the work of many designer/craftsmen in Finland and Scandinavia, Aalto products and furniture, also Tapio Wirkkala and Timo Sarpaneva, and younger furniture designers like Mogensen, Mathsson, and Hansen.

Then in 1958, like most designers of the world, I attended the Brussels World Fair, and gave special attention to the Finnish Pavilion by Pietalä. There, as I expected, I found an abundant display of classic and new Finnish craft designs, which I hungered to transport in toto for a complete floor exhibition of the nation's quality work, as I had done with Japan in 1956. And in the pavilion I encountered Printex, which I also determined to locate for Design Research on returning home.

Robert Eskridge We showed Ben Thompson a group of dresses bought from Armi's shop, and he asked us to contact her. Ben was organizing an exhibition of the Finnish craft wares he had seen in Brussels for D/R. Peggy designed the poster for the exhibition. She and I worked with Ben and store staff to organize the exhibit spaces and tables. At the very end, Armi's designer, Vuokko Nurmesniemi, arrived and took charge of integrating the exhibition materials into something special.

Photographed by TONY VACCARO

The U.S. goes for colorful, simple Finnish style

Bright Spirit of Marimekko

On giant woodpile, Finnish girls wear evening dresses. Dress with point in front costs $51, circle prints (right) cost $57.

In Finland where nature is often gray, color is a dictate of modern design. Finnish color—sometimes bold, sometimes muted, often set in strong geometrics and unfussy florals—is sweeping the world in the form of Marimekkos. These are the hand-printed cotton shifts that were first worn in the U.S. by young intellectual college girls. Marimekkos today constitute a kind of year-round uniform of sophisticated simplicity of hordes of snappy dressers across the country. The literal translation of Marimekko—which is also the name of the company that makes and exports the dress—is "little dress for Mary." But broadly speaking it is practically a philosophy of design that stresses freedom from fashion rather than fashion. It encompasses apparel for men, women and children as well as household articles. The pictures on these pages, showing the radiant array, were taken in Finland—and the listed prices are stateside.

"Bright Spirit of Marimekko," *LIFE*, June 1966. Photographed in Finland by Tony Vaccaro.

A "Uniform for Intellectuals"

78   Design Research

Flowers blooming on giant sun umbrella ($150) provide protection from Finland's summer sun which shines practically around the clock. The bikinis ($32), classically minimal, are in cotton prints.

Anja Vaccaro (right), Finnish wife of Photographer Tony Vaccaro, cycles in Porvoo in broadly striped pullover and slacks ($64). Every print is designed and hand printed in the Marimekko factory.

Clinging to their umbrellas like high-wire artists, three Finns walk across a barge in shift-shape dresses: red banded in blue (left, $33) white with vest-like bodice ($43) and half red, half blue design ($47).

A "Uniform for Intellectuals" 79

A pretty Finn wears a modern striped apron ($27). Its ruffled hem and cap sleeves are taken from the traditional aprons worn by the girls on either side. Many Marimekko designs are inspired by folk costumes.

80　Design Research

In striped dresses, barefoot girls (left) liven up stone-paved streets of Porvoo, a small city near Helsinki. Short-sleeved dress at left costs $42, long-sleeved one in the middle costs $45 and sleeveless version at right, with contrast panel, costs $44.

With her blue shirt ($28) tucked into her skirt, Erika Ratia, daughter of founder of Finnish company that makes Marimekko dresses, talks with friend in striped shirt ($20).

A "Uniform for Intellectuals" 81

In sturdy boots, Brigitte Juslin, a young painter, wears an at-home dress ($78) with puffed-up sleeves in a Finnish field. Burning to restore soil's vigor is centuries-old practice.

Wearing helmets of stitched cotton, girls peer out over farmland. The helmets, whether close fitting aviator style (left and right) or crusader-shaped (center), cost $14.

82   Design Research

Winsome Anne Pesonius pushes an antique baby carriage in a field of wheat nearly as tall as she. Her dress ($18) is a basic Marimekko shape. Because all Marimekkos are made without waistlines, some dissenters say the designs are for little girls and pregnant women only. Armi Ratia, the firm's founder, bristles at such a notion. "There is a Marimekko for every woman and of every type and age," he says. "From the beginning we had dresses designed for the very round little body we call the Happy Apple."

Ben Thompson, "Scenes from a Friendship," 1985 Together with Marimekko we made a little "selling" shop on the second floor of the old house on Brattle Street. Now we wanted to light the streets of Cambridge and Boston with color. The walls were white and pink. The exhibition was soon "alive" with customers and salesgirls in bold colors.

Lorraine De Wet Howes, D/R staff, 1957–60 All the dresses that Armi brought just walked right out the day of the exhibition opening. They just vanished that very day. We were all wearing them, and people were saying to the staff, "Is that yours or can we buy that?"

Then we started the little upstairs dress department, which I ran. I found that the rack of clothes was fabulous yet overwhelming to sell, so I would pick out two or three dresses every day and thumbtack them onto the wooden slats going up the stairs. As people came up they said, "I will have that one. I will have this one." You had to pull the chosen items out and set them aside—the demand was that tremendous.

Nancy Hemenway, D/R staff, 1968–76 With Armi and Ben, there was such a great friendship. It was wonderful to be introduced into that culture, because their way of living was so joyous. The work ran over into private life because the work was what they both loved to do most.

Margaret Turnbull Simon, D/R staff, 1969–75 At one early point Armi Ratia came to Ghirardelli on one of her not very common rounds. Of course we put in incredible energy to get the store absolutely beautiful and perfect. She came in and walked through the store as only she could do and looked around at everything. She came up to me and said, "Margaret, it looks perfectly beautiful. Now go and take something away." I looked at her and she said, "Life isn't perfection. Life isn't symmetry. There is a design principle in this. You line everything up like little toy soldiers and then you take something away."

Nancy Hemenway Armi just was. She lived a lifestyle and that's what she was. She led by example. She let her people come along, emerge, which is what Ben did too. Both Armi and Ben were larger-than-life kind of people. That's why they had so many great people around them—they gave room for growth and tons of responsibility.

The business was her personal aesthetic. That country house at Bökars on the Baltic was unbelievable. What she did there, her way of being, her sense of humor, the way she entertained, the food, the love of life. The furniture: she had a grand piano in her living room and three big rocking chairs. That was it for the living room, and you could just sit in the rocking chairs as she played the grand piano in a long flowing dress while someone served champagne. In another room there were two 10-foot-long couches with a table in between where large groups sat. The atmosphere was enchanting, like being in a movie. In the winter it gets dark in mid-afternoon, and Finnair pilots even land on snow. It is light twenty-four hours a day at midsummer in June. The Finns go crazy and don't sleep for two weeks, eating and drinking around the clock, playing and dancing. They store up the transient daylight.

The Life and Times of Marimekko and D/R, press release, 1960s "**Armi, as she will tell you at the drop of a 'trend' remark, doesn't give 'a gotemhell' about fashion.**"

Raymond Waites, D/R staff, 1975–78 I met Armi when she came to New York for Ben's "To Finland with Love" show in 1967. Helga, who worked on the Marimekko floor with Nancy, my wife, set up a dinner party for their arrival in America. It was going to be a small dinner party, four or five of us. But when word got around, it grew to a dinner for about fifty, all in our small apartment in Brooklyn Heights.

We wondered, "What in the world can we do for these international chic people?" We were kids from the South. We decided to fix the food that we grew up with — the fried chicken, the turnip greens, the corn bread, the black-eyed peas. It was a big Southern cookout dinner but very elegant.

As we watched them come up the three flights of stairs, we saw big arms filled with white roses. Armi, everywhere she went, brought big armloads of flowers. It is a beautiful memory to launch a wonderful evening. At the end, Armi and Risto came to us and said, "We want to see more of you." Every night for a week we went to a different restaurant, such as the new La Fonda del Sol, with her entourage of six to eight beautiful Finnish models brought for the show. She stayed at the St. Moritz on Central Park South. It was magic for two young kids just up from the South.

Lorna Dawson Elkus, D/R staff, 1961–70 Frances West [Gitter] was the Marimekko dress girl. She had been an actress. When I came to D/R she had long, dark, limp hair, wore cinch elastic belts, crinoline petticoats, and those big dirndl skirts with the ballerina flats and the pointy bras. That was the fashion. Armi Ratia, who was really clever, offered Frances a trip to Finland. They wined her, dined her, partied her, gave her all kinds of gifts, sent her back via Paris, where she bought Roger Vivier shoes. She went to London, where Mary Quant had just hit the news, and she got the miniskirt, the Vidal Sassoon haircut, and came back a changed person, with a completely new personal image.

Minkie West McKevitt, D/R staff, 1961–64, 1968 My sister Frances went several times a year to Finland to buy, and she was well treated. One time she brought a baby, her eldest daughter, and they were met at the airport with a nanny and a fur coat to wear. They had a very good relationship and it kept up for many years. She was an actor before she started at D/R in 1959 and she ended up doing wonderfully well with Shakespeare & Company in Lenox, Mass. She passed away in November 1999.

Ben and Armi's close relationship was reflected in all the correspondence, written and shipped, between the company and the store.

OPPOSITE: Dresses on display at 57 Brattle Street, hung to show the easy fit and possibility for movement (no girdle required).

A "Uniform for Intellectuals" 85

Eugenia Sheppard **"The Lilly may be fashion, but the Marimekko is design."**

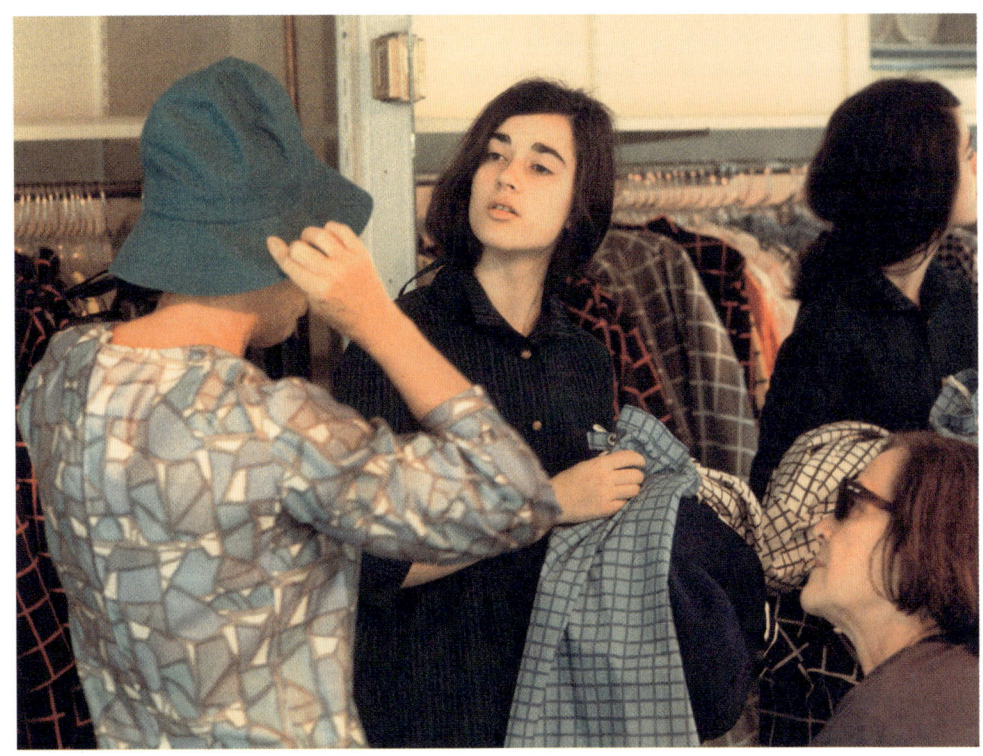

Eugenia Sheppard, fashion critic, *New York Herald Tribune*, 1963 What Lilly Pulitzer has done for socialites, a charming, fresh-faced Finnish woman, Armi Ratia, has done for intellectuals—given them a uniform. Though the Lilly is a slinky, slit Oriental-type sheath and the Marimekko, invented by Armi Ratia, is more generously cut, the two dresses are first cousins. They reduce fashion to a common denominator of simplicity. They are basic shapes made in a variety of fabrics so that, once sold, women can collect them, and how they dearly love to collect. Both dresses are relatively inexpensive, as fashions go, and often cost under $50.

Naturally, the Marimekko is a much more intellectual performance than the Lilly. Armi Ratia and her husband, Major Viljo Ratia, who run the factory together ten miles out of Helsinki, put their whole souls into the Marimekko. The hand-screened prints aren't just prints. "They have the value of thinking," according to Armi Ratia. Some are like paintings and others are graphic art. The Lilly may be fashion, but the Marimekko is design.

She would be the last to say that her design is a uniform for intellectuals. The way she puts it, the Marimekko is for women whose way of wearing clothes is to forget what they have on.

Her best customers are not only intellectuals but wives of intellectuals like architects, designers, and professors. In this country, the Marimekko got off to a flying start in Cambridge when it was introduced in the original Design Research shop started by a Cambridge architect, Benjamin Thompson. Hundreds of Radcliffe girls took it home to their mothers, and so the fad began.

The moment of transformation for Cambridge women of every age came in the upstairs dress department— a glance in the mirror confirmed how loose shifts liberated female figures. And for a place known for long, cold winters, the bright colors added natural warmth and festivity. The shapes and patterns matched wider social changes for women in the 1960s.

OPPOSITE: Hat and dress in the Suolampi pattern, designed by Vuokko Nurmesniemi.

A "Uniform for Intellectuals" 87

Revolutionary color combinations—saturated pink and orange, blue and green, red and purple—proved attention-getting for Marimekko customers, even in this relatively simple Rötti stripe.

OPPOSITE: Children were well treated by Marimekko, with their own corner at D/R for clothing and toy designs.

Lorraine De Wet Howes The biggest transition in the history of clothes was the sack chemise of 1957. As Yves Saint Laurent said, "You catch it like you catch a cold." In my mind it is the last universal fashion for women, after which there has been no one way to dress; from 1947 to 1957 we experienced the entire clothing cycle from what I call conservative retrograde—the tight waists, pointy bosoms, and round hips of the New Look to the sack chemise. When Marimekko arrived, the chemise had already happened, so women were not averse to wearing tentlike clothes, and the bright color palette was part of the new catch-it-like-you-catch-a-cold era.

Marimekko were the first apparel designers to put together blue and green. My grandmother, a famous dressmaker, used to say, "Blue and green shall never be seen." And I would say, "Why not? The sky is blue, the leaves are green. God knows what he is doing." Marimekko put pink and orange together, which was unthinkable. A fantastic revelation.

Astrid Vigeland, D/R staff, 1974–76 There were certainly very popular patterns, ones that sold better than others: Lokki, which was a wave pattern; Kaivo, the one with the elongated oval; and Melooni with the big circles.

Minkie West McKevitt The wonderful moment was when the boxes came from Finland. It was like Christmas opening the boxes and trying on dresses; all of us would gather to see what had arrived. The colors and the way they were combined were awesome—pink and orange, or purple and green, brown and purple. New ones came in every spring, even brighter and more cheerful.

Jane Thompson The clothes gave new freedom. The styles didn't demand of you, they permitted you: avoid the waist, play down the hips with a long line, show knees if you need to. Move easily—work, cook, make a splash at a party, throw it in the washer the next day. Save it for your grandchildren. In Cambridge, standards of dress went from "high proper" to "high casual"—at once to look good and feel good—that fit Cambridge just fine.

Telegram, Armi Ratia to Ben Thompson, September 10, 1963 *"Your Lyndon B Johnson bought 29 Marimekkos here."*

Cambridgians worked up the courage and appetite for this new frontier. Yes, it was trendy, but I didn't know a lot of people who did it only because others were doing it. They liked it for themselves, and still do.

Ben Thompson, Memoirs It took considerable education of salesgirls and customers to build the confidence to sell and appear in anything so "far out." Marimekko needed a sympathetic audience—and D/R, because of its prior six years of pioneering for quality, provided it at that critical moment.

Nancy Hemenway Marimekko customers were the kind of people Ben liked: really well educated and just a little off center. This was not mainstream clothing. All the women who wore this apparel, women and girls, looked fabulous. Ben loved the staff to wear long flowing dresses, the pinafores, aprons, and jumpsuits. When customers entered the store, the dressed staff was part of the whole setting. Human theater—that's what he liked.

Christa Marcelli, D/R staff, 1957–70 We couldn't get those Marimekko dresses fast enough! The shipment would come in and people would line up before we'd even opened. They'd rush in, and the dresses would fly off the racks like that!

Patricia Moore Sullivan, longtime D/R customer We were married and our family home was in West Newton. Going to Cambridge was something one just loved to do if one was quirky and eclectic and looking for something more than the plain old, plain old. I would be wearing a Mekko dress to a family gathering in the conservative Boston suburbs and my mother's comment would be, "Well, it is lovely dear, but did it come in blue?"

Minkie West McKevitt Before I had my baby I was working in the little New York store on Lexington Avenue. The managers didn't really want me there in my condition, because in those days we didn't want to identify Marimekko as a maternity dress. They were trying for a more chic image, not a pregnancy image, which many people concluded because dresses were so full. On the other hand, I knew the different stages of maternity, so I could look good at each stage, and I was selling like crazy.

Christa Marcelli One time, a woman came into the store and saw all of us in the Marimekko sack dresses, and she said, "Is this a place for fallen women?" Barefoot and pregnant—that was a comic moment.

Elizabeth (Biffy) Malko, D/R staff, 1966–68 There came a point in your life when you had to evolve. Sometimes you would swap dresses and trade. For those of us who started having children, Mekko became maternity dresses. You passed them on to your pregnant friends.

A "Uniform for Intellectuals"

From *Vogue*
April 2008

A Backward Glance
Elizabeth Kendall

recalls the moment—and the Marimekko dress—that changed her life forever.

It is a little painful to remember myself in the first gathering of college freshmen, in the fall of 1965, in the faded genteel living room of a Radcliffe dorm. The other girls, in drapey clothes, offered limp hands and languid smiles. I, Midwestern in wraparound skirt and shirt, all but pounced on my new classmates, quoting them back their middle names—Claire *Adriana* Nivola!—memorized from the photos in the freshman handbook.

By the end of that year I myself had become languid, or a facsimile of it—and that's a little painful to remember, too. I tried to speak in a bored breathy voice. I wore slingback heels to the library and a little tweed skirt suit smoothed inside by a severe Lycra girdle. That, I thought, was how you attracted a Harvard grad student. After all, I had been schooled by my mother to believe that my body's whole task in life was to avoid doing something shameful: never to bulge out of clothes, reveal underwear straps or leg hair, get too hungry, restless, or joyful. My body was not to be trusted.

Fortunately, a wave of new thinking was rolling in from the West Coast, a slow wave that would come to be called the sixties. My first taste of it came at the beginning of sophomore year, when a girl from California appeared on the front steps of my dorm wearing a sky-blue coat and a straw boater. I'd heard about Robin Von Breton from older girls. She'd taken a year off to work in L.A. for Charles and Ray Eames. She was a poet. But the jolt of this sky-blue coat (coats then were gray, black, brown), on this blonde earnest person, and the hat out of a Victorian novel—this sense of a *costume* that pleased her alone—was unlike anything I had ever seen. We proceeded inside together. She took off the coat. She was wearing a trim tent-shaped dress of stiff canvas, imprinted with huge red strawberries on a field of yellow.

There are moments that are watersheds in one's life—when a vast structure of assumptions shifts, opens, tumbles. Robin wasn't trying to look like an adornment to a Harvard man. She was a young woman whose every move proclaimed originality. And it wasn't just a pose. Her poems were clean and natural (although turquoise, from a turquoise typewriter ribbon). Robert Lowell had let her into his seminar. But the most potent of Robin's traits, to a dazzled me, was the boldness that had led to that dress. Actually, she had several such dresses, all with different patterns. "You don't know about Marimekko?" she said.

I did know vaguely about the small fabric company in faraway Finland, the source of these geometrically shaped canvas dresses with the wild patterns. They had become all the rage in fashion magazines. *Vogue's* pictorial had been positively sylvan: Marimekko-clad Finnish models posed on old wooden docks, among lakeside reeds, in forests. But I hadn't known about the store right here in Cambridge, on elegant Brattle Street, which was called Design Research, or DR.

Did I dare go there? My allowance was whatever my mother could squeeze out of the household budget (and I had five younger brothers and sisters and a father who sometimes gambled on the commodity market). But one sunny day I rode my bike to the old white-brick row house with the stark, bright interior. Upstairs, in their own pink-and-white selling space, were the dresses, ranged on blond-wood hangers. I can see myself, dark hair parted in the middle, wearing a trim navy skirt and white blouse, staring at these dresses, which were anything but well behaved. Each one was saying something like "Rejoice!" in a language of huge fruits, psychedelic stripes, flower explosions.

I was waitressing then at the faculty club. I stopped buying books; I saved all my tips. After a few months I went back to get "my" dress. It was a stiff canvas sheath with a mandarin collar whose top half featured plum-colored sea urchins swimming in a sea of rust, with rust sea urchins on plum on the bottom. I put it on, right in the store. I can still remember the feel of that canvas—so clean and crisp. I can feel again the relief of my body set free—the dress's geometry required no girdle.

The Marimekko didn't unleash the erotic me—that would come later. It stood for something even bigger than eros. When I think of the dress, I see myself in motion: racing to class, whizzing on my bike, in animated conversation about Edith Wharton (ignored then by Harvard) with a beautiful graduate student-teacher, Ann Douglas, who became my thesis adviser. It was as if the Marimekko dress emboldened me to write the thesis about women writers—and by extension, to dare to be a writer myself. I, who'd assumed (as my mother did) that under my faux suaveness lurked the inevitable marriage to a boy back in St. Louis, the ferrying of children to the country club, the volunteer work.

On a trip home, I gave the dress to my mother. Why? Because another girl in the dorm had given me *her* cast-off Marimekko, with its brazen black-and-white stripes. I could be generous—or rather defiant: "Here, Mom, in one dress, are all the things you said I couldn't be, yet somehow wanted me to be—a creature of pleasure, boldness, devil-may-care-ness."

But my mother loved the Marimekko. She'd already broken out of her own young-matron mold, it turned out, to become a passionate civil rights worker. She'd become bright like the dress, which she wore to meetings and rallies. She wrote to thank me in a new tone of voice—not as a mother but as a confidante.

Little did I know how short a time we would have to enjoy our new status. A few months later I flew home for spring break. As a surprise, she'd booked a beach cabin in Alabama for a family vacation. We set off in the car in the rain, she and I and four younger siblings; my father would join us later. As we headed south on Highway 61, the rain got heavier. I'd just replaced her as driver. A truck roared past, flooding the windshield. I braked hard; we smashed a low bridge; I blacked out. The kids in the back slammed knees, elbows, heads. In the passenger seat, my mother broke her neck.

I remember a rural hospital; bandages and wheelchairs; the nurse with the country twang who told me my mother was dead; my uncle shepherding in my shattered father—they'd flown down in a small plane. The rest of us, except for cuts and bruises, miraculously weren't injured—but how would we ever recover? We flew back through clouds and rain, to find our driveway suddenly full of cars, our house full of neighbors putting casseroles on the dining-room table. At the funeral, packed with people, the plain pine coffin stood alone on the altar steps.

I stayed home a week more, as aunts, grandparents, friends, and strangers passed through our living room, bestowing tearful hugs. I walked around in a daze, not sure, suddenly, of anything. When it came time to go back to college, I felt it as a relief. Packing on the eve of my departure, I went alone to her closet, which already smelled of neglect. In a row of somber dresses, the plum-and-rust Marimekko stood out. I put it in my suitcase.

From then on, I would wear it for both of us.

Anna Sui **"I love the optimism that Marimekko designs embody."**

Raymond Waites We might go to a restaurant; the girls would wear Marimekko dresses, I would wear a Marimekko shirt, and the host wouldn't seat us. It was revolutionary. It was edgy. At that time Courrèges and Pucci were popular. Fashion was breaking out of the boundaries of tradition.

Tizzie (Elizabeth) Lambert, D/R staff, 1962–64 At the magazines where I worked, like *Harper's Bazaar* with Diana Vreeland, fashion was very different in the sixties. Everything was created for older women, and Paris couture still reigned supreme. Americans who were buying in America licensed copies of styles from Paris collections, or from the American designers who were beginning to find their own sense of style. Designer clothes were for the wealthy, and the rest of us bought less-expensive copies.

D/R was different. Things weren't cheap by any means, but there was a different ethos entirely. Marimekko was itself, not dictated by anybody. The same dress would look different on different people because they were such flat little paper doll cut-out shapes. When Jackie Kennedy was wearing them in Hyannis, that was a turning point.

Dorothy Twining Globus, curator of exhibitions, Museum of Arts and Design I had a hat, an orange hat, which defined me in college. I had a friend who had a hat that was another color so we were the Marimekko hat girls. Even in that small way I felt part of it.

The clothes were very gutsy. They were more of an Asian design in the sense that they were clothes made to *display* the textiles rather than clothes that were made out of textiles and cut to fit in very complicated ways.

A testimony to the success of all that clothing came when people gave us their dresses for a Marimekko exhibition at FIT [Fashion Institute of Technology]. They all had the hemline marks on them, revealing that they would take them up and put them down as hemlines changed. I have one dress from my mother—she loved it, she treasured it—and it showed that telltale sign that she too couldn't bear to give it up.

Cara McCarty, curatorial director, Cooper-Hewitt, National Design Museum One of the reasons I am doing the work that I do is because of D/R. I lived down the street from the old store in Cambridge, and when I was twelve years old one of my classmates, a tall, slender girl from India, was one of their models. We would play in the store after school. It was an old house with rambling rooms, and there were sweeping views through it. It was filled with light and colors and the most exquisite contemporary design. I remember the colors and glass vases filled with flowers and birch furniture. Particularly the fabric section and the clothing.

I made a lot of my own clothes at the time, and I loved Marimekko fabric. In the fabric area, shelves ran from the counter up to the ceilings. They looked fabulous because the fabrics were organized by colors. My mother told me she would buy me all the fabric I wanted if I would finish what I was making and stop getting upset when I made a mistake. If I was willing to learn patience, she would provide me with fabric.

At the time, there was almost nothing like D/R, and part of the reason had to do with the Marimekko fabric. It gave the store a unique atmosphere. The palette and the size of the patterns, like those big flowers you could barely wrap your arms around, were so different from anything else. Imagine trying to match the pattern on a miniskirt that was fourteen inches long.

Anna Sui I remember the *Life* magazine with those gorgeous Marimekko dresses from when I was a kid. I didn't know what they were, but I saved the pages. Then in 1999 I did a whole collection inspired by Marimekko; after that I took a trip to Finland and went to Marimekko. I met Kristina Isola and toured the facilities. I love the optimism that Marimekko designs embody. They make you smile when you look at them. They make you so happy when you wear them.

I did a 1960s pop collection after my trip to Finland that had some prints and colors that were very Marimekko. It was so hard because those Marimekko prints are so distinct. You can't beat them.

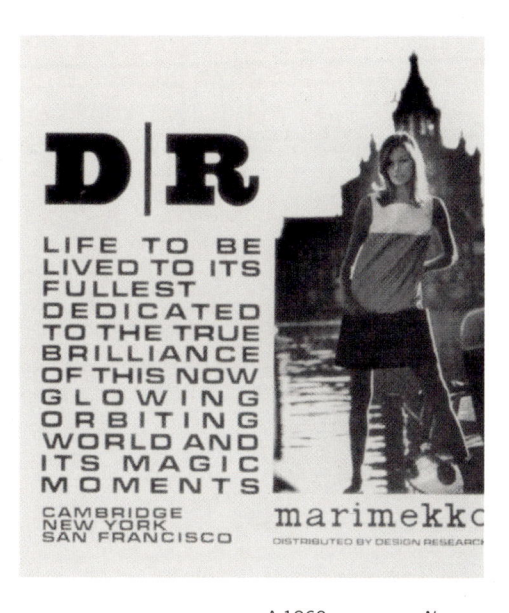

A 1960s space-age *New Yorker* ad invites customers to enjoy "this now glowing orbiting world and its magic moments."

A "Uniform for Intellectuals" 91

Armi Ratia and her principal designers, Maija Isola, Vuokko Nurmesniemi, and Annika Rimala, were all educated at the Helsinki Institute of Industrial Arts, where they acquired a common graphic sensibility. These examples are mostly Isola designs, including the botanical Putkinotko, 1957–59 (top row, center left), a purple version of the still-popular Ornamentti series of 1958–60 (top row, center right), leafy Ruusupuu, 1957 (bottom row, center left), and squiggly Joonas, 1961 (bottom row, center right).

OPPOSITE: A D/R sales sheet listing the new dress shapes, many created by Rimala, the company's premier designer in the 1960s.

Gordon Segal, cofounder, Crate & Barrel
The look was so fresh and new in the 1960s when it first came out. No one in U.S. business would have taken big bold colors and things of that nature and done what the Finns did. Obviously Warhol did it. If you look at Unikko and the Warhol flowers, they are very close. I have always said, "Did Warhol copy Isola or did Isola copy Warhol?" I have one Warhol on my wall right now, and I am laughing as I am looking at it. This was a period of time of rock music and acid and the Vietnam War, and then these wonderful wild color prints came out of Finland. Everything started happening.

Jane Thompson When did Warhol paint his flowers? In 1965, about the same time Maija Isola printed hers. Worlds apart, the supergraphics gripped global imaginations. The hand-painted, hand-screened spontaneity of Isola's designs spoke to the eye. This fabric is executed by an artist, not a machine. Likewise, Vuokko's hand-drawn stripes, and later Annika Rimala's bold geometrics, always conveyed their painterly origins and an intensity of color found only in oil paintings. Marimekko stands for the artists' dedication to craft skills translated into quality production.

M-963   KUTTERI

M-1001   SIIMA

M-1006   VIMPELI

M-974   TIIRA

M-965   REITTI

M-971   VIIRI

M-997   HAUKI

A "Uniform for Intellectuals"

Walking Around with My Colorful Totes
Or, The Mari-Sisterhood Is Still at Work

By Jane Thompson

I am a two-bag lady. There are burdens and paraphernalia of life and business that I must tote around daily, a "life-readiness kit" in anticipation of demands lying in wait, who knows where. Once it was the "mommy needs" for pacifiers and Band-Aids. Today it is backups—batteries, chargers, support for a veritable *batterie technologique.* So I split the weight and carry two bags: the manageable shoulder-strap pouch for wallet and lipstick, and a colorful canvas tote bag over the other arm for the heavy stuff. Both are bright, bold, and conspicuously Marimekko, if you are tuned in to the cult. The bags, I have found, operate somewhat like a high-frequency signal system, the sort only perceived by animals of high aural sensitivity. In my strolls, I have found that visual recognition of the bags opens a door to immediate conversation, and often to bonding.

In *The Tipping Point,* Malcolm Gladwell posits that certain events and occasions, even things, act as connectors among people. His case study grows out of a social phenomenon that he calls the "sisterhood effect," demonstrated by sales of the novel *The Divine Secrets of the Ya-Ya Sisterhood.* Sales of this book rose over time to what is termed an epidemic success, through what he describes as "The Power of Context," really the word-of-mouth power within groups of people, amplifying interpersonal bonds beyond any usual expectations.

I constantly am struck by the way I ignite the same connective experience just walking around with my bags boldly labeled *Marimekko.* First you ask, "Why is it called 'Marimekko'? Is that a musical nonsense word?"

No, it is a *good-*sense word: *Mekko,* in Finnish, means "little dress," or house dress, casual. *Mari* means Mary, which in Finnish denotes, generically, woman. A little dress for Mary is an everyday dress for every woman. Each Marimekko pattern on cotton is a handmade artwork painted onto a silk screen, originally printed with a hand-screening process. Since the 1950s, the originality of fabric, color, and pattern has carried an instant visual link to every piece in a unique family of products, even, or especially, tote bags.

Often it happens like this: Someone asks, "Isn't that a Marimekko bag?" Or, "Do you love it?" And, "I had a similar one ten/twenty/thirty years ago. Now my granddaughter has it and it makes her feel cool." There follows a discussion of other beloved products—a dress, how much it really meant, and the unusual store that sold it. Design Research . . . do you remember that jumping place? Dropping my Mari-labeled bag onto store counters, or on office desks, I hear amazing life stories volunteered breathlessly: "You cannot believe how important Design Research in New York was to my childhood and education! Mother brought us from Ohio once a year just to visit the store, so she could show us and explain about design and beauty. I learned everything there." Or, "Experiencing D/R in Cambridge as a young girl changed my life. It liberated my imagination."

Cambridge portrait photographer Elsa Dorfman, a D/R groupie since the 1960s, created a portrait series of people in Marimekko dresses, which includes many D/R participants wearing their enduring favorite garments. Her photographs are featured in the film *It Wasn't Just a Dress*, produced by Caroline Van Valkenburgh.

MEKKO FANS, LEFT TO RIGHT: Former DR staff members Minkie McKevitt, Anne Solley, Marja Lianko; Lexi Van Valkenburgh-Chiong, Grace Chiong, Caroline Van Valkenburgh; D/R customers Michael Van Valkenburgh, Karen Lewis, Colgate Searle; Sheila McCullough, Jane Thompson.

These encounters have not only continued over decades but have increased as Marimekko products have been seen less often in this country. This power of connectivity has built what I perceive is a Mari-Sisterhood, joined by some special awareness common to members of the 'hood. Today's members include seniors, 1960s veterans, and initiates enjoying the American upsurge of Marimekko shops in which all of us feel like members of a special alumnae association. (In large number, it is an alumnae association, but male fans can be fanatics too.)

What is the core of Mari-connectedness? It may be discovering visual values and pleasures for the first time; it may be stimulating personal abilities and self-confidence at a formative age. In the 1960s, each woman wearing a Marimekko garment was proud to signal boldness of spirit, audacious *cool:* something original had touched an inner button, beaming a defining message of independence as clearly as waving a flag of freedom.

The sisterhood of Marimekko owners still operates with a generosity of spirit we rarely find in the fashion world. For a sister, encountering someone wearing an identical dress is cause for good cheer, a bond of recognition. That is not an expected response in the world of high fashion when, say, two stylish women meet at a high-tone benefit decked out in identical Valentino gowns. Ach!

The ownership of one single piece in the Marimekko family of beautiful products—a bag, a pillow, a cotton hat, or striped towel— can link you to others as firmly as, say, a passion for gardening, cooking, reading, or even social causes. Marimekko fans frequently love all five. All are elective, all are fulfilling and expressive of individual interests. People so mutually involved are not strangers but immediate potential friends with shared tastes. Such parallel value-based preferences are the core of a social bonding.

Sisterhood also spurred a brotherhood that took off with men's shirts and ties. The leading model in D/R menswear was Ben Thompson, invariably in a striped Finn Farmer shirt of subtle contrast. Women came to appreciate (and promote) the Finn Farmer striped shirts not only for themselves but to liberate male friends (at that time) from the Brooks Brothers starched-collar uniform. They could discuss the flattering effects of color, stripes, and patterns, they could buy them as gifts for husbands and relatives, and they could vocally appreciate a good shirt worn by a strange man passing at a party: "Hmm, Mekko shirt! Good color with your eyes."

I suggest that the high-frequency Mari-signal is returning to American culture. It remains the mark of fashion and taste, unifying male and female appreciation of something unique, colorful, and eminently wearable, something always in some way beyond gender—a universal, yet strongly personal expression.

A "Uniform for Intellectuals" 95

Expansion Without Imitation, 1959-65

4

In 1960, as D/R Cambridge was enjoying explosive growth in sales and internal shop space, Ben Thompson was testing the mood of the market for a second store in New York. The company's agreement to be the exclusive American distributor for Marimekko broadened Ben's outlook not just on the geographic potential for goods but for retail operations too. In some ways, the quick acceptance of Finnish design had become a geographic imperative for expansion.

Retailing in the big city was a formidable challenge: Competitors in home goods, while not numerous, were established and well funded. They included such tony establishments as Bonniers, Georg Jensen, Baccarat, Bergdorf Goodman, even FAO Schwarz. Artek of Finland, representing the furniture designs of architect Alvar Aalto, had been a prewar entry into the market that served the very earliest owners of modern homes.

By comparison, D/R was a young, innovative enterprise with minimal capitalization, strained by meteoric growth over a decade. The store's Cambridge expansion, tripling the store's floor area across all three walk-ups, had been funded by reinvested operating profits, with occasional loans from Field. By 1960, the store's 1953 sales ($77,000) had multiplied ten times; by 1970, sales multiplied another ten times.

D/R on 57th Street in New York, the former Joseph Brummer mansion and art gallery seen on opening night, November 1963.

The two-story front window of the 57th Street D/R provided ample room for vertiginous displays of dresses and masses of same-color, same-variety flowers, as well as a view of the street's many modern shoppers.

98   Design Research

Ben, an intrinsically hands-on and face-to-face leader, was not an empire builder, but the enthusiasm driving accelerating sales in Cambridge gave him confidence in the reach of his niche business. The need for furnishings and accessories for comfortable home environments was now a national phenomenon: 77 million "boomer" babies had been born between 1947 and 1963. Millions of new homes had been built across the country from 1960 to 1963 alone, and growing families were pushing residential density in cities as well. New owners were in need of furniture and equipment to fit smaller spaces and busier lives in this new era. Ben's mission was to reach and satisfy some part of this palpable market demand, left unanswered by conventional home-goods stores. The Big Apple was the center of this market, with a large customer base of both architects and discriminating urban customers.

With shrewd retail vision, Ben launched two satellite stores to test the market. In late 1959, he opened a well-placed shop in Manhattan at 866 Lexington Avenue, at the corner of 65th Street. It provided excellent display opportunities with two full-height corner windows. Despite its diminutive size, its 700-square-foot interior was filled with a veritable forest of hanging wicker forms swathed in Marimekko dresses.

A few months later, Ben set up a D/R Summer Shop in an empty storefront on Main Street in Hyannis, Massachusetts. The town was an attractive retail location as the epicenter of Cape Cod seasonal tourism and the year-round hometown of affluent families. It was also a convenient five-mile drive from the Thompson family's summer place on Barnstable Harbor. It was in Hyannis that summer where future First Lady Jacqueline Kennedy, pregnant with John Jr., glimpsed Marimekko in the shop window.

Modern on 57th Street

Customer response to these two new boutiques, and the positive reflection in the cash register, bolstered Ben's intuition that it was time to join mainstream retailing in New York. His decision was certainly pushed by Marimekko's urge to reach a national audience.

With the help of a local broker, Ben came upon a small, handsome five-story townhouse—the former Joseph Brummer mansion and art gallery, most recently the exclusive showroom of Mr. John Hats. Its thin classical façade faced directly on East 57th Street, New York's most posh retail stretch.

The location 53 East 57 was a first-class address for a leading-edge design statement. But as a space it defied all rules of good retail experience and operation: rather than the conventional continuous open sales floor, it had five deep, narrow levels (20 feet wide by 100 feet deep) and a mezzanine, posing problems of inventory logistics, product display, and daily operation.

When D/R NYC opened to international fanfare in autumn 1963, it was classically the small frog in a big pond. By croaking loudly with stunning merchandise and ingenious window settings, it attracted leading professionals, top-flight customers, and celebrities. Many were cruising and looking to learn, as they might in a museum, but many more were making substantial and repeated purchases, and coming back regularly just to keep in touch with things.

D/R was not about "forever new" modernism but the "forever good" classicism of lasting design. "We are selling an attitude," said Ben, "not just about design but about living: the design became smaller, and living became rather large."

Expansion Without Imitation

Voices

Ben Thompson "**I want girls with freshness, vitality, and enthusiasm. I have chosen to work with girls. Not a difficult choice.**"

Lexington Avenue, New York, 1959

Julia McFarlane, D/R staff, 1963–69 The Lexington Avenue store was tiny, on two levels. You walked in over the same slate and cork combination floor used in the Cambridge store, and you stepped down. It had racks of Marimekko dresses and small home accessories.

Marianne Sundström Williams, D/R staff, 1962–65 New Yorkers tended to ask personal questions immediately, such as "Where are you from?" and "How long have you been here?" in the middle of trying on a dress or selecting glassware. One lady said she had been looking for the perfect glass for vermouth, and we found that the Kaj Franck straight-lined, thin, and smoky-colored glasses were the absolute match. Somehow it seemed ever so natural that this lady then happily invited me to join her, her family, and guests that evening to have vermouth out of these glasses. With a small bouquet of anemones in a matching Kaj Franck glass pitcher in hand, I found the exquisite apartment and spent a wonderful evening with "total strangers." Or, as I determined, a typical D/R customer in New York.

Kathy Keating, D/R staff, 1962–65 When I moved to New York I worked in both shops there. In addition to clothing, the small Lexington Avenue shop offered sweaters, knitted things from Bolivia, silver jewelry from Betty Cooke (I still have some of that), and Tunisian chain necklaces. We had wonderful boots, felted, not at all waterproof. Woolen stockings from Marimekko, pull-up tights that were also woolen, in great colors. And handwoven woolen dresses. It is easy to forget how rare this was in the 1960s.

Main Street, Hyannis, Mass., 1960

Nancy Gathercole Riaz, TAC assistant, summer 1953; D/R staff, 1953–64 The Hyannis store was one season only, selling only Marimekko. It was a short distance from Ben's Cape home in Barnstable and it was an excellent trial for a branch store. The town had a big market because of people taking the island ferries or flying in and out for holidays. Hyannis was a very commercial place, whereas nearby Hyannisport, where the Kennedys had their compound, was an uncommercial exclusive place. I think that's why Ben chose the location: It was a short trip from home and a stone's throw from the Kennedys.

53 East 57th Street, New York, 1963

Julia McFarlane Working there was a phenomenal experience. It was a very tall store with four floors and just that one doorway through which everything went. A 30-inch doorway, too. Everything came through the front door, often followed by incoming or outgoing half-trees, because more than the furniture came down from Cambridge. Every week in the fall there were huge tree branches and leaves for the seasonal setting.

Working in display, I worked at times with Ben, but mostly with Paul Dietrich and Lorna Dawson Elkus as Ben's right-hand person. Paul was a wonderful opposite for Ben. Paul could tell you about everything happening in a very explanatory way, which was great for the display team. He translated what Ben wanted. Ben himself was brilliant and sometimes a bit oblique; he made you see by questioning what you saw. "What did you see when you walked down the street? How did you look?" In terms of display, it all made so much sense. Ben hated to see a bowl of lemons. He asked, "Who has a huge bowl of lemons in their house? You eat apples, but lemons might stick around for months and get moldy." There was always a big barrel of apples somewhere in the store to grab and eat, sent down from the farms of Massachusetts.

LEFT: California supergraphic artist Barbara Stauffacher Solomon displayed her oversize enamel artworks in a 1968 D/R exhibition.

BELOW: An ad from *The New Yorker* announcing the opening of the big store in 1963.

Barbara Plumb, design critic, *New York Times*, 1963 To celebrate its tenth birthday, Design Research of Cambridge, Mass., has given itself an extravagant present: a new store in New York occupying the whole of a town house at 53 East 57th Street.

The name of the new store, D/R International, is already known to New Yorkers. It belongs to a small, sophisticated boutique at 866 Lexington Avenue (at 65th Street) where the stock-in-trade is Marimekko dresses from Finland. . . . The new store . . . is much more like its Cambridge counterpart, a shop internationally known for the well-designed modern furnishings it offers. It attempts to supply everything necessary to create a total visual environment for a home — from a coffee table to a pepper mill . . . .

Mr. Thompson designed the New York store in collaboration with Paul Dietrich. He attempted to capture the character of a town house in a very simple way. "We have dining furniture and accessories in the dining part, kitchen accessories in the kitchen, toys in the nursery, and Marimekko in the boudoir. Each space will be arranged to convey a different mood but it will feel related to the architecture," he said.

Barbara Stauffacher Solomon, artist "I feel like it's your coming-out party and I'm giving you away," Sibyl Moholy-Nagy said at Design Research on 57th Street, as she stood greeting design gurus and groupies. It was the opening of my show "SIGNS," in 1968. While intellectuals were reading signs for their readings, I made signs that said nothing. My "signs" for the sixties were hard-edge abstract designs in bright, glossy, porcelain enamel colors—vermilion, red, blue, yellow, black, and white on four-by-four-foot metal sheets, fabricated at an Oakland sign shop. Shiny slam-bang-sock-it-to-you assembly-line art, with squares hung from one corner as diamonds.

D/R was packed, the music loud, the lights bright, the booze free. Beautiful D/R salesgirls passed bowls of crème fraîche, powdered sugar, and enormous stemmed red strawberries.

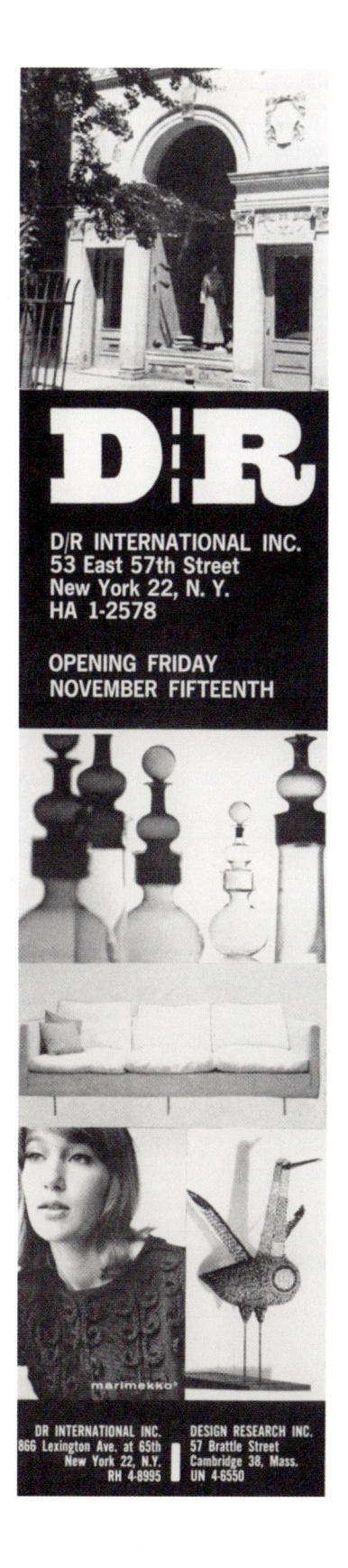

Expansion Without Imitation   101

Alan Heller **"When I first walked into the New York store, I almost got dizzy from the multisensory blast—music, aroma, pattern, color impacting all of my senses."**

Architectural Forum, **1964** At Design Research, Inc. . . . shopping, as the saying goes, is fun—partly because of the handsome and intriguing merchandise, and partly because of the way the building has been remodeled. Among the things that make D/R such an interesting store is its multilevel plan—for D/R is a shop on seven levels, with a split-level system of stairs connecting the seven . . . the interior of the store is in sharp contrast to the classical façade, which was left untouched. . . . For D/R, the basic spaces inside were kept intact. An open stairwell was removed, and an enclosed fire stair leading directly to the second floor was put in above the stairs to the mezzanine. The existing mezzanine was cut back to give more space to the entrance lobby. Throughout the store spotlighting is used. The walls are white plaster, except for a few areas where the brick party wall has been exposed for contrast.

Lorna Dawson Elkus, D/R staff, 1961–70 New York was an impossible location, in my view, because it had no street presence. Fortunately Paul Dietrich came down. We were walking down the street one day and saw that somebody had hung long banners out. He said, "Why not make up some Printex Marimekko banners and fly them from the front of the building for the opening?" So we started that whole tradition.

It seemed that D/R didn't have a chance of succeeding on its own terms in New York as a small, independent, albeit exclusive retailer. Ben was interviewed the day before opening. He was really mad after one newspaper interview because they asked, "So what's new here?" He said, "What's new? Do you go into a restaurant and ask them if they have invented a new vegetable?"

There was a lot of new design and design thinking brought by D/R, but New York is very fickle. There was a following, but it wasn't Cambridge, with that high level of appreciation and interest in becoming a part of that culture of hanging out.

Julia McFarlane The fourth floor had the furniture and another skylight too. The person minding that was Berthe Rudofsky—wife of Bernard Rudofsky, the wonderful Viennese architect—and such a character. She knew everyone, she knew Charles Eames. She would say, "I have to go early, I have to cook dinner for Tanguy, he's coming over." Lorna [Elkus] did most of the hiring but Ben would have hired Berthe. She was divinely eccentric. She might say to a customer, "Could you just come back a little bit later? I have so much paperwork."

Raymond Waites, D/R staff, 1975–78 I had a fellowship to study at Pratt. Arriving in New York, we saw an ad in the *New Yorker* for the TAC daybed at Design Research. It was a platform bed, very contemporary. We had come from the eighteenth-century South, sleeping in a mahogany four-poster bed. So we walked into Design Research and were immediately groupies. Our weekends were spent going to the store, just as customers at that point, young college kids. We bought the daybed. With Marimekko fabric, of course—all those expressive colors. Just two yards or three yards of fabric and you had decorated your whole room.

Nancy didn't have anything to do while I was painting and going to class. I said, "We really love this store, why don't you go apply for a job?" Which she did. Her grandmother had given her a full-length fur coat and she had the Vidal Sassoon asymmetrical haircut and she walked in. Many of the D/R girls were from a comfortable segment of society, probably didn't really need the job. They paid $65 a week if I remember. But it was *the* place to work in those days. She got the job. She started work in the little shop on 65th Street. I would drive in and pick her up after work and go back to Brooklyn Heights, with its TAC daybed.

Elizabeth (Biffy) Malko, D/R staff, 1966–68 What New Yorkers hadn't had was the sort of evening where the so-called lifestyle—the D/R lifestyle I will call it—was on display in presenting and honoring our special designers, Sam Smith, Joe Colombo, Barbara Stauffacher. Each was a generous event. There was food on the table, with offerings you hadn't seen before: bowls of strawberries and cherry tomatoes, good cheeses, a smorgasbord displayed on the china we were selling. For these special evenings the staff wore Marimekko dresses. Vidal Sassoon came to New York, pioneering a geometric look, and would often do the hair for staff who was modeling the clothes. That wasn't the Scandinavian blond hair, blue-eyed look; it was a crisp New York version.

Julia McFarlane Sam Smith was a wonderful toymaker, a sculptor of toys. We had an event for him when he came from England. Then there was Joe Colombo. Ben was the first person to show Joe's work in the United States when he gave him an exhibition at D/R New York in 1966. That was a bold, great move — and it was six years before Joe was shown in the big Italian design show at MoMA in 1972.

At D/R there were Malacca cane pieces — beautiful chairs with big cane seats and lacquered wood. Plastic as well, the Colombo Elda chair, lamps, which were metal and plastic. And the molded stacking chair — a classic. In those years Italian design was at the forefront. Ben was interested in contrasting this gorgeous Italian beauty to the wonderful but simple Danish and Finnish furniture we had in the store. I was surprised whenever we sold an Elda Chair, because it was more expensive than anything else at D/R. It was a big price jump and New York customers shopped for it.

Elizabeth (Biffy) Malko Ben used to have business dinner parties. He liked to go to the Four Seasons. Or the newest restaurant at that time, La Fonda del Sol, designed by Alexander Girard. Like Ben, Alexander Girard had a great eye for folk art and textiles, and designed a lot of textiles — Ben was on his wavelength, adoring the handmade folk carvings and weavings. It was a treat for all of us invited to be a part of those evenings, seeing places none of us would go to on a regular basis.

Entry view of the first floor, where furniture groupings divided the long space into sample living rooms. A D/R Down Seating Group in Haitian cotton, foreground, sets off a Mies van der Rohe glass coffee table. A Spanish Disa balsa wood lamp, rear left, echoes the ovals of a Marimekko fabric panel.

Expansion Without Imitation

Julia McFarlane Always, there was the front window to be done with new collections of Marimekko. At first we were using wicker dress forms that originated in Finland. Then simple bars on rope. The ceilings were maybe 50 feet with a double-height window, and the ceiling was even higher. Our display people, Robin Drake and Herbert Muschamp, had to go up the ladder to do the display, both of them equally terrified. I said, "I am more terrified than you, just on the ground watching."

Herbert was wild. He had lived in Berlin and gone to the Architectural Association in London. He was from a fantastic, other world. I am sure he had been even more flamboyant before he came to D/R. He lived in the East Village and told a funny story about being chased by a would-be mugger; he had on such a loose huge mohair sweater that when the guy drew the knife on him, it just caught his sweater. Herbert was zigzagging across the street screaming. I was delighted when he became the architecture critic for the *New York Times*.

David Wasco, D/R staff, 1975–78 Jim Schultz was the display guy at the New York store when they sent me to New York in 1977. One time he took a stack of cheap white grid outdoor patio chairs, like a little armchair, called the Emu chair. He made two piles, maybe 15 feet high, and then he took the tops of the stacks and bent them over, so they became like an arch in a church. That was it!

Lu Wendel Lyndon, D/R staff, 1965–73 We always tried to make the space feel believable, so that everything coordinated realistically. When I was working in New York, we decided to group the product not by function but by material. So the whole front of the store was all neutral, natural wood and pottery. In the middle were brightly colored things and toys. The back room was a precursor of the high-tech look, turned into a silver and white and natural wood environment.

Kathy Keating After Cambridge, the sense of the New York store to me was even more exciting. I would pick out one item—a day, or a week, or a month—and that was the thing I would sell. If somebody wanted

104 Design Research

a wedding present, that was the thing I would point them to. It was fun to see how many I could sell in a week—Finel bowls or whatever it was.

Raymond Waites Nancy had clients like Joanne Woodward and Jackie Onassis and Mrs. Frank Stanton from CBS. Even missionaries in Africa would come in, and Nancy would know what styles they liked so she could send them out. I remember one of the missionaries saying that you couldn't ever beat the dresses up, which she knew because they were washed on the rocks in the river.

Nancy Waites, D/R staff, 1965–70 I remember Mrs. Valentine Macy. She was a large woman, and we would special order Marimekko dresses for her. They made the 5-pocket dress up special for her, with a different fabric for each pocket. Despite her size, she always carried little pocketbooks.

Julia McFarlane Once Jackie O came in with the director Mike Nichols, in the mid-1960s. I remember the day Johnny Mercer came in. We made sure his music was playing. He was sort of a dandy and he was definitely shopping, but I don't remember what he finally selected.

I was the one who took Marcel Breuer's order for a Ben Thompson down sofa on the day the store opened. I suspect it was all set up in advance, since he was Ben and Gropius's old associate in Cambridge. It seemed entirely natural that Breuer was in the store to have a look around. I also remember when Georgia O'Keeffe, the painter from New Mexico, came in. She was fantastic and acted so iconic. She was pretty dour, but she sat in a Thonet rocking chair, knowing full well how it suited her. She sat on the fourth floor and rocked and they discussed the chair under the skylight.

Blase Gallo, D/R display, product development, 1971–78 I saw Jackie O and John Lindsay—who wasn't mayor at the time—on the same day. And Gregory Peck, who was incredible to see in person. I waited on Carly Simon when she first married James Taylor and bought the house on the Vineyard. We had received a shipment in from Iittala of Aalto vases. I put all the new vases on the platform in the front window and filled them with yellow tulips—100 vases and 100 dozen yellow tulips. I was doing the last one when Carly Simon walked in and commented on the display.

OPPOSITE, ABOVE: The kitchenwares department showcasing colored enamel Le Creuset pots on open shelves and the full line of Braun appliances designed by Dieter Rams, introduced in the U.S. by D/R.

OPPOSITE, BELOW: The entry reconfigured for glass and china display.

At the rear of the deep first floor, kitchenwares are used for a food tasting on a round table, with a line of Thonet café chairs behind and vernacular Italian rush stools a level up. A hanging panel of Kaivo fabric separates the two levels.

Expansion Without Imitation 105

From *Berlin-New York, Like and Unlike*
1993
In Search of the Lost Research
By Herbert Muschamp

With architecture the problem was somewhat different. Modern architects had always seen their mission as one operating in the field of mass culture. The Museum of Modern Art's "Good Design" shows had been mounted to encourage public consumption of well-designed objects. Even so, though clearly founded for promotional purposes—to gain public acceptance of a particular vision of modern culture, MOMA was supposed to be above the crass values of the marketplace; part of the myth of museums is that they stand outside the normal course of contemporary events. At MOMA, we were supposed to focus on the intrinsic qualities of designed objects and overlook the systems designed to place these objects in circulation. But at what point would it become obvious that modern design, an aesthetic based on mechanical production, was now a matter of promotion?

Moreover, as Linda Nochlin observed, the canons of modern design "functioned to separate the 'tasteful' sheep from the 'philistine' goats." More than one script was provided for each object; there was the socialist narrative of mass redemption through reason and a capitalist script of status through privileged acquisition. At what point would it become clear that the acceptance of an aesthetic based on the ideal of mass culture depended on the taste of an elite? At what point would the art historical sense of the work style merge with the word's fashionable denotation?

In the late 1960s, I spent a year working at a place where an attempt was made to reconcile these two scripts: the New York branch of Design Research, a store that had been founded in the 1950s by Benjamin Thompson, an architect from Cambridge, Massachusetts. Describing the store in its 1967 edition, the *AIA Guide to New York City* came right to the point: "A modern architect's dream. Collected in one four-storied store are furniture, kitchen equipment, cutlery, dresses—in fact, everything that has been touched by the wand of good design. It could well be an exhibition for the Museum of Modern Art; but in this case the exhibits are for sale."

DR was literally "a modern architect's dream." Thompson was (and is) an architect of impeccable modern credentials. He was one of the young Americans who gathered around Walter Gropius when the Bauhaus founder emigrated to the United States to become chair of Harvard's Graduate School of Design. An associate of Gropius's at the Architects' Collaborative, Thompson later assumed that chair himself. His own architecture, even in recent years, has never strayed from the modern canon.

A few years ago, I ran into Thompson at the Design Conference in Aspen, one of the few places where unreconstructed modernists still set the tone. He didn't remember me, but I introduced myself and thanked him for one of the happiest years of my life. And it was. I loved working at Design Research. I worked in the store's display department; my job was to make sure that the exhibits looked good enough that they would sell. At the end of the year, I went off to architecture school, learned a lot about ideas and about the way architects talk to each other; but I never learned more about forms and about the ways we see them in context than I did that year at DR. I played with the classics as though they were toys: tables and chairs by Mies, Breuer, Aalto, Eames. I made sale signs with Le Corbusier's beautiful metal stencils. I ran around tacking panels of Marimekko fabric behind the new Italian designs. It made me proud to make these things sell—changing a light filter, moving a spot around, putting a bright dress at the front of a rack, going down to Little Italy to buy a particular kind of pasta to fill some glass jars.

Like other modernists, Thompson believed there was an affinity between the machine-made and anonymous handicraft; prominent among his wares were country chairs, Bennington pottery. For a while, the walls were hung with large pictures of Bernard Rudofsky's vernacular architecture, salvaged from the Museum of Modern Art's exhibition "Architecture Without Architects."

I loved to stay late on Friday nights to get the store ready for the Saturday crowds. I was often there until way past midnight; sometimes I would stop by on a Saturday afternoon, though it was my day off, just to see how sales were doing. It was a challenge to make the front window so beautiful that whatever was on display there—especially stock that hadn't moved for months—would sell out completely by the end of the day.

D/R San Francisco offered a front door on Ghirardelli Square.

BELOW: Invitation to the 1965 opening showing the elaborate architecture of the West Coast outpost—just as distinctive as the East Coast venues in industrially scaled spaces.

San Francisco: Opening of D/R West

While D/R was getting its land legs on 57th Street, it was also propelled—indeed seduced—into a distant pioneering adventure. The invitation came from Bill Roth, a visionary entrepreneur who recognized D/R's unique fit for one of the first large private redevelopments of urban industrial buildings for new retail use, a move that was both creative preservation and innovative urban progress.

Roth was a leading Democrat, scion of a shipping enterprise, and a free-thinking urbanist. He had recently acquired a block-square nineteenth-century factory facing San Francisco Bay, sited on a sloping property like a hillside village. The factory, which had long produced Ghirardelli chocolates, was in danger of the high-rise development encroaching on this quieter postindustrial area of Buena Vista Park. With his mind on development plans being worked on with architect William Wurster, Roth, on a visit to D/R in Cambridge with his family, sought out Ben and asked him directly if he would like to open a new store in San Francisco. "I told him I could not afford that," Ben said. "But Roth talked me into believing I could do it."

Here was the third of Thompson's antique "found spaces" to display modernity. Like the others, this one took on the character of its special place in the West. In 1965, its twelfth year of operation, Design Research Inc. opened as Ghirardelli Square's anchor tenant, largest among numerous owner-operated specialty shops. Ghirardelli Square reawakened the tradition of personal retailing that was to attract a new generation of entrepreneurs in America's emerging maker-oriented mobile enterprise, the pushcart marketplace.

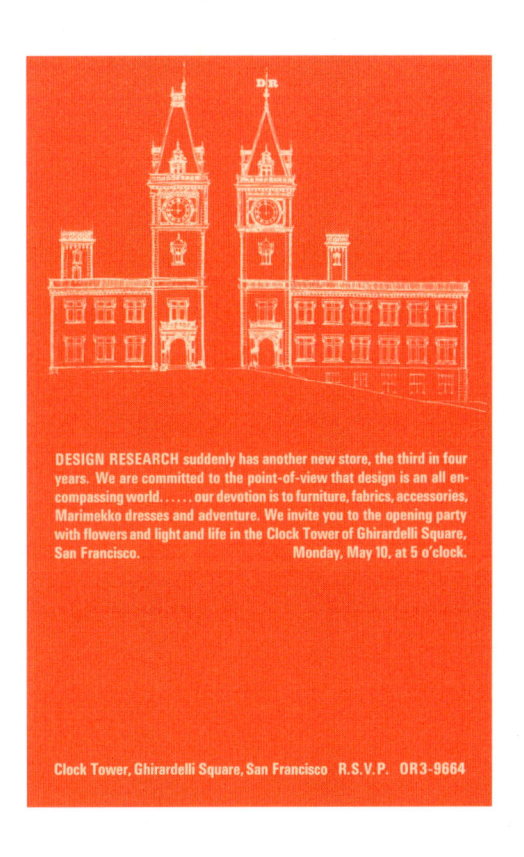

Expansion Without Imitation   107

Ghirardelli Square, San Francisco, 1965

William Roth, owner and developer, Ghirardelli Square; D/R board member 1968–70 My primary aim was to save the historic factory buildings. I'd always felt guilty because I saw the destruction of the Montgomery Center; a parking lot was being put in there, which had then been sold to a real estate person. I had some cash, so I had an architect go look at the center; there were a lot of problems so I didn't go ahead with buying it. There was a very famous restaurant there called The Murals, probably the most famous Gold Rush building that could have been saved. I didn't go there, so I thought I should do Ghirardelli.

Interiors, 1965 Designed by Wurster, Bernardi and Emmons, in conjunction with landscape architect Lawrence Halprin, Ghirardelli Square has not been shellacked for tourist consumption, but remains what it was: open, forthright, filled with sunlight, geraniums, and views of San Francisco Bay.

That D/R should end up on Ghirardelli Square is as natural as a Marimekko dress itself. San Franciscans are the ultimate customers of D/R; the godfather of Ghirardelli Square, William Roth, and Ben Thompson, architect and owner of D/R, both have definitive and somewhat parallel points of view on how life should be lived — unfettered, filled with sunlight, sea-washed air, pretty girls, and flowers.

Thus when D/R leased the lower floor of the Ghirardelli chocolate factory (the other half still produces some of the world's richest, blackest chocolate), Thompson practiced the essence of good design: using natural materials and leaving good things alone. He simply knocked out the partitions of the former shipping office, removed acoustical ceiling tile, and left the pillars and unadorned windows with their snatched views of the sea. He sanded the original oak floors with gray pumice and whitewashed the cement cavern which was left.

Interior details included hooks that were sunk into the concrete ceiling to provide for continuously changing furniture groupings, which can be divided by fabrics or panels hung from the ceiling. . . . The marine feeling of the space was complemented by dress racks hanging from marine ropes, knotted into monkey fists.

Ben Thompson, Memoirs I came to know Bill Roth as a store customer the day he came into the store looking for me. It was the beginning of our cross-country adventure. He became a close friend and supporter, a director of Design Research during our difficult time.

William Roth In those days there was nothing else like Design Research. I always felt it was positive when a city like Rome took its older buildings, including the Colosseum, and reused them for new things without destroying the building. To me, it was important that an older building be resurrected into appropriate new uses, using the best modern architect that you can get.

Sandra Smith Griswold, D/R staff, 1966–74 A very open space plan was created with huge windows. The openings were original, but Ben had replaced them with a sash that pivoted to open, which was a chore because they were so heavy.

Margaret Turnbull Simon, D/R staff, 1969–75 The chocolate factory had really high ceilings, like a warehouse space. The shell was always painted white. From time to time we would paint a colored accent wall but it was a basic white and glass interior in an old brick building that carried its own weight architecturally.

New York Times, 1968 In their renaissance the two sites [Ghirardelli Square and the Cannery] are rambling, multilevel marketplaces where the shopper can eat a crepe, sip a margarita, take in a play, examine a painting, buy a pair of sandals or a Rudi Gernrich dress, or soak up the sun and sniff the San Francisco Bay breeze. . . . Unlike the Cannery designers, who gutted the Del Monte plant, retaining only the outer shell of brick, the Ghirardelli Square architects . . . left the buildings intact. The structures, which bear names like the Mustard, Cocoa and Chocolate Buildings, are linked by outside stairways, balconies and walks . . . . The hungry i, the theater restaurant, several women's specialty stores, and Almond Plaza, the California Almond Growers Exchange, are among the new tenants. . . . Other tenants are radio station KFOG-FM, Design Research, two art galleries and American, Mexican, and Scandinavian craft shops.

In 1984, BTA remodeled the square's retail and public spaces, adding an exterior stair with a bandstand viewing platform and new paving and circulation routes.

OPPOSITE: The D/R van—a moving advertisement as it made daily deliveries around San Francisco.

William Roth I like to think that most things you do are entertaining as well as something else. Ghirardelli Square was done neither as an entertainment nor entirely as a business venture but to prove that it could be done, in part—that you could take old structures and reuse them and not go to high-rise in a particular area.

Ben Thompson, Memoirs In 1964 Bernard Rudofsky had given me the photo panels retired from his traveling MoMA exhibition, "Architecture Without Architects," which showed parts of great cities and sites around the world. We hung them as a thematic statement of vernacular urban design and folk tradition to dramatize the store's design idea: living in the given natural environment by ingenious use of indigenous resources.

Sandra Smith Griswold Ben took the old factory space and made it so beautiful. They stained the floors white and painted the interior white. There was open-track lighting on the 14-foot ceiling. When we built the Embarcadero store in 1972–73 we built a grid system in the ceiling so that it was easier to move around lighting and shelving.

Blase Gallo With large arched windows on three sides, open air moved through the space. Everything always felt fresh there.

Expansion Without Imitation

Margaret Turnbull Simon

"Ben started retailing for a good professional reason – for consumers who wanted to furnish their spaces with more than the family antiques."

Sibyl Wahl Hanson in a moment of rest during the first frantic weeks at Ghirardelli Square.

OPPOSITE: Two views of the renovated factory floor. Top, a D/R Down Seating Group, Mies coffee table, and two Thonet chairs, with an Aalto bar cart in the background. Bottom: Paul Dietrich's TAC daybed, American vernacular Clore chairs, and the hanging cone lamp made by Louis Poulsen, which was also used for thirty years as task lamps in the BTA office.

Sibyl Wahl Hanson, D/R staff, 1962–66
I came from California, went to Cambridge, and then drove back to San Francisco for the opening of the Ghirardelli Square store ahead of the truck with all the Design Research goodies. I was in charge of the opening. I think I sent an invitation to all the rich people I knew. Armi was there, all the social types, and the social reporter from the *San Francisco Chronicle* came. We bought the paper the next day to see which social types had been there and found a huge photo of the food spread. I had gone down to wholesale food places and bought entire sausages and baskets of cheeses and bowls of fruit. Everything whole, masses of fruit. So many things D/R did seem common now, but they had never seen anything like that before.

Sandra Smith Griswold They hired me to work in the dress department selling Marimekko dresses. After three weeks, Lorna Dawson made me store manager. I was twenty-seven at that point. I had people older than me and barely younger than me that I was managing. It was my dream job.

Everybody wanted to work for us, as they do for the Gap or Banana or J. Crew today. Applicants ranged from debutantes to architecture students to art historians. Ben's advice was important: "Never hire an ugly employee." He didn't mean ugly in a physical sense. He wanted attractive personalities able to convey enthusiasm.

I was so lucky in my hires. There was a girl from the fabric department, Wendy Tsuji, who became Larry Ellison's architect. Jeanne Allen and Marc Grant now own the Jeanne Marc clothing company. The last person I hired for Embarcadero was Randy Delahanty, who is one of San Francisco's best-known architectural historians. He ran the California Historical Society. He was my stock boy.

Margaret Turnbull Simon We used Marimekko panels to create visual blocks to stop your eye and reorient you to furniture or fabric or housewares or furniture settings. We had open shelving that was just four-by-four redwood verticals with screws on either end to tighten them. When we started in 1965, we just had wood shelving, redwood or pine boards cut to size for whatever products were on display. The constants of display were shelving and fabric and the fabric-cutting counters, painted white with butcher-board tops. A few sales counters were modular so that we could turn them into squares or into long cutting areas.

Kathleen Parks Perry, D/R staff, 1975–77
Armi Ratia came once and gave a talk. Someone asked her why she would choose a particular pattern to produce. She said, "I am always looking for something that is slightly uncomfortable," which I thought was fascinating and very right on. There was something provocative about her fabrics that made you stop. There was a kind of skewed symmetry about it. There was an evenness to the designs but there was always something slightly off. Positive space was a very big deal in her fabrics. That boldness of the form. All of those things. Other fabrics were more timid, and hers were not timid at all.

Sandra Smith Griswold The stores I admire usually have a single philosophy. It is not complicated. You know exactly who they are. If you look at the furniture from Denmark that was carried at D/R in the mid-1960s, Ben picked Poul Kjaerholm and Hans Wegner, and the *pieces* he chose are the only ones still in production. The store always drew you back to see what was up. It was informative, it was interesting, it evolved.

110   Design Research

Expansion Without Imitation 111

Lu Wendel Lyndon When Ben would come out, we would go into a frenzy. Then came the walk-through. Ben delighted in trying to turn things upside down. It was always fun to move departments around, to put one part of the store in a totally different place. Regrouping the products to create different room settings obviously stimulated customers — frustrated some — but generally generated much more business. Objects always look different in the context of different things.

I remember telling Ben my idea that the California lifestyle was so different from the East Coast's, and he was rather brusque with me. He didn't see that much difference in style. I ended up agreeing with him. What D/R offered was a way of living and a way of looking at things that was not bound by one side of the continent and part of the world, which is why so many people here responded to it.

Sandra Smith Griswold It was significant that every single object in the store, with the exception of the truly vernacular, was identified for us. We knew the designer's name, country of origin, the history of everything we carried. A clock, a glass pig, a piece of fabric, a rug, a toy. That was an amazing education. Second thing, it was the first store to show furniture in complete rooms. Even stores like Gump's in San Francisco, then a good source, had a furniture floor with a sea of stuff. They never put a coffee table with a sofa with a lounge chair in a room environment with fresh flowers and great music.

Marian Parmenter (Wintersteen), D/R staff, 1972–77 All that furniture was so elegant but very light compared to the antique furniture we had all grown up with. Except for the Eames chair, the leather one that is stuffed. I loved selling those. Now they seem quite beautiful, but to me at the time I thought it was a funny design. It has become such a classic because it fits well with old furniture. It is more interesting to have a mixture of things, not everything spare and minimal.

Emma-Gail Lombardi, D/R staff, 1965–78 I had no training but I didn't need it, I just exaggerated everything. I had an unlimited budget for flowers. It was not a flower here and a flower there; it was like a mass of this and a mass of that. So you got the real impact of the color and the flowers. I would take at least five gallon buckets and fill them with flowers of all one kind and put them in the front window. As you walked in the store, which was very light and wonderful, there would be a repeat of this. I would also put them in a large Aalto vase. I would use the merchandise. It was never so precious that it couldn't be used.

Lu Wendel Lyndon It used to be that for glassware, we displayed one glass of each size and pattern out on a shelf. Then came the day when Ben said, "I see that grocery markets have so much impact and make you want to buy; the trick is piling up a lot of each box or can on the shelf. Try this as an approach to display." It was 1967 or 1968 when Ben conveyed this epiphany to us in San Francisco. So the rule became to use eight or twelve glasses or cups. Each item's impact was expanded, and it could be seen as something right for your house or your kitchen cabinet. Gordon Segal took this a step further at Crate & Barrel when said, "Let's put out all we own."

OPPOSITE, ABOVE: Kitchenwares displayed in custom-made wooden boxes, which were easy to move around or remerchandise.

OPPOSITE, BELOW: Pillows arranged as a full-spectrum wall-size array of color and texture.

A summer living room setting. Suspended from the ceiling are panels from the 1964 exhibition "Architecture Without Architects," created by author-architect Bernard Rudofsky for MoMA in New York. This was shown in D/R stores in San Francisco, New York, and Cambridge, and was a gift to Ben from Rudofsky.

Expansion Without Imitation

Sandra Smith Griswold "Ben had a perfect eye for what was good and would endure."

Lu Wendel Lyndon We decided, which Ben also felt, that people bought by color. Customers had a certain affinity for certain colors and others just didn't inspire them. So to put things into a color/textural context rather than a functional one made things look very different, and also stimulated them to buy more than one object. "I need this to go with that." It worked.

In the Marimekko department, you grouped dresses by pattern and by color, not by size. I received a Marimekko display manual in the mail a couple months ago and realized that we developed those rules. Pillows were done by "color spread," Ben's guidelines in doing the cubby displays. Rows of cubbies had the same thing in variation: One row of three cubbies was all pillows, for instance. Another row was, perhaps, filled with the wonderful glass goblets that Marimekko made. Another row held stuffed Marimekko toys. But instead of three rigid rows across of the same thing, you would take one away to substitute a contrasting form that would catch your eye. Big things would go on the bottom, lighter colors would go on the top, tall things would go on the very top or bottom but not in the middle. It had a lot to do with balanced composition with visual arresting points.

The process was always inventive. It wasn't ever a "No." It was, "Have you ever thought of . . . ?" When someone tried to write it down as "the D/R way," it became a little obnoxious. Ben never wrote it down. He would change his mind based on looking at things as they were, or might be.

Margaret Turnbull Simon When I started in display we began color-coding things for grouping. Starting in with kitchenware, china, and glass, we would display merchandise by color. Then that took on a greater effect, and we would do color themes, such as a yellow-and-orange theme, or black-and-white theme. My favorite displays used multiple primary colors and used black and white to really pop those into prominence.

We had Heller windows with orange plates stacked with the graphic Heller boxes. We did a toy window filled with sock hobby horses. They were suspended, thousands of horses galloping along on their poles.

Things happened all over the store. There was a Sam Smith show. It was Plexiglas cubes holding up his handmade boats. There would be a special setting on a coffee table at Christmas with flowers and with lovely Niederer glass ornaments stacked up with glass bowls and vases. This turned into a magical glass kingdom of ornaments with flowers. You name it, we did it.

Emma-Gail Lombardi The way I used the fabric so I wouldn't waste it was to take a bolt of fabric, run it across the table, and take the remaining bolt and put it on a chair at the table. Then I would use all different kinds of things, whatever we had to sell. Usually some nice china and glassware, but it wasn't elegant. It was simple and it was a knockout. I would put together Kaj Franck art pieces and make that a feature. I used Valencia, for example, mixed with other Arabia patterns. But I would never mix Ruska with Valencia. We had so many wonderful things, you know, and it was so new to San Francisco. People would come into the store and say, "I want the whole thing, the fabric and everything on the table."

Kathleen Parks Perry Emma-Gail was baroque in terms of her aesthetic. She made very full, over-the-top, luscious flower arrangements and unpredictable combinations. There was something really lush and much more rich than if you had done a tabletop that was tasteful. If you had done something really predictable it would have been like, okay, tasteful, boring.

There was something a little bit about the Armi Ratia aesthetic that Emma-Gail's tables had too. They made you feel like you couldn't leave without having one of each at least. I think from a merchandising point of view it was brilliant.

Sandra Smith Griswold We used to stack plastic letter trays twenty-five feet high in all the different colors. That's a bit of dramatic whimsy.

Margaret Turnbull Simon Ghirardelli was a tourist location. We were in a wonderful position to expose people who had never seen modern design. They would be awed by the color and the graphics and the ambience of the place. That's where having smaller, more accessible products was appealing. Visitors could take home with them things that registered a new way of looking at things, some token of the new experience. Having the store in an old building, in reused "found space," was also important. In a modern building some people wouldn't relate to it. They could relate to modernism in the bricks and mortar of a historic setting.

D/R and the architecture community of the 1960s were pretty symbiotic. Ben started retailing for a good professional reason—for consumers who wanted to furnish their spaces with more than the family antiques. Before D/R there was only the design floor of Gump's, which was clean Oriental stuff. Designers and architects would send in their associates and their clients, as it made their work easier. Pretty much the whole architectural community—David Robinson and Heinrich Boll, certainly Bill Turnbull and Charles Moore and Donlyn Lyndon—were very much a part of Design Research.

OPPOSITE: Color always meant more color at D/R—here an Indian cotton rug is used as a bedspread, vibrating against orange director's chairs. Ben brought a sophistication to an existing inexpensive traditional camping chair by making seat covers in bright new hues. The standing lamp is by Nessen.

Marimekko fabrics could be adapted for more and more uses, such as these stuffed toys and soft slippers, shown at D/R piled and stacked, never singly.

Expansion Without Imitation 115

A General Store of Good Design

5

Ben Thompson spent a lot of time explaining Design Research. What it was: "an attitude about design." What it wasn't: a museum of the new and exclusive. "Almost everything we had, someone else had too. The difference was the way we were using it and the combinations of well-designed things we were putting together in the store." He tried using the metaphor of the outdoor food market, a place where we all buy the same things and yet put them together in remarkably different ways back home. He tried using the then-bizarre term "environment" to indicate that Design Research was more than surface decorating; rather, it was a way of life. He rejected both the idea of *the* aesthetic — beautiful, not necessarily useful things — and also the idea of *an* aesthetic — his way or no way. But perhaps the clearest formulation was one he wrote in D/R's 1968 Christmas catalogue: "Simply put, D/R is a General Store of good design."

   A general store is a place for daily needs and for special treats. It is a landmark on the high street. Its owner is known to all. And it succeeds or fails on the variety and quality of its goods. No one should be able to leave a general store disappointed or empty handed. The essence of

The traditional Viennese café chair, light and versatile, introduced by Thonet in 1859, was updated when Ben ordered them in hot contemporary colors. They became a perennial best-selling item in the store.

As seen in D/R catalogue, products in the store were never alone: Basics like coffeepots, sugar shakers, and pepper mills were massed, while tables were dressed with pop linens, bright flowers, and china and melamine. Interplay of form and strong, clear colors was key to the effect.

Design Research, therefore, lay first in the special qualities and diversity of its products, then in the way they were laid out for the customer.

Though Marimekko and D/R would always be visually synonymous, Maija Isola's supersize prints were only the splashiest items Ben Thompson introduced to America. To discover new products, Ben avoided the national trade shows and instead went abroad, hunting down designers and artisans, and blazing a personal trail from one studio to the next, led by each craftsman's recommendation to the next destination. He found D/R-worthy goods in the ateliers of famous architects, of course, like Alvar Aalto and Arne Jacobsen. But he also found them in the workshops of artisans working in centuries-old traditions like the glassblowers of Venini, or in the radical new ways of Swiss glass designer Roberto Niederer. And in vernacular wares like American canvas camp chairs or Bolivian alpaca sweaters. And in true discoveries, like the hanging carved monkeys by Kay Bojesen or the articulated toy-sculptures of British artist Sam Smith. He worked with many artisans during production, shaping groups of products with the requisite dimensions or capacities required by American users. They all soon became friends.

In this way, he quietly and effectively achieved the exact qualities he desired for the harmonious mix of ingredients at his store. Ben introduced the work of some designers established in Scandinavia for decades, plus a new generation of Europeans, premiering and promoting each product as a major news event for American consumers. He never bought one designer's whole line, as that would have turned D/R into a mere showroom. And he never locked his suppliers into full-line exclusives; instead, he cherry-picked the best items and designed others as additions to D/R's family of furnishings. The following products provide a visual account of D/R's shelves and attempt to show the range and mixture of items high and low, and delicate and indestructible. Although they can be understood as belonging to three main product categories — modern, vernacular, and toys and folk art — in the next pages we've arranged them naturally in the home: living room, dining room, kitchen, and home office, and in a couple of cases by material or use.

Modern

This category includes a number of designs that are familiar today, even overly familiar, such as Iittala glassware, Aalto stools, Wegner wishbone chairs, and the first glass-and-steel coffee table (the pedigreed version, by Mies van der Rohe). In the 1950s, however, these pieces were not widely available in the United States, and Design Research and its retail contemporaries introduced them to a wider public. That most of them are still popular, and still look modern, is a testament to Ben's selective eye. What were once novelties are now staples, available online everywhere and thus easy to overlook. No longer news, they endure as classics.

First in this category of the once revolutionary would be the sturdy furniture designed by Ben Thompson and his associates, Paul Dietrich, Phoebe Mason Bruck, and Claud Bunyard. Ben's great discovery was butcher board, originally an industrial laminated-wood product, which he moved beyond its factory origins as a heavy-duty chopping block. He developed laminated table tops using the wood grain visibly and decoratively, with inset tapered wood legs held in place by a walnut wedge in many shapes and sizes, perfect in maple for breakfasting, drafting, or writing, or in fruitwood and mahogany as dining and coffee tables. He found fine-grained Finnish birch laminates with elegant striated edges left exposed on open shelves and cabinetry and countertops. Pushing the envelope, BTA's new dormitories for Colby College in Maine opened in 1967 furnished with a new line of furniture entirely composed of laminated slabs, including couches, side chairs, tables, desks, and low table-benches for the common rooms. Then his D/R group designed a suite of sturdy oak furniture—dressers, desks, and shelves—for the dormitory rooms of the new Kirkland College (BTA 1968, Clinton, N.Y.).

In the stores, a rolling kitchen island with a butcher-board top—popular for on-site omelet pan demonstrations in D/R's kitchen departments—simultaneously solved chefs' counter-space problems and made their cooking the center of any party. Ben again upped the ante with a design for a mobile bar cart with handsome bicycle wheels and a laminated maple top. In all, he established the value of laminated wood in many forms as a new domestic material throughout America.

Equally important were Thompson's discoveries abroad. He found side chairs by Hans Wegner and an ergonomically superior traditional Finnish rocker. In his Vienna workshop, Carl Aubock honed shapely home tools—cork pulls, brushes, cap lifters—of brass, bone, and leather, irresistible to the eye and hand. At a smaller scale, there was glassware striking for its sheen and shape, both high-end handblown pieces from Roberto Niederer in Switzerland and Nanny Still, Kaj Franck, and Timo Sarpaneva in Finland, alongside textured glassware by Oiva Toikka and Vuokko Nurmesniemi. These artisans, as well as many others, had a

A General Store of Good Design 119

The simplest version of Thompson's taste for the unaffected vernacular: kitchen jelly glasses—inexpensive but substantial in the hand—on a sunny Unikko-covered table.

major impact on postwar American design practice in glass, ceramics, wood, brass, and other natural materials. The names Niederer and Aubock, two of Thompson's favorites, carry on today in studios operated by their sons and grandsons.

Ben Thompson was also visionary in accepting new materials for improved performance, especially the high-quality, strong, hard melamine and polypropylene plastics that emerged from Italy in the 1960s, opening enormous new design possibilities. D/R, like the culture, was changing, and even the advanced forms of a designer like Wegner in wood began to look conventional. Joe Colombo's pioneering polypropylene injection-molded Universale stacking chairs offered changeable leg sizes for adult- and children's-size seats. Shown alongside products like his mobile kitchen, they evoked a new, quick, lightweight, and (unfortunately) disposable lifestyle for the 1970s. Dinner could be eaten off not only hand-painted cobalt-blue-and-white Arabia, but also off Massimo Vignelli's Max I melamine dinnerware, which was stackable, sturdy enough for the dishwasher, and in colors unknown in the natural world. Choices expanded.

Even in the twenty-five-year life span of the store, the definition of classic transformed. In period photographs of the store, one spots products that still seem novel, strange, intriguing. Børge Mogensen's useful line of teak furniture was challenged by the lighter, more linear, and more affordable German beds and cabinets by Dieter Rams and by Finnish designer Pirkko Stenros's modular, stackable, and small-scale Muurame chests and beds. Striking individual designs can be forgotten with the closing of factories and changing careers. Some of these items, introduced five decades ago, are of a quality worthy of reevaluation and perhaps reconsideration.

Vernacular

D/R's standard for quality and value was not based on costly materials or the makers' upmarket aspirations. There were a significant number of highly affordable generic products that could be found in the everyday marketplace, accepted as ordinary but readily transformed by coats of bright paint (the 1876 Thonet bentwood Vienna café chair) or dyed canvas (the director's chair), or merely by the company they kept on D/R's shelves and floors. Beside handmade, precious pieces, there were mass-produced American "jelly jars" and pressed-glass goblets, the Chemex coffeemaker, and a slim ladderback chair as appropriate to an 1850 farmhouse as to a Gropius house.

Thompson had a particular fondness for lightness and transportability—an easily moved chair, as he often demonstrated, is one that encourages people to form social groups for conversation. He picked a group of light but sturdy chairs and stools, like the Italian rush benches and the Yugoslavian folding chair, which could collapse or be stacked for use as casual perches. Also important to his notion of flexibility were multifunctioning pieces like the German willow daybed, a woven piece that doubled as sofa and guest bed accommodations, without the weight of a fold-out. Another staple was the well-made sailor's hammock, native to Pawley's Island, South Carolina, which traveled from D/R into many distinguished gardens. The hammock, not incidentally, looked fabulous in the Brattle Street stairwell piled with Marimekko pillows, adjacent to multicolored bamboo lounge chairs from the islands.

Toys and Folk Art

Despite his appreciation for the newest material and the latest designers, Ben remained a traditionalist in his admiration for the workable products of the earth—clay, stone, fiber, silica, reed, rush and grasses, and wood of every kind. Wood was favored for its warm tactility, its natural aging, and its plasticity in taking many forms and finishes, allowing the artist's hand to be subtly present. He believed the mark of a tool or the irregular surface of a turned clay pot made the surface attract the eye and touch the imagination. Imperfections made the product more perfect because it felt more human. Ben saw these qualities as yin to the yang of the clean spaces of modern architecture. Folk objects were eagerly sought to bring tactility and color to white walls and glass houses, a feel of timeless tradition to their inhabitants.

Ben scoured the animated markets of Mexican cities and country regularly for wooden toys, woven mats and belts, carved animals, and celebratory ornaments for *Semana Santa.* One dedicated craft representative worked with natives in the Bolivian Andes to produce luxurious alpaca wool sweaters, which she shipped to Ben in batches (but only when both sleeve lengths matched and the dimensions approximated an American size). From Denmark and Switzerland there were Christmas decorations used year-round: delicate hanging foil and paper snowflakes, or glass drops filled with colored water, amazing in depth and texture when hung en masse. Ben found remarkable Navajo rugs and Indian blankets in the West, kilims and Berber carpets in North Africa. As a native Minnesotan, Ben knew the cold-weather tradition of fur hats and personally sported and sold the classic Alaskan unisex sealskin cap with flaps (legal at the time). An ironic Eskimo craftsman used his fur scraps to create a tiny toy seal, which was irresistible to the touch and became a wildly popular gift.

There was no common ground in material, in make, in complexity, or roughness. Rather, the role of folk art objects at D/R was to disrupt the sometimes too-smooth surface of good design, introducing through handwork the quality of play and fantasy that comes through travel but is often so difficult to take home.

Living Room
Bentwood, wicker, and leather, plus worn-in textiles and airy lamps, fostered a modern, relaxed atmosphere

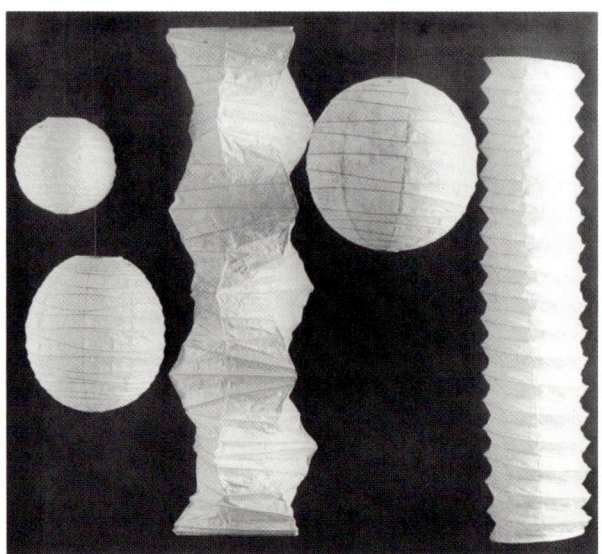

TOP LEFT: **Alvar Aalto,** Finland, Tea Trolley 900, Artek, 1937

BOTTOM: **Jorge Ferrari Hardoy,** Argentina, Butterfly Chair, Artek-Pascoe, 1938/Knoll, 1947

TOP RIGHT: **Yki Nummi,** Finland, Modern Art Table Lamp, Orno, 1955

CENTER: **H. Magg,** Germany, Willow Sofabed, 1950; **Joan Forrester Sprague for D/R,** USA, Birch Cube Table, D/R Workshop, 1965

BOTTOM: **Isamu Noguchi,** USA, Akari Light Sculptures, c. 1951

Design Research

now available in USA
FRITZ HANSEN AX CHAIR
the tennis racket chair

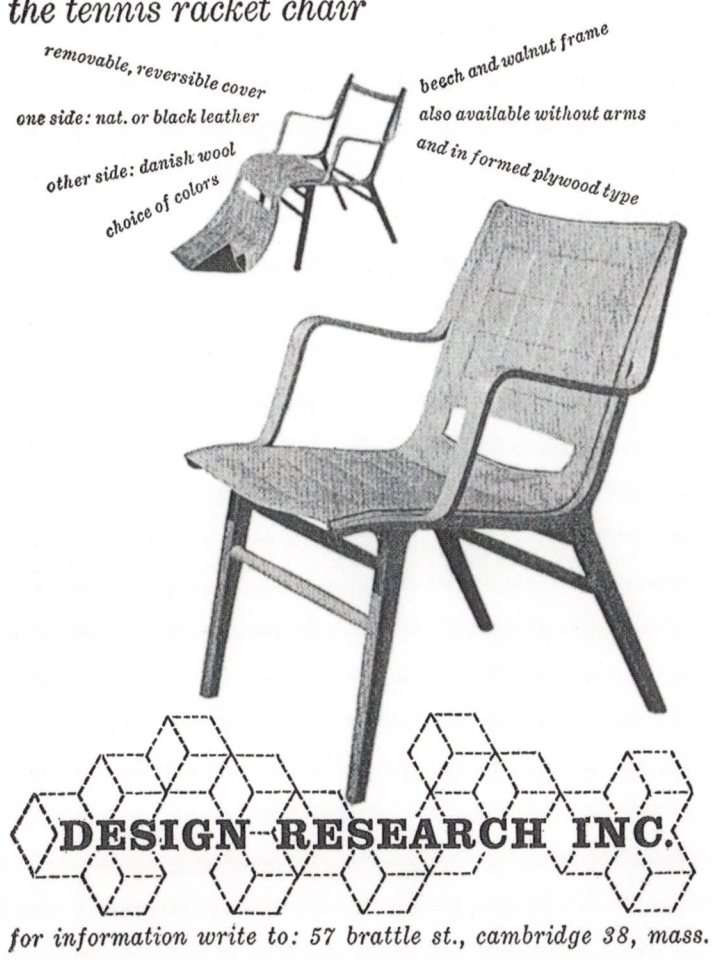

removable, reversible cover
one side: nat. or black leather
other side: danish wool
choice of colors

beech and walnut frame
also available without arms
and in formed plywood type

DESIGN RESEARCH INC.

for information write to: 57 brattle st., cambridge 38, mass.

TOP LEFT: **Peter Hvidt** and **Orla Mølgaard-Nielsen,** Denmark, AX Chair, Fritz Hansen, 1950

CENTER: **Bruno Mathsson,** Sweden, T. 108 Pernilla 3 Lounge Chair, Firma Karl Mathsson, 1944

BOTTOM: **Ludwig Mies van der Rohe,** USA (born Germany), Tugendhat Table, Knoll, 1930

TOP RIGHT: **Franco Albini,** Italy, Margherita Chair, Vittorio Bonacina, 1951

CENTER: Maltese Rug, Malta, n.d.

BOTTOM: Berber Rugs, Morocco, n.d.

A General Store of Good Design   123

Dining Room

American classics (Clore chairs, Arthur goblets) mingled with multicolor Arabia dinnerware and daring Disa lamps

CLOCKWISE, TOP LEFT:
Kaj Franck, Finland, Kilta Table Service, Arabia, 1952

Alvar Aalto, Finland, Tables 81A, 83 (casters added), Artek, 1933–35

Finel Enamel Bowls, Finland, Wärtsilä, 1958

124 Design Research

TOP LEFT: **Arne Jacobsen,** Denmark, Ant Chair, Fritz Hansen, 1951–52

BOTTOM: E. A. Clore & Sons, USA, Ladderback Chairs, c. 1830

TOP RIGHT: Disa Lamp, Spain, c. 1960

CENTER: **Ulla Procopé,** Finland, Valencia Table Service, Arabia, 1960

BOTTOM: Indiana Glass Co., USA, Arthur Goblet, c. 1900

A General Store of Good Design 125

Cooking

Braun appliances, stove-to-table Vallauris casseroles, and elegant Aubock bar tools were part of the lived-in kitchen stocked with goods from all over the world

CLOCKWISE, TOP RIGHT:
Peter Schlumbohm, Germany, Coffee Maker, Chemex, 1941

Vallauris Casseroles, France, n.d.

Hans (Nick) Roericht, Germany, TC 100 Table Service, Rosenthal (Thomas), 1959

Timo Sarpaneva, Finland, Cast-Iron Casserole, Rosenlew, 1959

Gerd Alfred Müller, Germany, M121 Portable Mixer, Braun, 1964

126   Design Research

CLOCKWISE, TOP RIGHT:
Antti Nurmesniemi, Finland, Enamel Coffee Pot, Wärtsilä, 1957

Carl Aubock, Austria, Bottle Opener, c. 1962

H. A. Mack & Company, USA, Collapsible Salad Basket, before 1953

D/R Sauté Pan, France, 1965

Joe Colombo, Italy, Rolling Kitchen, Boffi, 1964

A General Store of Good Design   127

Glass
Masters from Switzerland, Italy, and Finland created new forms for daily use

LEFT, TOP TO BOTTOM:
Saara Hopea, Finland, Stacking Tumblers, Nuutajärvi, 1955

Saara Hopea, Finland, Camilla Goblets, Nuutajärvi, c. 1955

Oiva Toikka, Finland, Kastehelmi Plate, Nuutajärvi, 1964

CENTER, TOP TO BOTTOM:
Timo Sarpaneva, Finland, I-Line Stacking Bottles, Iittala, 1959

Timo Sarpaneva, Finland, Varireuma Bowl, Iittala, 1956

RIGHT, TOP TO BOTTOM:
Venini, Italy, Decanter, c. 1960

Tapio Wirkkala, Finland, Bolle (decanters), Venini, 1967

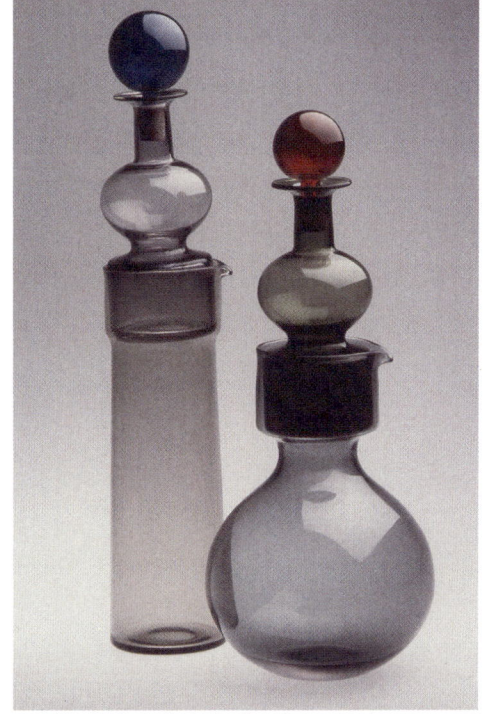

LEFT, TOP TO BOTTOM:
Roberto Niederer, Switzerland, Handblown Glass Ornament, 1959

Roberto Niederer, Switzerland, Blow-Molded Ash Trays, 1959

Alvar Aalto, Finland, Vase 3031, Iittala, 1936

CENTER, TOP TO BOTTOM:
Kaj Franck, Finland, Kremlin Bells Double Decanters, Nuutajärvi, 1957

Kaj Franck, Finland, Candlesticks, Nuutajärvi, c. 1965

Kaj Franck, Finland, Turn-Molded Filigree Glass Jars, Nuutajärvi, 1964

RIGHT, TOP TO BOTTOM:
Oiva Toikka, Finland, Handblown Bird Ornament, c. 1960

Tapio Wirkkala, Finland, Ultima Thule Glasses, Iittala, 1968

Tapio Wirkkala, Finland, Romantica Decanter and Glasses, Iittala, 1960

A General Store of Good Design 129

D/R Originals
Thompson and company filled in the gaps with soft sofas, elegant tables, and sturdy butcher block

MATERIALS: Frame: Solid ash, doweled and glued. Seat: Hand tied coil springs on jute webbing. Back: Sinuous springs with hair padding. Cushions interchangeable to equalize wear, filled with white goose down mixture, stitched and channeled. Fully upholstered or slipcovered over muslin in any fabric. Legs: Either chrome, walnut, or teak. (Pictured with Barcelona Table.) Also available with Poly/Dacron cushions, fully upholstered only.

DIMENSIONS:

		Upholstered	Slipcovered
Ottoman:	28" Wide, 22" Deep, 19" High	3 yards	3 yards
Chair:	31" Wide, 35" Deep, 28" High	6½ yards	8½ yards
Loveseat:	60" Wide, 36" Deep, 27" High	11 yards	13 yards
3-Seat:	88" Wide, 38" Deep, 27" High	16 yards	18 yards
4-Seat:	108" Wide, 38" Deep, 27" High	22 yards	24 yards

DESIGNER: Benjamin Thompson, 1953
MANUFACTURED IN: U.S.A.

D/R SOFA

D|R

CLOCKWISE, TOP RIGHT:
B. Wood Sanders for D/R, USA, Bicycle Wheel Bar Cart, 1966

Benjamin Thompson, USA, Down Seating Group, D/R Workshop, 1953

BTA, USA, Kirkland Dresser, D/R Workshop, 1969; **Marco Zanuso,** Italy, 275 Table Lamp, Oluce, 1963

Joan Forrester Sprague for D/R, USA, Butcher-board Table, 1953; **Marcel Breuer,** USA (born Hungary), B5 Chair, Standard-Möbel, 1927

130 Design Research

CLOCKWISE, TOP:
Benjamin Thompson, USA, Butcherboard Series: Sofa and Coffee Table, D/R Workshop, 1966; **Vico Magistretti,** Italy, Carimate Lounge Chair, Cassina, 1959

BTA, USA, Butcherboard Pedestal Table, D/R Workshop, 1968

Claud Bunyard for D/R, USA, Quartic Oval Dining Table, D/R Workshop, 1962; **Josef Hoffmann,** Austria, 811 Side Chair, Gebrüder Thonet, c. 1920

A General Store of Good Design   131

Working

The postwar home also became a place of work with lightweight engineered products from Fiskars, Luxo, and Vitsoe

EAMES CHAIR AND OTTOMAN

This world famous chair is on permanent exhibition in the Museum of Modern Art and proclaims the ultimate in comfort.

The core of each cushion is resilient foam, surrounded by a layer of feathers and down, and covered by the finest leather procurable, the "Best Auch" from Scotland. The seat and ottoman cushions are identical and can be reversed to equalize wear as can the two back cushions.

MATERIALS: Down filled leather cushions on a moulded rosewood veneer shell, mounted on a five-point cast aluminum pedestal.
DIMENSIONS: Chair: 33 3/8" High, 32 1/2" Wide, 32 3/4" Deep, Seat Height: 15"
Ottoman: 15" High, 26" Wide, 21" Deep
DESIGNER: Charles Eames, 1956
MANUFACTURED IN: U.S.A.

D|R

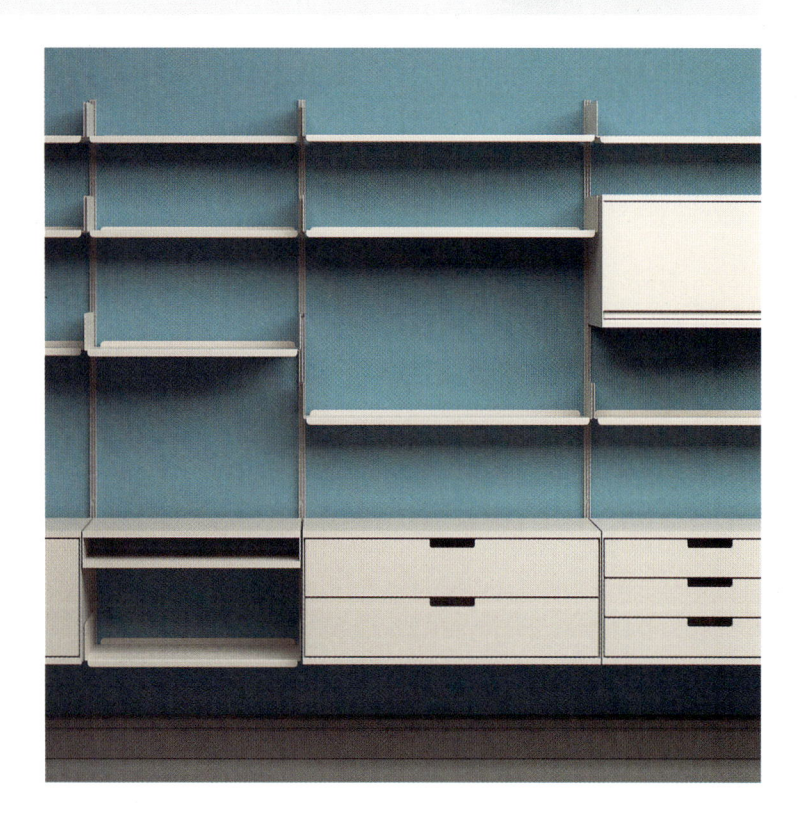

CLOCKWISE, TOP RIGHT:
Charles and Ray Eames, USA, Lounge Chair and Ottoman, Herman Miller, 1956

Dieter Rams, Germany, 606 Universal Shelving System, Vitsoe, 1960

R. Baltensweiler, Switzerland, Model 60 Adjustable Lamp, 1965

Bruno Munari, Italy, Cubo Ashtray, Danese, 1957

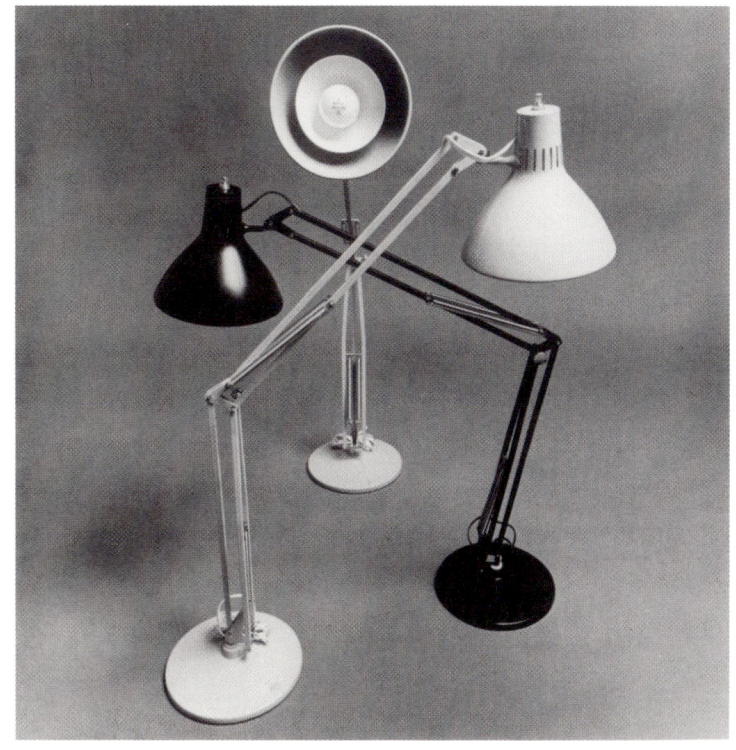

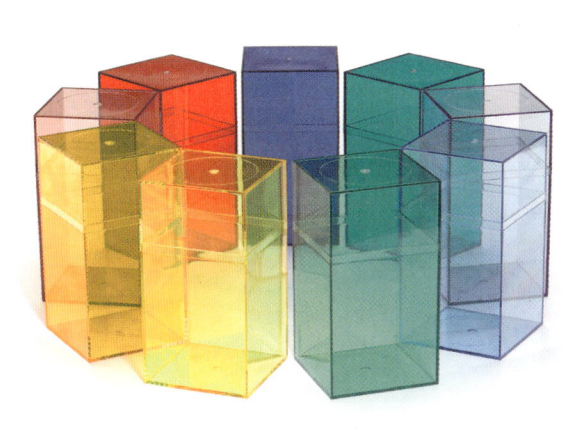

CLOCKWISE, TOP LEFT:
Olof Bäckström, Finland, Self-Sharpening Scissors, Fiskars, 1960

Jacob Jacobsen, Norway, LS1 Lamp, Luxo, 1937

Marimekko, Finland, Canvas Tote Bags, Unikko and solid colors, 1964

Gene Hurwitt, USA, M Series Storage Boxes, AMAC, c. 1965

Jørgen Rasmussen, Denmark, Drafting Chair, Kevi, 1961

A General Store of Good Design

Plastics

They stack, they inflate, they light, they shelter—the new materials added color, convenience, and comfort

CLOCKWISE, TOP RIGHT:
Giancarlo Mattioli, Italy, Nesso Table Lamp, Artemide, 1964

Massimo Vignelli, Italy, Max 1 Stacking Dinnerware, Heller, 1969

Vico Magistretti, Italy, Eclisse Table Lamp, Artemide, 1966

De Pas, D'Urbino & Lomazzi, Italy, Blow (inflatable chair), Zanotta, 1967

134   Design Research

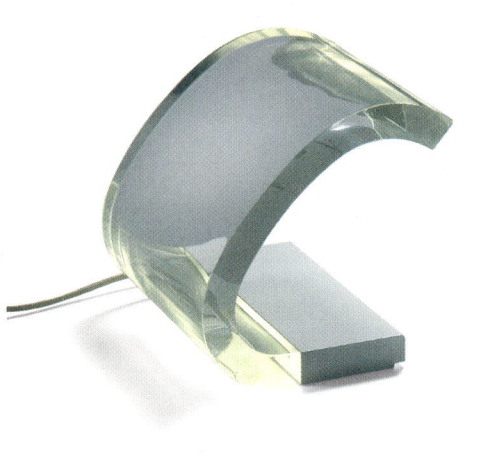

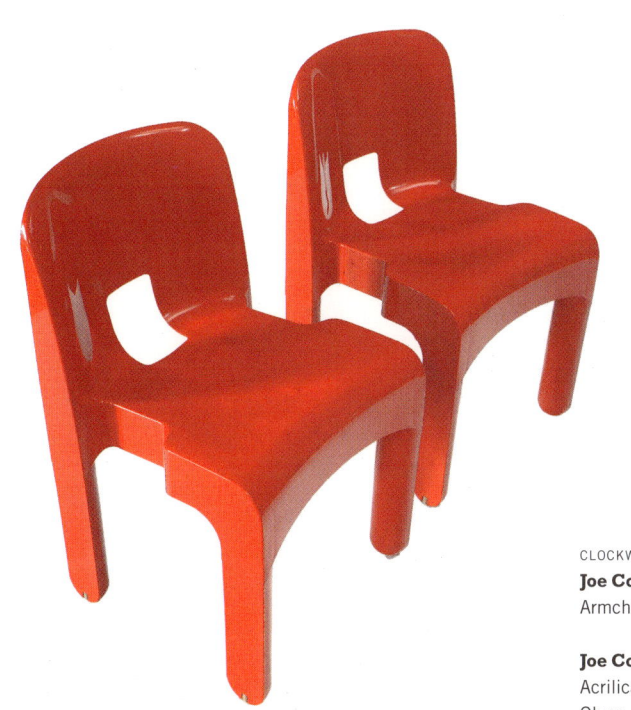

CLOCKWISE, TOP LEFT:
Joe Colombo, Italy, Elda Armchair, Comfort, 1963

Joe Colombo, Italy, 281 Acrilica Table Lamp, Oluce, 1962

Joe Colombo, Italy, Boby 3 Portable Storage System, Bieffeplast, 1969

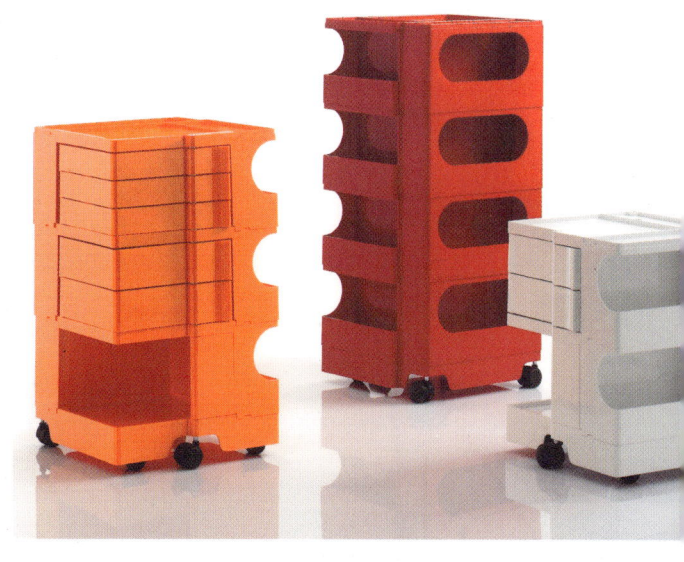

Joe Colombo, Italy, Universale Chair, Kartell, 1965

A General Store of Good Design   135

Seating

Modern classics from Aalto, Breuer, Thonet, and Wegner met postwar designs by Bertoia, Magistretti, Saarinen, and Wirth

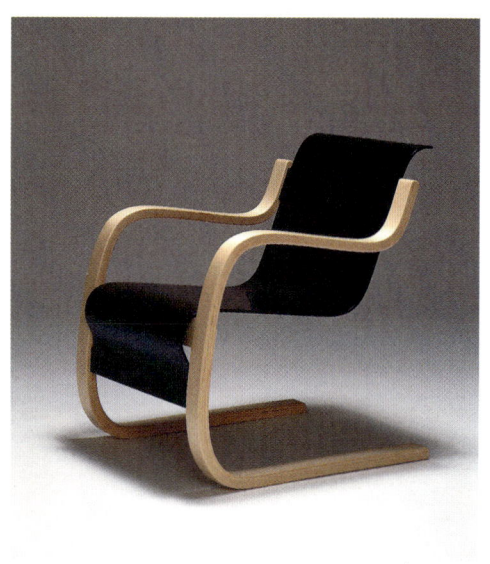

LEFT, TOP TO BOTTOM:
Marcel Breuer, USA (born Hungary), Cesca Side Chair, Gebrüder Thonet, 1928/Knoll, 1968

Marcel Breuer, USA (born Hungary), Wassily Chair, Standard-Möbel and Gebrüder Thonet, 1925/Knoll, 1968

CENTER, TOP TO BOTTOM:
Hans Wegner, Denmark, The Chair, Johannes Hansen, 1949

Hans Wegner, Denmark, The Peacock Chair, Johannes Hansen, 1947

Hans Wegner, Denmark, The Swivel Chair, Fritz Hansen, 1955

Hans Wegner, Denmark, The Folding Chair, Johannes Hansen, 1949

RIGHT, TOP TO BOTTOM:
Alvar Aalto, Finland, Stool 60, Artek, 1932–33

Alvar Aalto, Finland, Armchair 42, Artek, 1932

Alvar Aalto, Finland, Stool X601, Artek, 1954

136   Design Research

LEFT, TOP TO BOTTOM:
Gebrüder Thonet, Austria, Bentwood Rocking Chair No. 10, c. 1880

Gebrüder Thonet, Austria, Hoffmann Armchair No. 811, c. 1920

August Thonet, Austria, Corbusier Chair No. B9, Gebrüder Thonet, 1900

CENTER, TOP TO BOTTOM:
Heinz Wirth, Germany, Zurich Arm Chair, Erlau AG, 1963

Harry Bertoia, USA (born Italy), Side Chair, Knoll, 1952

Vico Magistretti, Italy, Carimate Chair, Cassina, 1959

FAR RIGHT: **Eero Saarinen,** USA (born Finland), Womb Chair, Knoll, 1947–48

A General Store of Good Design 137

Playing

No plastic here, but toys and furniture made to delight and to last by European craftsmen

MUURAME BED AND CHESTS

MATERIALS: Baked enamel finish on pressed pine. Pincore latex foam rubber mattresses.
DIMENSIONS:
#267 Bunkbed 801, 35½" Wide, 54½" High; Mattress 751, 30" Wide, 4" Thick
  Available in white/yellow and white/red
#455 Underbed Drawers, 29" Wide, 27" Deep, 10" High
  Available in white, red, and yellow
#400 4-Drawer Chest, 31½" Wide, 21½" Deep, 25½" High
  Available in white/red, yellow, and white/natural
#401 3-Drawer Chest, 15½" Wide, 21½" Deep, 25½" High
  Available in white, white/red, and yellow
#406 3-Dresser Chest, 23½" Wide, 21½" Deep, 25½" High
  Available in white, red, and yellow
#616 Table Top 631, 21" Wide
  Available in white and yellow
DESIGNER: Pirrko Stenros
MANUFACTURED IN: Finland

D|R

CLOCKWISE, TOP LEFT:
Marimekko, Finland, Puketti Critter, 1964

Pirkko Stenros, Finland, Bunkbed with Storage, Modular Chests, Muurame, c. 1951

J. K. Adams for D/R, USA, Marble Slide, D/R Workshop, 1963

Juho Jussila, Finland, Wood Toys, Jussila, c. 1946

138 Design Research

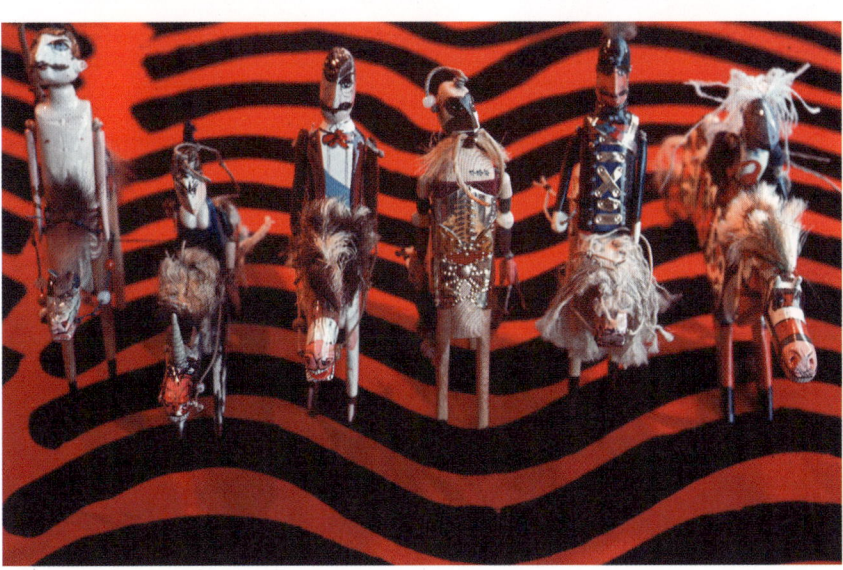

CLOCKWISE, TOP LEFT:
Marimekko, Finland, Stuffed Monkey, 1967

Sam Smith, Britain, Handmade Model Ship, 1964

Kay Bojesen, Denmark, Monkey, Rosendahl, 1951

Oaxacan Carved Animals, Mexico, n.d.

Sam Smith, Britain, Hand-Painted Horsemen, c. 1964

A General Store of Good Design 139

D/R catalogue pages, 1965

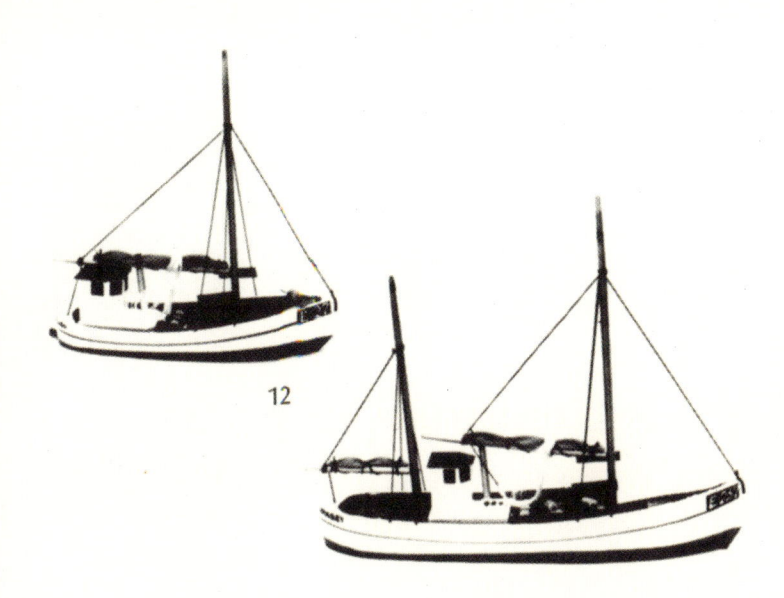

12   Model boats from Denmark. *Dana* 5". $3.   *Haabet* 8". $7

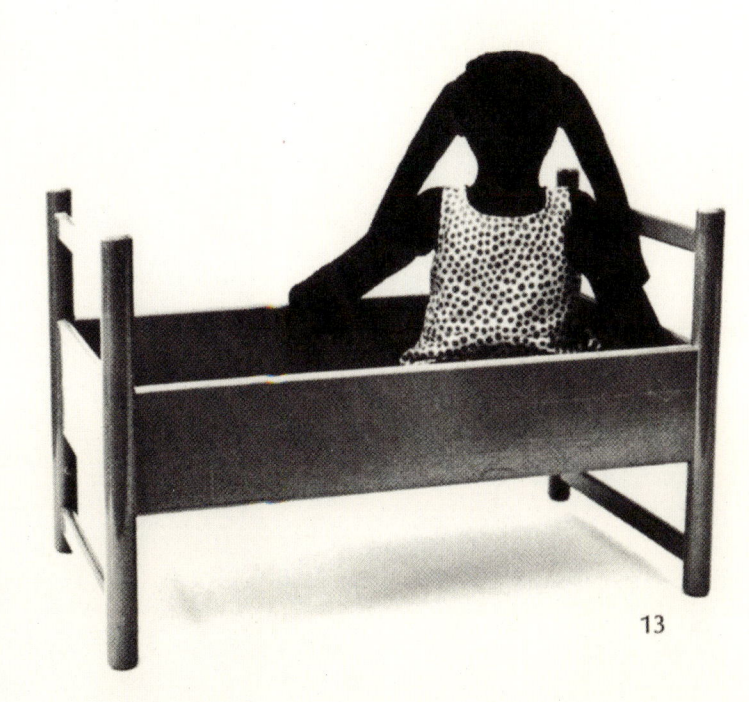

13   Doll's bunk bed from Finland can be stacked and also used for toys or clothes or even vegetable storage. Red, blue or yellow. 20" long x 12" high x 11" wide, $9, REA collect. The Marimekko® cotton doll has six parts to hang on to. $10.75

14   A Finnish pull-along and hop-along grasshopper, with spring antennae. $3

A General Store of Good Design   141

142   Design Research

4 Nut cracker General from Austria, painted wood $8.75

5 Cocktail shaker from Austria, designed by Carl Aubock. Stainless steel and black or tan leather top. $27.75

6 Undecorated Florentine leather cigar and cigarette cylinders. Solid extra-fine baby calf, red, black or tan. Small $6.25 Large $21

7 Stew pot designed by Timo Sarpaneva of Finland. Red or black enamelled cast iron with teak handle and lid-lifter. 2½ quarts. $20

8 Perpetual calendar designed by Enzo Mari of Italy. Aluminum or enamelled black back; white plastic cards with orange or black lettering, 13" x 13". $16

9 Italian paper weights designed by Enzo Mari of Italy. Colored cube or sphere within clear perspex cube. 2¾" cube $16.75 and 1½" cube $6.

10 Candles intended to melt in pools of Marimekko color. Lemon, pink, white, red, orange, dark green, blue and purple. 3½ to 8 inches high. $4 $5 $7 $9

11 Italian wine carafes of traditional style in rough glass with measure seal. Clear, blue, green or amber. ½ litre $2.25, ¾ litre $2.75, 1 litre $3.25

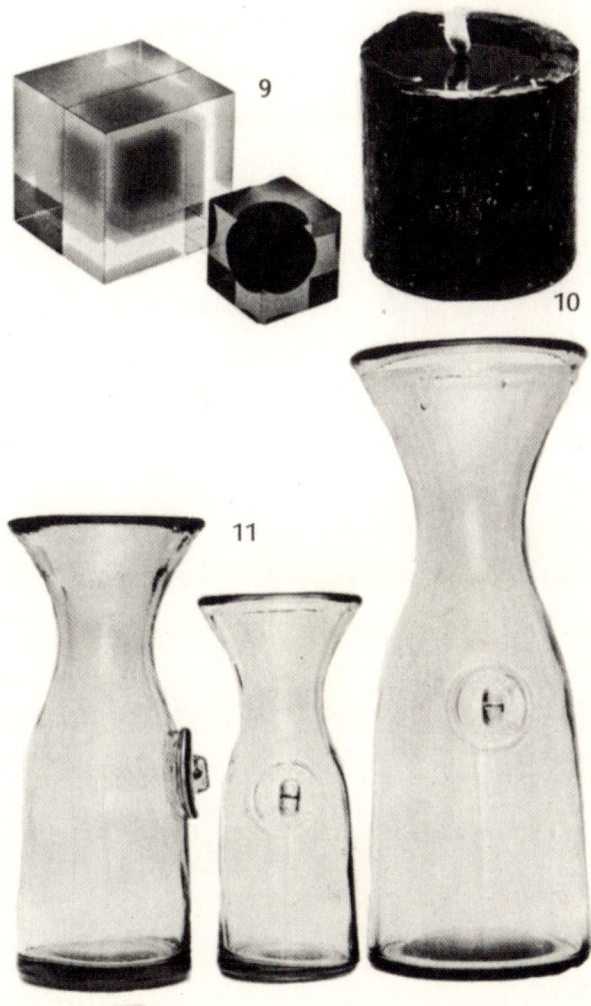

A General Store of Good Design   143

D/R's Glass Bazaar
New Headquarters, 1969

6

When Harvard claimed 57 Brattle as a site for its new Graduate School of Education, Ben seized the opportunity to design a new home for D/R and to merge his life as a merchant with his life as an architect. It was 1968 when the design process began. The yeasty urban spirit of Cambridge and Boston was soon to collide with the despair of student activists over two tragic American assassinations and the United States's faraway war in Vietnam. In this unsettled climate, Ben tried to create an architecture of hope and joy. His ideas for the new building illustrated the environments of the best city places and markets he had visited—Lausanne, Marrakech, Venice, Helsinki, Paris—as models for "The City of Man," the images set to Bob Dylan's "Blowin' in the Wind."

The building he designed was positively revolutionary. A transparent enclosure, with unframed glass running from concrete floor to concrete ceiling, it removed any barrier between shop and street. You could see the players inside from down the block. It radiated light and color and drew you in. Staffed by enthusiastic and educated women adorned in bright and often outrageous dresses, this was the perfect spot for the see-and-be-seen theater of life. At night it was a gem set amid Brattle Street's dark brick and

The glass headquarters building, opened in December 1969, was the first building for which Ben was both designer and client.

The many levels of the new D/R's open interior echoed the mezzanines of the original store at 57 Brattle Street, which was replaced by Harvard's Graduate School of Education, also designed by BTA.

clapboard volumes, an ideal showcase for all the beauty that lit up its windows. D/R transcended retail and became a perpetually rotating exhibition of the art of design: a museum without the walls and without the hush.

Ben had carefully considered the relationship of a modern building to the clapboard precinct of Longfellow's Spreading Chestnut Tree. But he had harmony in mind when he wrote: "Just as Harvard Square is an agora and Boylston Street a fair, Design Research lives in the tradition of the marketplace. Because good markets and fairs thrive on movement and action, they don't happen in architectural 'masterpieces' but in lively spaces that mix people and functions." The building's theatrics had a purpose, however. Social interaction continued to be the reason the store was so compelling. It was fun even for those without any intention of buying anything. Once ensconced on one of D/R's signature down sofas, you would likely run into someone you knew, or someone you needed to know, and would strike up a conversation over candlesticks or children's furniture. When the new store opened in December 1969, it set in motion the community-retailing revolution that Ben and Jane Thompson would continue with the redevelopment of Faneuil Hall on the other side of the Charles River.

With its open plan—the brick sidewalk just flowed inside, stepping up and down to stacked levels of colorful goods—the glass bazaar looked vulnerable. But when antiwar protesters hit Harvard Square shops with a hailstorm of rocks in 1970, D/R was the only store with no windows broken. The young rebels felt D/R was on their side. It suggested the new life they were leading, one with jugs of wine and floor-cushion entertaining, walls draped with fabric or with psychedelic posters. D/R was not corporate, but it was also no longer on the fringe.

Ben had his masterpiece, with glorious, multipage coverage in every design magazine. The *New Yorker* came up to see what the fuss was about, and in 1970 the American Institute of Architects gave it the Honor Award. At a time when architects were seeking the style that would come after modernism, the D/R headquarters offered a potential solution in a deceptively simple package: concrete without brutalism, glass without glossiness, contextual without imitation. In 2003, the building's enduring quality was recognized with the AIA's Twenty-five Year Award. It would become the defining work for Ben's career as an architect, completed just before he lost control of D/R and turned his design mind to adaptive reuse rather than new construction. Harvard Square lost the landmark neon D/R sign in 1978, but the glass bazaar lived on, subsequently showcasing the wares at Crate & Barrel, one of the store's many retail offspring.

Moving Day

Pauline Dora "We should have had movers and packed it up, but of course that's not the way it happened. That was part of the fun of it, to make it a carnival."

Staff, family, friends—even members of BTA—made the short but happy pilgrimage carrying goods from D/R's original store to Ben's new glass headquarters.

148 Design Research

Voices

Jane Thompson When moving day arrived in December 1969, the entire inventory of 57 Brattle was transported to 48 Brattle by an army of store staff and architects from Benjamin Thompson & Associates. It was a traffic stopper as Marimekko bolsters and butcher-block sofas, plus a multitude of plastic chairs and tables paraded across the street to the new glass building.

Pauline Dora D/R staff, 1968–77

He had us dress in these Marimekko dresses. It was the silliest dress, called Nina's Apron. It was sleeveless and went all the way to the ground but it had an oversize ruffle on the arm opening and on the bottom and silver buttons going down the back. And he had us carrying pillows across Brattle Street. He was taking pictures. It was fun, it was frustrating, it was exasperating, but it was great. I remember it after all this time.

We should have had movers and packed it up, but of course that's not the way it happened. It was just across the street. That was part of the fun of it, to make it a carnival.

D/R's Glass Bazaar 149

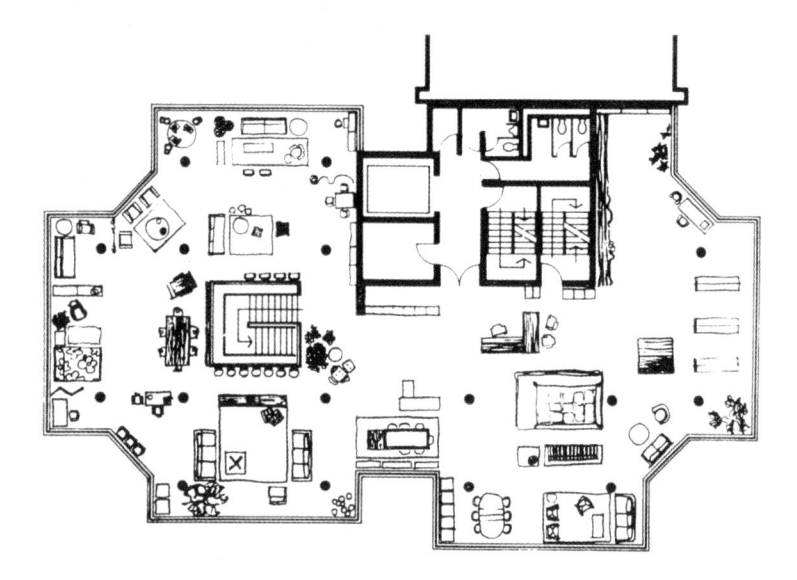

A plan of the headquarters' second floor. The main entrance was one level down, at lower right in the drawing.

OPPOSITE: The first floor brought in the brick paving from the sidewalk, providing a seamless transition from outside to inside. The building was a transparent wrap, without mullions or window hardware; windows were never cluttered with merchandise but left open to allow views from both inside and outside.

Ben Thompson, *Boston Sunday Globe,* 1971
So the task of building anew on Brattle Street, with its beautiful residential scale and bustling intensity around Harvard Square, was a complex prospect. Could we share the new D/R with the outer world, yet keep the sense of intimacy within? Could we achieve crystalline openness without the icy purity of most glass façades? Could we blend today's structure with Longfellow's neighborhood, mix children and elders, old and new, store and street into a comfortable continuity of color and optimism that life is naturally all about?

Tom Green, partner, Benjamin Thompson & Associates, 1966–80, 1988–2001
The TAC building on Story Street, on a site adjacent to our headquarters site on the corner of Brattle Street, was being designed at the same time as we were beginning the D/R building, but the TAC building was built first. It is a simple four-story building with a concrete frame, brick infill, and windows column-to-column. That was a vocabulary we started using at the Harvard Law School so it was within our tradition. When we began designing the Design Research building we assumed the same vocabulary, with columns on the outside and concrete spandrels.

When we started a new project at BTA, we would talk about the possibilities. Then Joe Maybank and I, as senior associates, would each develop an approach to the design. In this particular case Joe's approach was almost identical to the TAC building, but mine had bigger windows befitting a retail use. Ben selected my design, and as I developed it we pulled the columns inside, behind the glass, and cantilevered the floors out. We then developed the diagonal corners that looked back at the old D/R building and placed the main entrance on that corner, rather than along either street. The open chamfered corner symbolized an entrance for Ben, and welcomed people from all directions.

Ben Thompson, *Contract,* 1970 The inset corner entrance . . . picks up both the Story Street and Brattle Street corners, an inviting and protected access to the lobby. The open diagonal leads into a large space from every angle. It is a multi-directional extension of the street. We wanted the effect of a plaza, or a bazaar, in a town square.

Tom Green As the scheme developed, our window walls were four-foot windows with a steel mullion between each pane, which seemed technically required, though we wished for an uninterrupted glass wall. When drawings were almost finished, a salesman from Virginia Glass happened to walk in the office. The moment he showed me their new glass system, the butted glass without frames, I said, "Oh my God, this is what we're looking for. This is going to do it." I rushed to show it to Ben and he got very excited. We immediately brought our contractor to meet with Virginia Glass and develop the desired details for the building; until then, we had been told it could not be done.

That frameless glass detail allowed D/R to be a building almost "without architecture." Basically the whole building became a show window. It was as transparent as possible; all the lighting was designed so that the entire interior would be on display, seen from the street during the day and the night.

Ben Thompson, *Boston Sunday Globe,* 1971
We decided to try a working prototype, to demonstrate how a private shop can belong to the public street. The goal would be a quiet architectural framework for public theatre-in-the-round. The form would be elemental simplicity, a non-building whose structure would fade and reemerge as a warm busy world inside, or at times as a kaleidoscope of people, shadows, buildings, and clouds.

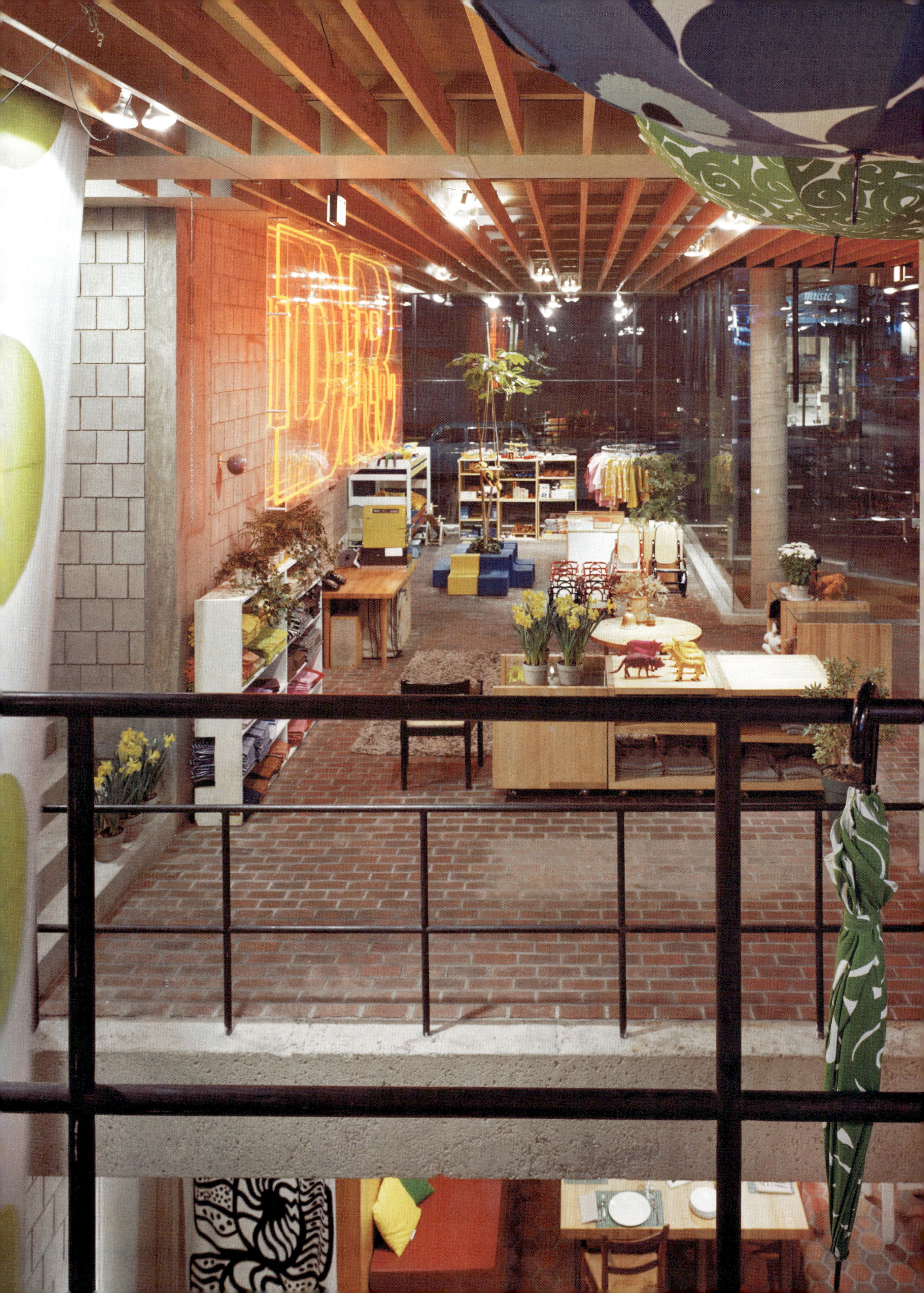
music

The frameless glass acted like a mirror during the day, reflecting the building's neighbors, both historic and contemporary.

Ralph Caplan "I think the building is great because somehow it didn't look like anything else in Cambridge. Yet it did not look out of place in Cambridge."

Larry Kroin **"When the new store opened... it was shining, sparkling, clean, and beautiful."**

Paola Antonelli, Curator, Department of Architecture and Design, Museum of Modern Art The building is a clear example of American modern architecture, but at the same time there is a lot of the Scandinavian thirst for sun. Maybe these are subtle suggestions: Once you know that the Thompsons are connected to Scandinavia, you look for the elements that remind you of Scandinavia. There's the combination of concrete with wood. And the glass façade that is not a curtain façade, so it is not an office building, but is somewhere between a residence and a retail place.

Ralph Caplan, design writer and author In the old house there had always been a certain kind of atmosphere, and you couldn't bottle it and move it into a big urban-looking shop, but you could use some of the same concepts. The lighting and the music—there was always music. I remember it was pretty hip music.

Mildred F. Schmertz, architecture writer The continuous glass. Let's just look at it. You see this all the time now in buildings, but the absolute truth is, I never saw a building like this before D/R, with the exterior surface entirely of glass, and the panels of glass clipped together in an almost invisible way. In his architecture, Ben was always trying to simplify and make the floors distinct and the walls distinct and not have spandrels and complications. This was just about as pure as he could make it. Also, consider the way it is totally on display. You are not looking into display windows, you are not looking into separate shops, you are looking into this great floor-through. You look into this building and you know you are looking at floor upon floor of well-lit, uninterrupted space.

Tom Green One of the problems of the internal organization of the store was creating a multilevel retail space, because when people come in at one single point, they don't typically move down or up easily. We tried to break up the interior of the store so it didn't seem like a four-story building. By playing with the floor levels, and having the staircase in the middle of the store bridging an open well, we could connect the bottom three levels, make them all visible to each other, and try to make it work visually as one space.

A new building, particularly if it were too slick, would be inappropriate and destroy the character the D/R stores had developed over the years. So from the inside we were trying to be as *un*-architectural and as un-buildinglike as possible. From the outside we wanted to have a continuous show window, with as little awareness as possible of actual "architecture."

Contract, 1970 The interior plan is based on a five-level, open-space arrangement. The ceiling treatment makes an important design contribution with store-length fir fins. From these are suspended free-hanging dress racks of metal bars, straight and circular; display and decorative items, such as strikingly patterned umbrellas; and specially created flexible lighting that allows brace-mounted incandescent spots and floods to be clipped easily on fins anywhere in the store.

Tom Green We investigated half-a-dozen different ways of making ceiling grids—Unistrut, three or four others—but they all seemed, well, too slick. What we needed was something flexible and fairly low cost. We decided on natural fir, which is quite sturdy, and it gave us the feeling of warmth we were after, as well as texture, and concealed a lot of hardware. It was a multipurpose solution for sure.

Larry Kroin, D/R staff, 1968–75 Products were spot-lit by this U-shaped flange that would house the spotlight. It had wings on it that sat on top of the fins, so you could position the lighting anywhere you wanted to highlight a product. So it not only showcased them, but fit within the architecture of the store. This was also done by hanging a hammock in the center of the well or Marimekko fabric on the high wall that went up three stories. When the new store opened there were dancing dresses hanging in the well. Flowers and candles played on everything. It was shining, sparkling, clean, and beautiful.

Pat Terry, *Home Furnishings Daily,* 1969
The entire store, which cost "under one million dollars to build," embodies the Thompsons' love of natural materials such as pine, oak, birch plywood. Manila hemp from Holland, with a doormat texture and a tweedy appearance, is inset in wood-framed staircases and covers one floor; otherwise brick, cork, or tile skims the unfinished cement, which is left exposed on ceilings and some walls.

Anne Flynt Amory Solley, D/R staff, 1960–67
Ben had a great idea for the dressing rooms in the Marimekko department. He used Sonotubes, the forms used for pouring concrete columns, which they were already using to pour columns during construction. Ben had the idea to get new ones and cut a door in them to make dressing rooms; they could be positioned anywhere on the apparel floor, curtained, and could move around as displays changed. If you were not a size 0 it was pretty tight in there and it was hard not to knock your elbows when you were trying on dresses. We painted them bright colors and they worked.

Jane Thompson The brighter colors inside the tubes, contrasting with the khaki color outside, makes the inside warm and sort of comfortable, iconic.

Pat Terry In the Marimekko department—on an open mezzanine one level up from the lobby—straight and circular buffed steel display racks swing from wires hooked over one of the ceiling's exposed beams and can easily be moved. Clean-lined oak storage display chests, which can sell as furniture, scoot around the cork floor on their casters.

Accessories, such as umbrellas, may be hung over the railing or suspended from the ceiling while a white-enameled unit, shaped like a flat-headed mushroom with drawers, shows off jewelry under glass (and locked away from temptation).

Darryl Pomicter, Benjamin Thompson & Associates field engineer, *Contract,* July 1970 The pillow display units are like building blocks; even when used at the windows you can see activity outside and beyond. The same boxes are used at the entrance level for the toy display.

Contractor's Sonotubes, used to mold concrete columns, became freestanding curtained dressing rooms in the Marimekko dress department. A Magistretti bench gave shoppers a place to rest.

Looking east along the window wall, with the two mezzanines in view, the glass disappears and one sees the seamless transition from street to interior. Also visible is Ben's palette of materials—natural (wood stairs) and industrial (round concrete columns) in the interior.

Peter Wheeler, D/R staff, 1972–77 The building itself was so useful, so utilitarian. There weren't a lot of tools, there weren't mannequins. There were so many modular things. The dress racks were basically just black iron pipe on airplane cable suspended from flat S-hooks suspended from the fins. We also had four-by-fours with adjustable jacks that are usually used in construction. Because the ceilings and floors were concrete you could put uprights in there and tighten them, then add brackets and put shelves on them. You could create a wall anywhere you wanted. We had U-shaped shelves with bookends, so you could put shelves on both sides and place pots and pans, dinnerware, vases, fabric, shoes, and candles on them. There were a lot of modular white Formica cubes. It was a little bit like having an Erector Set for me. I still think of it as playtime.

Darryl Pomicter On the wheeled display tables, we used 2-inch-thick maple butcher block. The legs are steel pipe—polished, buffed, and lacquered—with large ball casters. The table is easily moved around for continuously changing merchandise display.

Ben Thompson, Contract, 1970 I want to mention the sign for just a minute. Where was the D/R sign to go on an all-glass building? How could you advertise the name of the store without spoiling the smooth effect of the glass façade? We decided it had to go inside—on a wall deep inside the store—a fairly offbeat idea for a retail store. The sign is made up of two sheets of clear plastic, sandwiching slender neon tubes. The glass bays pick up the orange letters and bounce off them at every angle—the sign is extremely visible up and down the street.

Jane Thompson D/R made a different use of display space. By not crowding the window glass with merchandise facing out, it opened up space that invites you in and lets you see up, down, and see everything around in many dimensions. It was a see-through, see-around experience.

Larry Kroin Ben didn't want the merchandise up against the windows. Reflecting on it now, it's clear he was more interested in watching the building *life* move than in watching the product stand still. There was something about attractive people, smiling, against the product that, looking up from the street, made the building come alive. It wasn't just a jewel box to put products in but a place for people to experience products, and they were part of the show.

James Rouse, developer, Rouse Companies, *Architectural Record,* 1977 Ben is a merchant. He understands with us the things that are essential to a marketplace — how to stimulate certain kinds of traffic so that one type of purchase leads to another. Shops must be easy to find and enjoyable to be in. Shopping can be entertaining, and he knows how to make that happen.

Larry Kroin The front windows on Brattle Street changed once a week, so people who came in regularly never saw things in the same place. Merchandise wasn't just put on a shelf and shown, it was displayed on stock—on other merchandise, the same or different from what we were selling.

I can remember working with Pirjo Laine, a Finnish designer who did the displays, until midnight — at least midnight — moving furniture around. (That was one of the disadvantages of being one of only two men on the staff.) One time, around 1 AM, Ben came walking in with Agnete Kalckar. He was holding a drink, which he gave to Agnete, and he started showing Pirjo and me how to do what we were trying to do. Whatever he did, it just turned it into magic. Every item in the vignette held its own. Nothing necessarily matched but it all came together so organically in a display.

Olga Gueft, *Interiors,* 1970 But the shop where the people are, occupying three floors on the long façade on Brattle Street and the shorter façade on Story Street is, on the contrary, so extroverted that the people inside it never cease to see Harvard Square. While looking at the wooden tables piled with glassware, they exchange greetings with their friends on the street. While inspecting Marimekko dresses they find the passersby and the shops across the street within their field of vision just beyond the racks — which hang on thin wires. In the course of their Harvard Square stroll they have somehow begun to explore the colorful fabrics, the stacks of toys. They find stairs to reach what they see over their heads — suspended dresses and fabrics, pillows in racks, and furniture — and beneath their feet — kitchenware. The stairs are open and hung free, but of sturdy wood and railed with plain black-painted iron pipes. The floors are sometimes brick, sometimes concrete, sometimes wood. A few slender, whitish concrete columns, coil-marked by their forms and as tall as trees, hold up decks of raw concrete whose unfinished undersides are lines with thick fins of ruddy wood, to which lamps and wires — for hanging things — are attached. The basic materials of the place have a rough-and-ready look one expects on a street rather than in an interior.

OVERLEAF: A view from the lower mezzanine over the housewares floor reveals the range of moods in D/R's design inventory as seen in three dinner table set-ups, each a different arrangement of chairs, tables, and dining accessories. Ben's primary aim as a retailer was to gather the best and let each customer create a personal home environment.

Olga Gueft *"Only the masses of flourishing potted trees that contrast with the winter snow outside tell the visitor that he is definitely not out of doors, and that the sheer glass shell which wraps around this most delightful part of Harvard Square is an exceedingly effective weather barrier."*

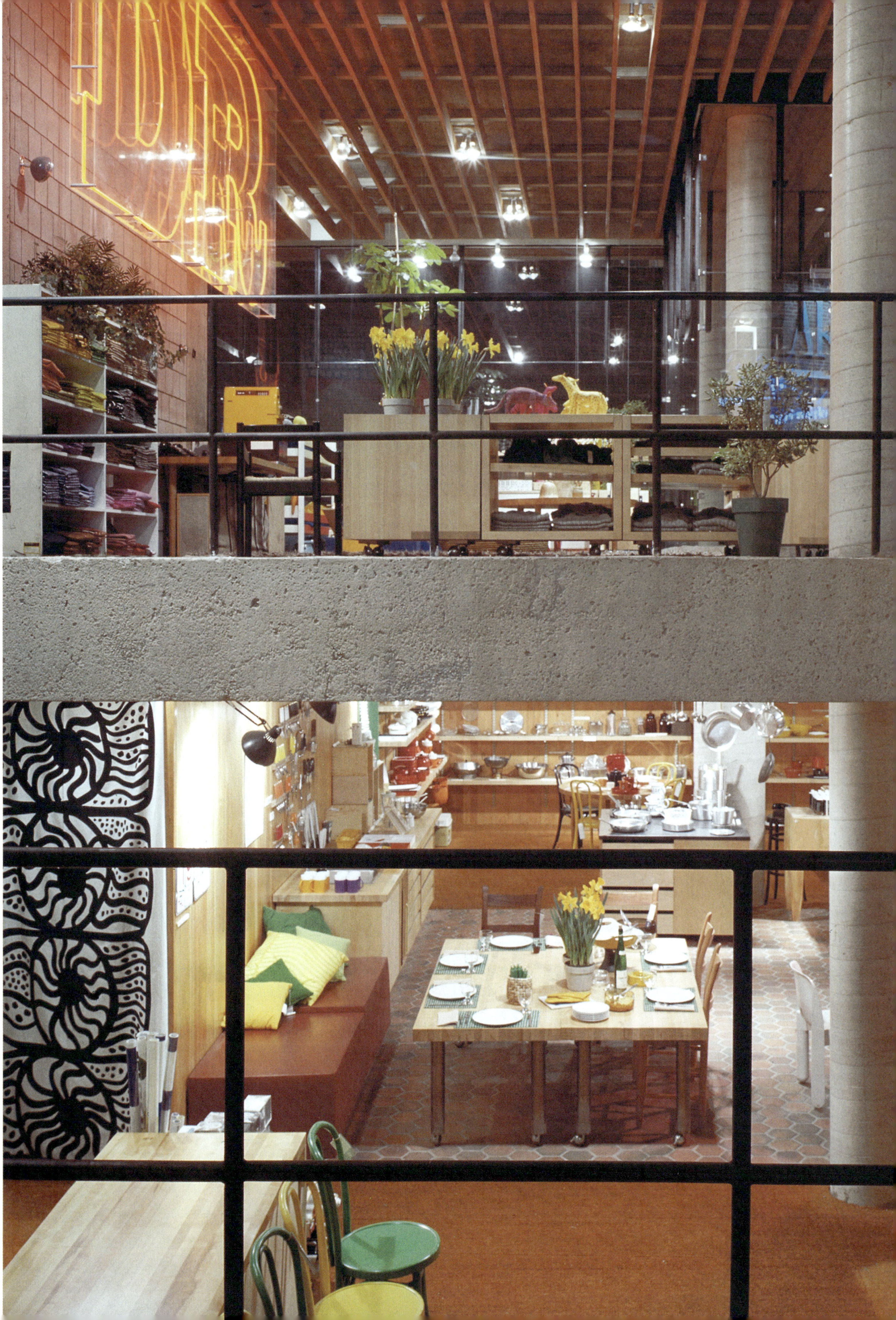

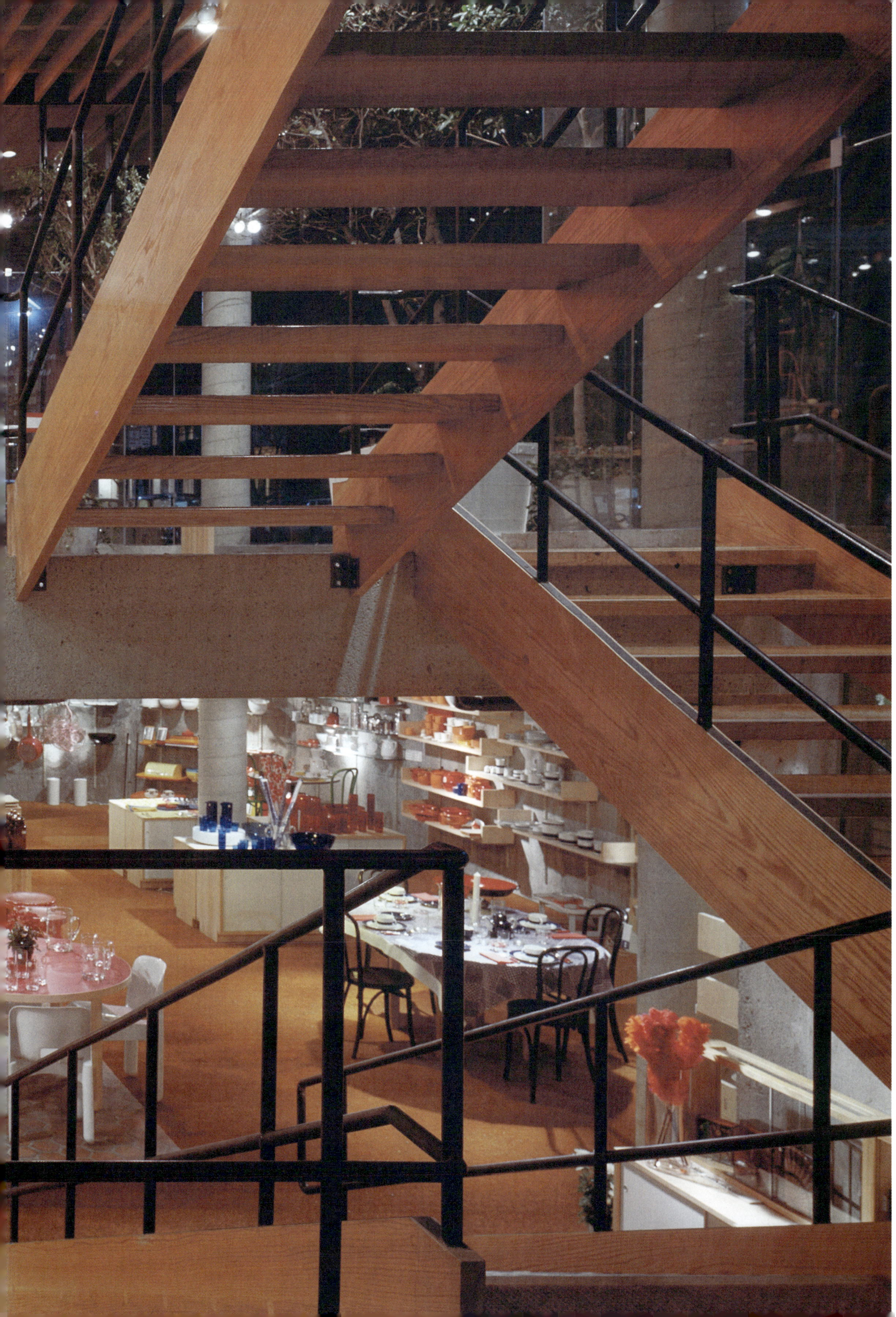

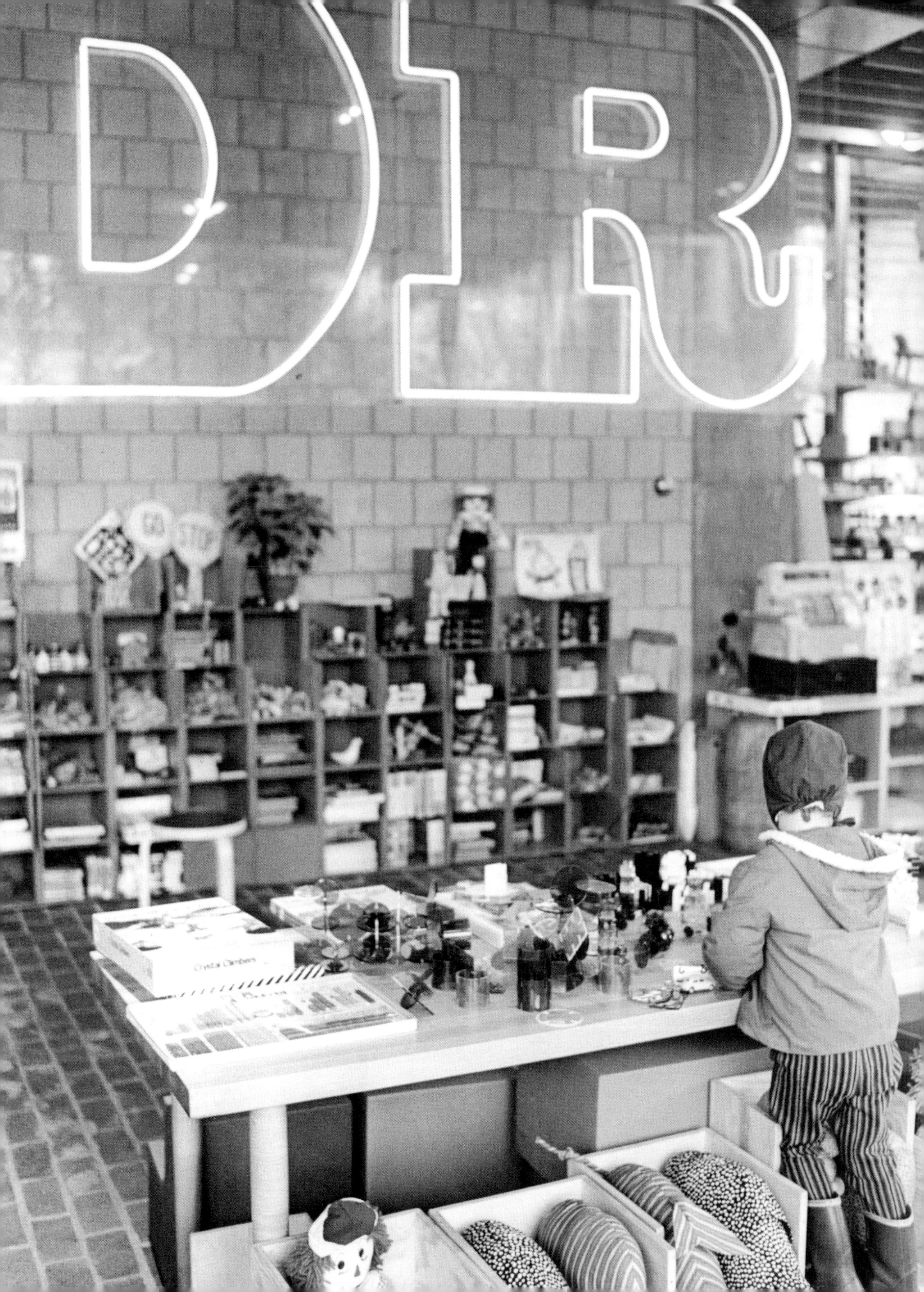
DR
GO
STOP
Crystal Climbers

Pauline Dora Today, most retailers shut off the outside world and create an inner environment just as they do in Las Vegas — when you are gambling, God forbid you should see the sun or the time. To let in the outdoors creates problems: the sun comes in, it hurts the merchandise, you have less wall space to work off. You have to work from within the space. That's how we did it.

Blase Gallo, D/R staff, 1971–78 We didn't just move a few products around, we moved whole departments from one floor to another. We had to be open on Saturday, but at closing time Saturday night there would be people running to get as much done by Monday morning as possible. It was like setting up for a show, getting ready for the opening curtain. Full department changes would happen on weekends four times a year, and we would have a giant potluck beforehand; D/R staff had incredible cooks. There would be jugs of wine and a big employee party, and then we would start working on the store.

Lu Wendel Lyndon, D/R staff, 1965–73 Most of us who worked at D/R, *lived* D/R. We lived what we were selling, this attitude about our homes. And we wanted to share that with customers. It wasn't an exclusive club; it was, "Come enjoy this *with* us."

Larry Kroin Ben hired young people with no bad habits aesthetically. He taught us all how to be in that space, and not in a didactic way, but in a way that permitted us to think as individuals.

There were shortcomings. Today I can't buy a hose for the garden without going to six stores. I have thrown everything out that isn't good design. I have grown up to live the part. And it is a beautiful way to live. Ben has brought that to me and to thousands of people.

Ben Thompson, *Boston Sunday Globe,* 1971 By night, lighted from within, interior color floods the street as if from the depths of a glowing jewel. By day, the inner arena of products and people draws in passersby becoming, as we hoped, a pocket marketplace adding texture to the city fabric. The natural pageantry of crowds and goods, of meat, fish, and crops from the fields, of things made and things grown, all to be tasted, smelled, seen, and touched, are the prime source of sensations, experience, and amusement in the daily lives of whole populations — were and still are, in most nations except our own.

Paola Antonelli Just the introduction of that kind of store, in Cambridge, on many floors — what today we would call *lifestyle* — was very innovative. It was at a moment when the culture was receptive to novelty. I also think that particular non-utopia was in Scandinavian living — almost a utopia, but not a utopia because they were really implementing it, building communes and so forth. There was a deep fascination with D/R and it became a deep cultural phenomenon.

High ceilings with a lighting and display system concealed by wooden slats encouraged vertical display and provided vertiginous views. Here, the downstairs cash-wrap area becomes a time-lapse film, and dresses dangle as ornaments at Christmas.

OPPOSITE: The neon D/R sign was not hung on the façade, but was mounted on the back wall of the main floor — fully visible to those outside because sight lines from the street were left clear of tall cases.

D/R's Glass Bazaar   161

An upper-floor bedroom display, with a Charles Webb spindle bed, soft rugs from Greece and Bolivia, and seating ranging from a Thonet rocker to Joe Colombo plastic chairs to molded foam banquettes.

OPPOSITE: Draft of a sign for Ben and Jane's first restaurant, Harvest, which opened directly behind the store in 1975.

Pauline Dora The contrast between the style of the old building and the new products was terrific. It heightened and dramatized the difference, how extraordinary the product collection was. In the new glass store, the building almost competed with the product mix. In other ways, it was great. We had the big neon sign, which was very dramatic. The building was amazing: it brought people in and then people bought our things. That's retailing.

Sandy Reynolds-Wasco, D/R staff, 1976–78 D/R was a place where customers could walk in and pick up great furniture for their houses without a middleman. They could mix it any way they wanted. In any one of the stores you could find a Barcelona table with all its contained style next to something really exuberant and almost folklike in the Mekko fabric or Mexican painted tinware.

David Wasco, D/R staff, 1975–78 We were working with a lot of things that were just exploding colors. The Heller line of their Massimo Vignelli plastic dinnerware came out in eye-popping colors. I blew up portraits of Massimo and Lella and mounted them on foam-core boards and hung those over the huge volume display of the bright colored plastic.

Larry Kroin The most important part of Christmas was the kids' toy display, which filled the front part of the store. Hundreds of glass ornaments from Niederer—cylinders and glass balls—were hung in the front window on fishing line. People would come in, look, and their jaws would drop. That moment was somewhere between falling in love and crying.

Sandy Reynolds-Wasco D/R was a leader in the food revolution brought on by Julia Child. D/R provided the more exotic—and versatile—stove-to-table equipment integrated with the new cooking-dining environment. By the time Macy's Cellar [in New York] started in 1971, D/R had pioneered gourmet kitchenware for a decade.

162   Design Research

Alexander Julian **"Design Research allowed you to combine intelligent design with self-expression and a joie de vivre that captured everyone's imagination."**

Jane Thompson We were actually involved in the redesign of American cooking itself, exchanging traditional, rich, sauced dishes for fresh local foods in simpler, lighter combinations. In 1975, Ben and I started The Harvest Restaurant next to the store, exploring the possibilities of fresh, imaginative American cuisine enriched by new ethnic tastes and blends: Asian, Scandinavian, Italian, Hispanic ingredients all introduced a welcome diversity to America's more casual and comfortable style of life—as they continue to do.

Sara Moulton, executive chef, *Gourmet* magazine After the new D/R opened, I went to work at the Harvest, the restaurant and café that Ben and Jane Thompson opened in 1975 next door to the store. There was an obvious connection to Design Research in the Marimekko upholstery and hangings throughout, and in the fresh seasonal approach to the menu.

I see the 1970s as the very, very beginning of America starting to discover itself food-wise. We hit the worst of the frozen food movement in the 1960s. Unlike New York, which was in the grip of the French restaurant mafia, Cambridge was more forward-thinking. Women could be chefs and were chefs. Maybe that had to do with Julia, but Cambridge was a much freer place, more open. Some years later, I met Julia Child. She hired me in the spring of 1979 to work on the television program *Julia Child and More Company* and the cookbook that went with it.

Peter Wheeler In the late 1960s to early 1970s, more sophisticated kitchen equipment was catching on. People were trying to figure out what's an asparagus peeler, what's an espresso maker. We had a movable kitchen, a Joe Colombo design with a refrigerator and cooktop on wheels, about four feet square. If things got slow, we would say, "Let's make omelets and sell omelet pans." We would practice flipping omelets and see who could do it. It always paid off.

Susi Cooper, D/R staff, 1975–78 I used to set up cooking demonstrations with local restaurants in Harvard Square. Chefs from La Piñata gave lessons in the store in tacos, enchiladas, and gazpacho; Tony Powers from Grendel's Den juice bar did a class called "Come See the Dance of the Fruits"; and Judy Rosenburg at Baby Watson made cheesecake. That was just one summer.

David Wasco I do remember showing how the Chemex coffeepot worked. That's another American product out of Pittsfield. And the Melior French press coffeepot with the Braun grinder. That was pre the whole big coffee explosion. We smelled the coffee!

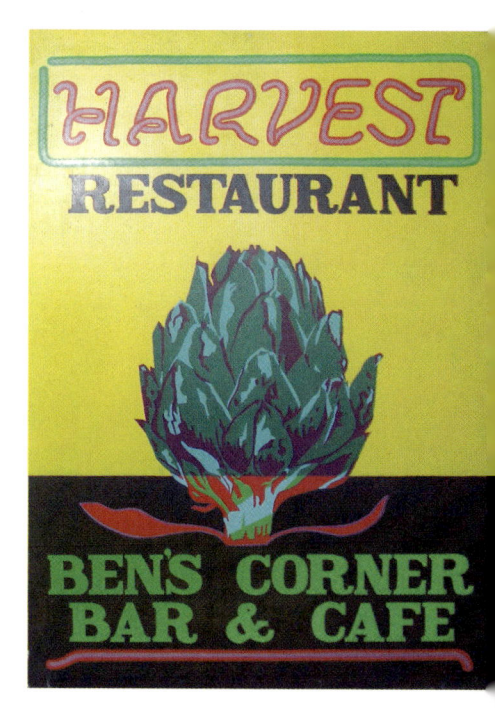

Design Research makes your heart happy with all its bright colors.

Barbara Westman documented Cambridge in the 1960s in a book of drawings, *The Beard and the Braid*. One of these became a D/R Christmas card, sent out the year the new building opened, which captured the store's Brattle Street corner and memorialized the Brattle Theater beyond.

OVERLEAF: At night the whole store became a display window, with everything from housewares (basement) to Marimekko (mezzanine) to furniture (third floor) on view, just as Thompson intended.

David Wasco It seemed to be our job to educate the public. In all the stores we would have classes with visiting chefs or artists, and we would explain new products to the public. There were different community events, such as weaving and silk-screening classes. D/R transcended a retail store. It felt like the items sold themselves and you were just helping the public understand the many possibilities.

Alexander Julian, designer, fashion, textiles, home furnishings I looked at the store's audience as people who were more intellectual about design, more educated, and more—I want to say *free-spirited* in a careful way. It could be very calculated. Design Research allowed you to combine intelligent design with self-expression and a joie de vivre that captured everyone's imagination. Other places seemed to take themselves too seriously: they lacked the spirit of fun and enjoyment that you got when you walked into D/R.

Chee Perlman, design writer and editor When I was nine or ten my mom would take me to Design Research in Cambridge in its new glass building. I was just besotted. Not many years later, one of my girlfriends and I would take the T into Cambridge and hang out there on a Saturday afternoon. It shaped a lot of my sensibility about design and my passion about design. How many people remember hanging out in this magic palace which was this store?

The curatorial point of view was there, but it wasn't precious. There was a sensibility that unified the whole place, a sensibility about supergraphics and infusing graphic design into product design, a sensibility about new materials like plastics and using plastics for unexpected things like furniture. Not everything in it was Marimekko. There was a half-bazaar quality, like an outdoor market. There was something about that building—the transparency of the building itself—that said, "You can come in here."

Pauline Dora **"The building was amazing: it brought people in and then people bought our things. That's retailing."**

From *The New Yorker*
November 7, 1970

On and Off the Avenue: About the House
By Janet Malcolm

If Knoll is representative of the best in today's public interiors, D/R International occupies the same exalted position in regard to private ones. Since its start, sixteen years ago, in Cambridge, Massachusetts (a branch store in New York and one in San Francisco came along in the early sixties), D/R has been noted for the consistent excellence of its furniture and fabrics and household objects, and for its remarkable sense of style. The initials "D/R" conjure up a picture of an interior as definite as the one evoked by the terms "Early American" or "French Provincial." Although everything at D/R is modern, not every well-designed modern object fits the store's notion of what is to be sold there. D/R's principle of selection resembles that used by people furnishing their homes. The store seems to ask of each object not "Will it sell?"—or even "Is it good?"—but "Is it for us?" Characteristic of the D/R style are square-cut furniture made of natural-finished maple of pine or butcherblock; china and glass of a plain, solid persuasion; heavy cotton fabrics printed with vivid, lucid geometric designs; a preference for the substantial and rough-edged over the delicate and highly polished, and for natural materials over synthetic ones (though D/R sells plastics, they take on a kind of "organic" look in the store's context). The D/R style is especially appealing to, and seems especially right for, young families who have little or no domestic help and who use their living rooms as well as admire them. The clutter of family life can be absorbed by a room filled with D/R things. (A room in the Knoll style seems to depend for its effect on the absence of such things as animal-cracker boxes and *TV Guides* left lying about.)

I recently visited D/R's new main store, on Brattle Street, in Cambridge, which occupies three floors of a new five-story cantilevered glass building that also houses the company's offices. The architect is Benjamin Thompson, D/R's owner and founder and probably the only storekeeper in America who has been chairman of the Department of Architecture of the Harvard Graduate School of Design. (Mr. Thompson occupied that position between 1963 and 1967; he now heads the Cambridge architectural firm of Benjamin Thompson & Associates.) The façade is an expanse of sheet glass broken only by horizontal slabs of concrete that mark the floors. The glass has no vertical supports; the panes are joined together by invisible epoxy cement and small metal clips. Cylindrical concrete columns, visible through the glass, support the structure. Because of the colorful merchandise that is also visible, the façade has a gay and lively aspect rather than the bleakness of the usual glass building. For all that, and for all its air (and the fact) of being a tour de force, the building is oddly disappointing as one regards it from across the street. One feels that one has seen buildings like this before, and that this is an exercise—a good one to be sure, but only an exercise—in well-worn architectural conventions, rather than an original departure. One wonders what all the commotion that has brought one to Harvard Square was about. On stepping into the store, one receives the answer. This is like no store one has ever seen. The extraordinary amount of natural light that fills the interior imparts to the merchandise something of the preternatural clarity and purity that the world assumes on the day the windows are washed; we are not accustomed to seeing furniture and fabrics and household objects in such a light, and the effect is breathtaking. We are also not accustomed to the conjunction of light and airiness with an almost Victorian richness and copiousness. The picture windows of the forties and fifties invariably went with the sparsely furnished and quite bare-looking rooms, and we still tend to associate light with a kind of emptiness; the lucent D/R rooms are crammed with furniture and objects: pots of plants—not one or two but great clusters of geranium, ivy, fern, chrysanthemums—appear at every turn; banners of Marimekko fabric and white-plastic mobiles hang from ceilings; mugs and goblets are displayed by the several dozen; toys, games, dolls, dresses, pillows, fabrics, casseroles, bowls, teapots, Braun electric mixers, cutlery, and writing paper fill shelves and cubbyholes and display counters. Like the Aulenti showroom, the D/R store has an open design; every vantage point provides vistas of other parts of the store, though here one is conscious of things above and below as well as around and about. A feeling of brightness and cheerfulness pervades the interior. Open wooden stairs, wide enough for two or three abreast, connect the various levels, to each of which a category of merchandise has been assigned: the main floor offers toys; the second floor has clothes; the third has furniture; and a sublevel floor deals in cooking equipment, glass and china, fabrics, and assorted accessories. The structural and decorative materials used within the store are of the sort one associates with vacation houses rather than with stores: natural-finished fir slats hang from ceilings; floors are tiled with natural brick or covered with warm brown rough carpeting or cork; shelves and display cases are square-cut and, again, of natural-finished wood. The crux of the feeling of pleasure that the store gives the visitor is, of course, the merchandise itself; the same store filled with "Mediterranean" furniture and gift-shop trivia would be no treat, and D/R's things would still be wonderful in a dusty warehouse. But a setting such as the new D/R store provides sharpens one's appreciation of the objects for sale and presents shopping as a kind of aesthetic experience rather than as an irksome necessity. Our own small D/R store on 57th Street is no dump—shopping there is always a pleasure—but for a full sense of D/R's great contribution to American design one has to go to Cambridge.

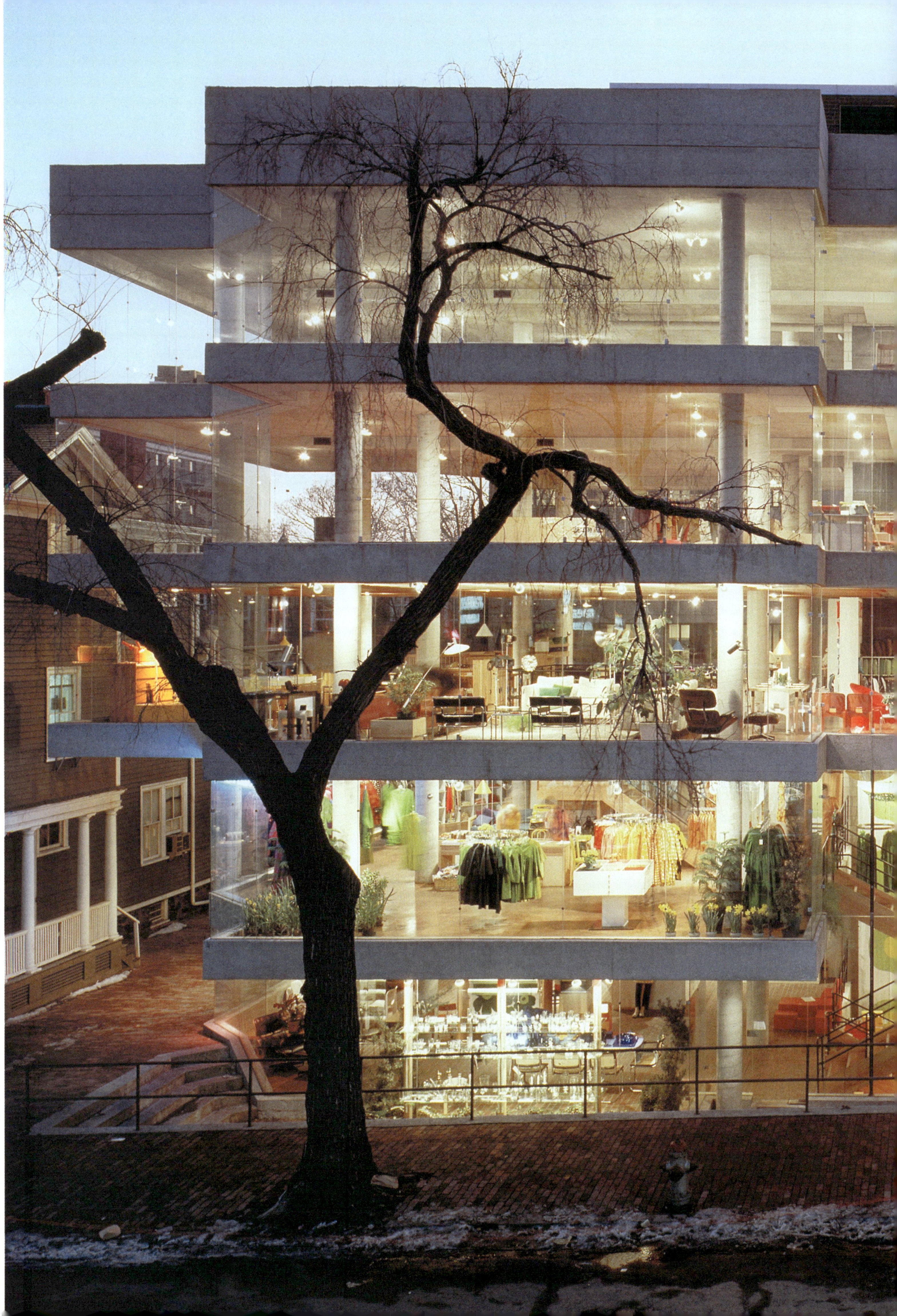

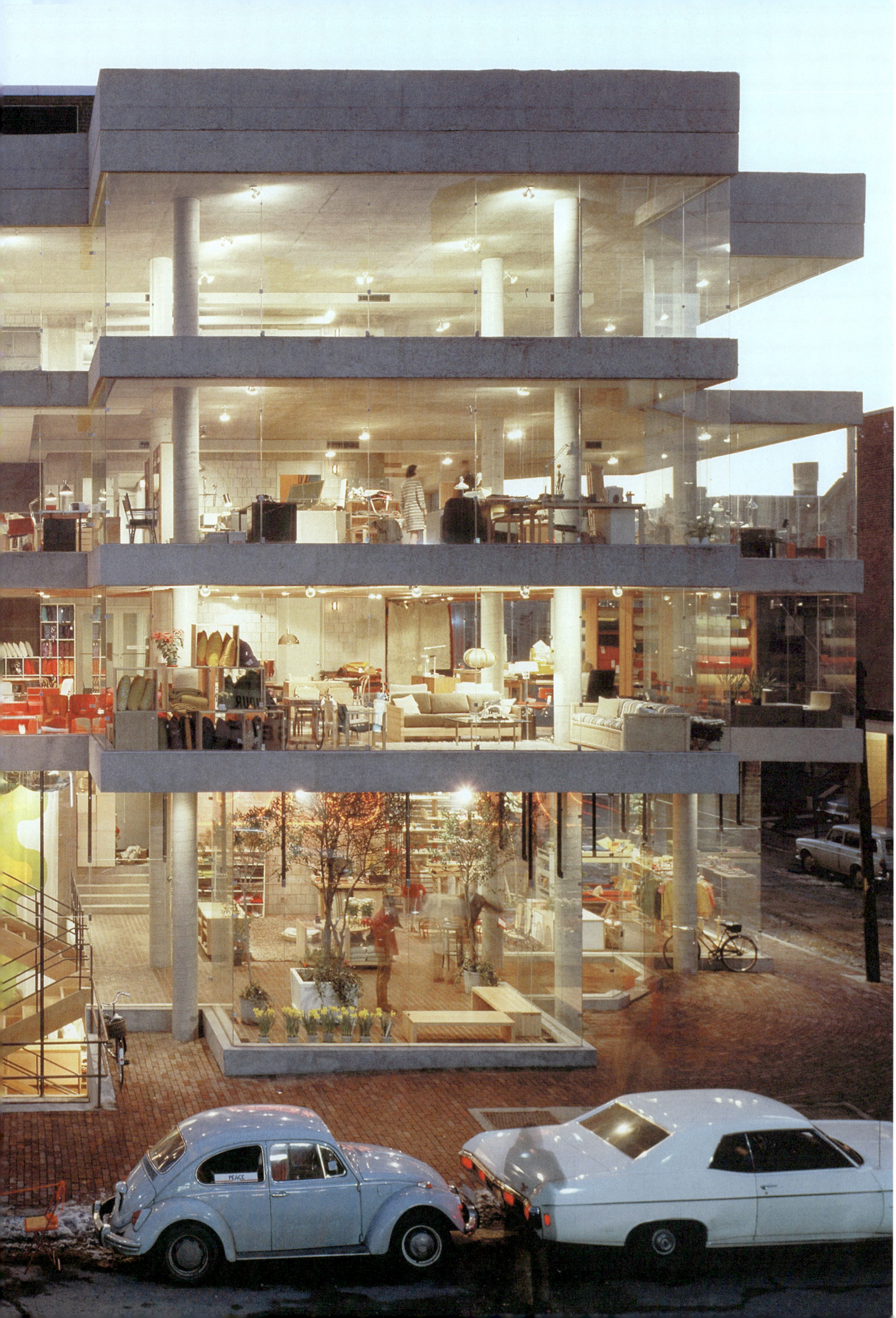
PEACE

D/R in the Seventies: Other Stores

After Ben Thompson lost control of D/R, new controlling stockholder Peter Sprague embarked on an aggressive expansion strategy, eventually adding eight stores to the original three for a total of eleven on the East and West Coasts. In one notable case, Sprague followed Thompson's "found space" strategy for selecting locations for Design Research stores when he chose to renovate the 1897 Van Rensselaer Mansion on Philadelphia's Rittenhouse Square. In another case, Sprague followed the tougher, glassier aesthetic of Thompson's own D/R headquarters in building out the 1973 Embarcadero store (designed by MLTW/Turnbull Associates) in a John Portman retail center. His primary focus, however, was on mall locations for expansion in California.

Certain key D/R principles of display carried through, whatever the architecture: open shelving with color-coded displays of soft and hard goods; fabric dividers for roomlike setups of furniture and accessories; and dramatic internal views (sometimes highlighted with neon, and real and fake interior arches), with interior staircases transformed from a typical retail disaster to a working focal point.

Embarcadero Center Two
San Francisco, California, 1973
William Turnbull Jr.,
MLTW/Turnbull Associates

Sandra Smith Griswold, D/R staff, 1966–74
With 13,000 square feet, Embarcadero was the biggest retail location on the West Coast. I looked at the site when Building Two was still under construction; a real estate developer was looking for an anchor store for the second building in John Portman's Embarcadero development. He had gone to I. Magnin, Saks, but nobody wanted to nibble. It was a two-level structure with dark bronze glass and no connecting stair. I said two things wouldn't work for us: we needed the glass changed to clear and a freight elevator.

Bill Turnbull solved the problem of getting people up to the second floor by building a scissor staircase that looked like escalators. They hammered an 18-by-28-foot skylight out of the concrete roof above. It made such a huge hole in the floor that people were drawn upstairs and down. What made Embarcadero amazing were the levels of people watching people.

Chestnut Hill Shopping Mall
Chestnut Hill, Massachusetts, 1974
Architectural Resources Cambridge, Inc.
Interior design and display,
Blase Gallo, Peter Constable

Colin Smith, architect, BTA, 1966–69
It wasn't difficult at all working with D/R. Chestnut Hill was a typical mall box, 140 feet-by-40 feet-by-17 feet. To add a little dynamic tension to the space we put the whole plan on the diagonal. We did a version of Ben's suspended hemlock ceiling grid from Cambridge, which hid the lighting and the air-conditioning ducts. It was a screen. Two triangular platforms at either end of the store, carpeted in green, showcased the Marimekko department and created a zigzag path through the space, which made people wander. Because the displays were changing all the time the fixtures were flexible.

On the front of the store, facing into the mall, we used the frameless glass detail from the new D/R on Brattle Street. Chestnut Hill was like looking into an open box with lovely things inside. At the time, a wall only of glass was quite new. Since then retailers have used miles and miles of it.

Rittenhouse Square
Philadelphia, Pennsylvania, 1976
Architectural Resources Cambridge, Inc.
Interior design and display,
Blase Gallo, Peter Constable

Raymond Waites, D/R staff, 1975–78 Part of the D/R philosophy was picking historical architecture and saving it. When we took over the Van Rensselaer Mansion, it was still controversial to put a modern environment in a historic building. We saved the Tiffany stained-glass dome and the antique Italian medallions on the ceiling in the Doges' Room. Without that the building was going to be torn down and turned into a parking lot.

ARC gutted the west wing of the mansion, preserving the three stories of the east wing (including the Doges' Room), and created 11,000 square feet of selling space. A new open-tread staircase was built up through the center under the stained-glass dome. If you were on the second level you could look through the staircase and see a piece of furniture displayed on the floor on the other side. We also used the big drops of fabric, as in the Cambridge store, and hung posters from the scaffolding. There were not any big exterior display windows—we couldn't touch the exterior—so we hung the dresses in the old windows.

I designed the opening invitation, which had an architectural drawing of the façade made into an advent calendar. Every window opened up and showed a different product for every day leading up to the grand opening.

OPPOSITE, ABOVE: Marimekko pillows on Willow daybeds, lit by a Luxo lamp, and with a bicycle wheel bar cart standing by at D/R Chestnut Hill. Kitchenwares are displayed in modular cubes designed by Ristomatti Ratia for his Décembre line.

OPPOSITE, BELOW: D/R Philadelphia, where Architectural Resources Cambridge renovated the historic and opulent Van Rensselaer Mansion.

Raymond Waites **"Part of the D/R philosophy was picking historical architecture and saving it."**

D/R's Glass Bazaar

Thompson House, Cambridge, Mass., 1969

It would be ten years before Ben and Jane Thompson's restoration of Boston's Faneuil Hall Marketplace would come to fruition, but the Thompsons' ideas about adaptive reuse got a trial run in their own hundred-year-old Cambridge house, renovated in 1969. Their goal was to create the kind of open, untraditional plan seen in Ben's built-from-scratch work within a historic shell. To do this, they removed most of the existing interior walls to create an open living space and removed one staircase and used its square footage to add a bathroom, laundry room, and sewing nook. A master suite on the top floor included a study as well as a double soaking tub with a view of the backyard treetops; the second floor had small children's bedrooms and a communal TV-game room, and the first floor had a flow of public spaces.

The kitchen took pride of place, occupying half the ground floor, with a view of the back garden through a three-sided glass plant room. Ben Thompson wrote:

> In Gropius's house in Lincoln the kitchen was just a very functional work room. Certainly Mies and Johnson showed that same more formal attitude when they entertained. That is carrying an aesthetic too far, into a life different from the one most people, or at least TAC's clients and D/R's customers, knew in those democratic postwar years. We became an eat-and-entertain-in-the-kitchen family.

Almost every aspect of the kitchen was out in the open, from the built-in mixer to the acrylic wine racks to long birch plywood shelves that held glass jars of staples, multicolored Benningtonware and glass and ceramic serving pieces from Iittala and Arabia—just like shelves in the Design Research stores. The house's original chimney, freestanding after the walls disappeared, now divides prep from dining areas. The dining area has built-in banquettes with Marimekko cushions, a yellow wall, and more Marimekko oilcloth protecting the mahogany Aalto table from the many children. The chairs are Joe Colombo's Universale plastic stacking chair, a product and designer that Ben introduced to the United States.

At the Thompson House in Cambridge, the rear wall is entirely glass, with a view of the deck and verdant garden. The open kitchen, running from the front to the back of the house, combines a dining table and a rear prep kitchen, with a central grill and cooking center accessible from both sides. Open birch plywood shelving keeps tools visible, while butcher-block counters and a wood-burning Franklin stove provide a warm hearth in a comfortable family kitchen. The living room, opposite, also centers on a Franklin stove, with piano and harpsichord as focuses of activity for the Thompsons' large merged family.

The D/R Legacy

7

The 1950s proved to be a celebration of innovation and entrepreneurship when design achieved new prominence both as a profession and as a consumable. Soon after the V-J Day celebration of 1947, architects and designers, schools, museums, and businesses began to redirect their resources to address the national peacetime needs of individuals and the transforming society. It was a decade of firsts in redefining house and home in postwar America, sparking demand for furnishings of nontraditional style, of small-house scale, and of quality to endure the field-testing of active family life.

The peacetime bonus of war production was a burst of innovative materials and techniques: experiments in steel, wood, glass, and plastic; new methods for bending and joining plywood solids and veneers. Flexible adhesive joints allowed combinations of materials never imagined before, as seen in the rubber shock mounts used by Charles Eames to connect the wood and metal parts of his early molded plywood chairs. Among an emerging generation of modern architects, some made parallel careers as product designers, developing a range of new domestic furniture, particularly chairs, introduced by the Eameses, George Nelson,

Placewares, run by Lu and Maynard Lyndon in a new West Coast location in Gualala, California, features timeless good design in the D/R tradition: still-in-production Aalto vases on a new Marimekko tablecloth.

Eero Saarinen, Ralph Rapson, and others. The leading producers (Knoll, Herman Miller, and Finland's Artek), working with these progressive architect-designers, stepped up the marketing of modernism. Few traditional suppliers of mass-produced furniture moved to pursue these new designer lines, although Baker Furniture was an exception when it introduced a line by Danish architect Finn Juhl in 1951.

Propelled by the public's growing interest in modern architecture and interiors, a crop of small shops was opened by independent retailers who were often designers without retail experience. They assembled furnishings that appealed to a market which they understood from personal experience — everyday customers with a taste for leading-edge living. They rounded up inventories from the few "designer" firms in the United States and from innovative European sources known before the war. Alvar Aalto's pioneering bentwood, Marcel Breuer's curved steel tubing, and Mies van der Rohe's masculine steel and leather pieces — all created for custom modern homes built in the 1920s and early 1930s — were imported for the first wave of American modern houses in the 1950s.

The pioneers' knowledge, and certainly their taste, were informed by a handful of leading design-oriented schools and universities, among them Harvard's Graduate School of Design and MIT in Cambridge, Massachusetts, the New Bauhaus and the Institute of Design in Chicago, and the experimental Black Mountain College in North Carolina. In these acknowledged outposts of Bauhaus teaching, masters from the Bauhaus workshops such as Joseph Albers, Lázló Moholy-Nagy, Walter Gropius, and Marcel Breuer helped shape graduate programs in architecture, design, and planning. It was natural that an entrepreneurial retail spirit was first expressed in those cities: places where design creators were working became the places where customers were soon discovering a taste for modernism.

The following material pays tribute to the three American generations that make up modern retailing's postwar evolution: D/R contemporaries — individual shops from the first postwar decade; D/R colleagues and rivals, including national businesses that still flourish; and D/R family, staff from the original D/R stores who have created successor businesses that reflect their owners' prior D/R experience.

Pioneers of American Modernism

Among the earliest modern design entrepreneurs were Sarah Pillsbury Harkness, a future partner at TAC, and Louisa Vaughan Conrad, who opened the Pillsbury & Vaughan shop on Boylston Street in Boston in 1940. They sold the furniture of Aino and Alvar Aalto, and were the exclusive Massachusetts reps for Artek-Pascoe from 1940 to 1942. Both women were graduates of Smith College and the Cambridge School of Architecture and Landscape Architecture. Baldwin Kingrey, established in 1947 in Chicago, was another American outlet for imported European functionalist furniture and Herman Miller and Knoll, selected by architect Harry Weese (MIT, 1938; Cranbrook Academy, 1939), his wife, Kitty Baldwin, and partner Jody Kingrey. Roughly parallel in impetus and history to D/R, Baldwin Kingrey had a very different aesthetic, displaying objects in a gallery-like setting more akin to a high modernist house. BK continued until 1957.

Boston had the eponymous store of architect Ralph Rapson (faculty of the New Bauhaus, 1942–46; MIT, 1946–54), which opened in 1950. Rapson and wife, Mary, sold his own furniture, manufactured by Knoll, as well as other pieces from the Knoll and Herman Miller lines. In Connecticut, Edith Twining, Alan Buck, and Elodie Osborne, a friend from the prewar days at MoMA, opened a small shop in Salisbury, publicized nationally with a breakthrough mail-order catalogue showcasing their imaginative collection of useful household objects, most of them imported. Twining and Buck spread the word about modernism far beyond Salisbury from 1950 until 1959.

On the West Coast, the Frank Brothers furnished the architect-designed Case Study houses from their Long Beach, California, store. Known internationally via their publication in *Arts & Architecture* magazine, the houses' carefully arranged furniture, as much as the glass walls and indoor-outdoor flows, sold the architects' vision of a casual West Coast lifestyle.

In New York, there was New Design, organized by Harvard GSD graduates Dorothy Noyes and Robert Rosenberg and his wife, Harriet, correlating Aalto and Hardoy (the soon-ubiquitous butterfly chair) with daring Betty Cooke silver jewelry and Danish glassware. Otherwise in Manhattan, most international retailing was limited to a few midtown blocks—Bonniers, Georg Jensen, and Form and Function.

The hub for cross-fertilization among designers and disciplines was the Museum of Modern Art, on West 53rd Street, close to many midtown retailers. Modernism was its reason for existence; its mission was propelling public interest in fine art as well as applied (industrial) art through design contests, most famously the 1941 Organic Design in Home Furnishings competition. These led to books and exhibitions that trumpeted a new philosophy: art as a means to a better way of life. MoMA had been founded in 1929 as a model of a modern multidisciplinary museum representing art and design as equals. The daring vision of its founding director, the young art historian Alfred Barr, was based on insights from the workshop curriculum of the Bauhaus. In addition to painting and sculpture departments, Barr's museum formed departments of architecture and design, film and photography, prints, theater, and dance. In 1947, newly appointed curator Philip Johnson presented Mies van der Rohe to the American public in a comprehensive exhibition. In 1948, Johnson commissioned a full-scale butterfly-roofed house designed by Marcel Breuer for the museum's garden, which became for many visitors their first experience of modern space and structure, one they could walk into and touch.

Consistent with the museum's belief that art is found in man-made and manufactured useful objects, MoMA's design curator, Edgar Kaufmann, Jr., launched its Good Design program in 1950, throwing its reputation behind the still-revolutionary notion that most common household objects—flatware, coffeepots, chairs, wastebaskets, even the kitchen table—could be works of art. MoMA provided a Good Design tag for display on selected products, a list of where to buy the best, and the show traveled to commercial venues in other cities, such as Chicago's Merchandise Mart, where store buyers from across the country selected their wares. Today the Good Design tradition is incorporated in MoMA's famed and extensive Permanent Collection of Objects of Design.

Design Research, then, was part of an era and a movement of like-minded men and women who lived the modern life by example and wanted to make it easier for others to do so too. All the original shops, while small and personal, made important statements locally. But in an era of slow communications and limited travel, only a few pioneers managed to grow, evolve, and survive as firms of national stature.

Edgar Kaufmann, Jr., launched the Museum of Modern Art's "Good Design" shows in 1950. Like D/R, the exhibits featured stylish, functional everyday objects at multiple price points. Today, the museum's collection contains numerous objects first introduced to the U.S. at D/R stores.

The D/R Legacy 175

National Enterprises

As the D/R idea was formulating on Ben's notepad, other entrepreneurs independently established sophisticated lifestyle stores that have thrived and survived over many decades. If the term *entrepreneur* means someone with a drive for new ideas and conviction in the face of risk, it describes how each of these founders seized the opportunity to bring products of superior quality to the still-isolated American marketplace. Among notable entries into specialty retail after the 1960s (including Pottery Barn, Workbench, Smith & Hawken), there are three—Design Research, Conran, and Williams-Sonoma—with early contemporaneous influence, albeit with interesting distinctions. They operated in different geographic arenas; and emphasized quality, efficiency, profit, and customer experience in different ways. Along the way, they rubbed shoulders, communicated informally, and exerted some collective market influence.

This trio was joined in 1962 by Crate & Barrel and was paid homage in 1999 by the upstart Design Within Reach. DWR pioneered selling serious designer furniture directly to the public via catalogue. DWR's success represents a new millennium leap in a retailing format whose success has improved the interface between far-flung consumers and well-designed interiors.

Habitat and the Conran Shop

The best contemporary parallel to D/R's diversity is probably found at Sir Terence Conran's two UK-based international chains, The Conran Shop and the lower-priced Habitat. Conran, trained as an architect—and knighted Sir Terence in 1983—began his retail career with the food orientation that Ben Thompson ended up with, as a restaurateur opening the Soup Kitchen in 1953. His first design company created furniture, textiles, and interiors and eventually offered complete design programs for corporate clients. In the early 1960s, Sir Terence sought an outlet for Conran-designed furniture whose production he could control, developing the first Habitat store in London in 1964. His lines were organized as a well-coordinated kit-of-parts for the interior, to be selected cafeteria-style and self-assembled. Whereas D/R's girls wore Marimekko, Habitat's wore Mary Quant, although the spirit was the same: As Conran's biography, *50 Years in Design,* puts it: "People seemed readily to identify with the style of life that Habitat embodied, a world in which more women worked and people increasingly took holidays abroad." And, "customers responded enthusiastically to furniture they could take away and assemble themselves, just as they did to the labour-saving duvet and the simple chicken-brick." By the 1970s there were eighteen Habitats, and in 1973 the first Conran Shop opened in London, with a higher price point and objects of design both classic and newly discovered.

Like Ben Thompson, Conran continued to seek new goods and new designers internationally, never rejecting the midcentury pieces that were his first loves. Also like Thompson, Sir Terence carried his merchandising ambitions into other corners of domestic life, including Mothercare, the child-care company that merged with Habitat in 1982, on one side, and gourmet restaurants and new town development on the other.

Williams-Sonoma

Chuck Williams entered retailing as a personal quest for quality in the life of the kitchen. Although Williams did not begin with an architect's concern for design or modern living as whole, conceptually his approach was similar to Thompson's: a desire for quality and a high level of information and interaction. Williams was a home builder and a dedicated chef who found his retail inspiration in a trip to Europe.

In his own words, Chuck describes the experience: "In 1956, with three friends, I made my first trip to Europe. Knowing that American pots and pans were made of thin aluminium that bent out of shape, that you couldn't buy a really good knife, I was fascinated in France to see heavy copper pots, the beginning of enameled cast-iron, great knives of carbon steel. It spoke to my passion. I thought, 'Since nobody has brought this amazing *batterie* to the U.S., maybe I will.'

"In Sonoma in 1956, I bought a building to subdivide and remodeled it into smaller shops, even doing the cabinetwork myself. In 1958 I moved all the cabinets into San Francisco on Sutter Street, where W-S remained my single store for seventeen years. We sold best-quality goods, backed by my knowledge of how to cook. We introduced omelet pans, sauté pans, and we showed customers how they could be used. Having knowledge and talking about it—that was what built the clientele. When Julia Child's first cookbook was introduced in the West, Julia and Simone Beck came for a visit, and we were the first non-bookstore permitted to sell *Mastering the Art of French Cooking*.

"I opened the Beverly Hills store in 1972, then more down the peninsula. And I started a catalogue—quite an innovation. In 1978 we were ready to expand beyond four stores, and it was challenging to manage the financing and opening of new locations. I sold to someone who understood expansion and who made W-S into a sound national company.

"I remember D/R when it became *the* new store in San Francisco. It was an amazing place. It had all the equipment for your life, and sold modern living to a new group of people after the war—just as I did."

OPPOSITE: The Conran Shop carries on in New York in a spectacular location underneath the 59th Street Bridge, where it opened in 1999.

Chuck Williams built the original San Francisco Williams-Sonoma store on Sutter Street himself in 1958, where it thrived for seventeen years before he added new shops. Williams's dedication to bringing fine equipment to good cooks paralleled Ben's search for diverse new furnishings for American homes.

The D/R Legacy

Gordon Segal's first Crate & Barrel store in Chicago opened in 1963. Shown above is one of Crate & Barrel's typical mall locations, which average 40,000 square feet and contain a comprehensive inventory of furniture and accessories.

Crate & Barrel

Gordon Segal, cofounder and former president: "In April 1965 I went to Cambridge with one of my key design people. Design Research was then in the clapboard house on Brattle Street. It was a spring day, trees were blossoming, lawns were green. We walk into this house and there are two beautiful Finnish girls behind a table with a big bowl of oranges with fresh orange juice nearby for visitors. In the kitchen you had the cookware, the dishes, and the glasses. In the bedroom you had apparel, including all these modern dresses. Marimekko fabrics were hung throughout the house. In the backyard, a Finnish rowboat was on some wooden sawhorses.

"The whole scene was spectacular and was so unlike any other retail. For a young retailer like me—I was maybe thirty years old—to walk in and see somebody else's very different take on retail was just a knockout. I said, 'My God, there are things to learn here.' It started my neurosis about trying to create a business in which people's feeling when they walked into a store—the visual display, the music, the *environment*—was going to be much more important."

Segal began buying Marimekko textiles wholesale from Thompson, which he sold at his original 1962 store in Chicago. By 1968 he had two stores, and by 1971 he opened his first Cambridge Crate & Barrel in Putnam Square. The two stores were competitors, although Segal remained a Marimekko wholesale customer. When D/R closed in 1978, Crate & Barrel moved into the D/R glass headquarters. To Segal, "Ben Thompson designed a remarkable piece of architecture, but with all glass and no walls to put stuff on, it was a very difficult place to sell in. And it had a totally different quality from the house, which had the residential sense, the warmth." But C & B adapted and for more than thirty years made 48 Brattle its own successful iconic store.

Design Within Reach

Rob Forbes, founder: "I first fell under the spell of modern design in 1968, when I walked into a friend's house in Laguna Beach, designed by Lamont Langworthy. The three-story house spanned a ravine, had glass, slanted redwood siding, with extraordinary views. In it were all sorts of objects my friend's parents had picked up at a store called Design Research. I was a teenager, not a consumer. But I knew this was the coolest place in my world to hang out.

"I conceived Design Within Reach in 1998 after living in Europe, when I became aware of a basic problem: there were no sources in the United States for well-designed chairs, lamps, or sofas other than showrooms. (I learned later that this same frustration motivated Ben Thompson to become a merchant in 1953.) My concept was that simple: make stylish products easily available, price them fairly. I did not see much risk in that. In fact it took off like a rocket, and in our first full year we more than doubled our plan. People still say you cannot sell chairs without letting people sit on them. I have learned that you can sell *anything* if you create an appealing context. People need objects with meaning in their lives. At DWR we presented customers with the story of the designer(s) for each product before giving them the price."

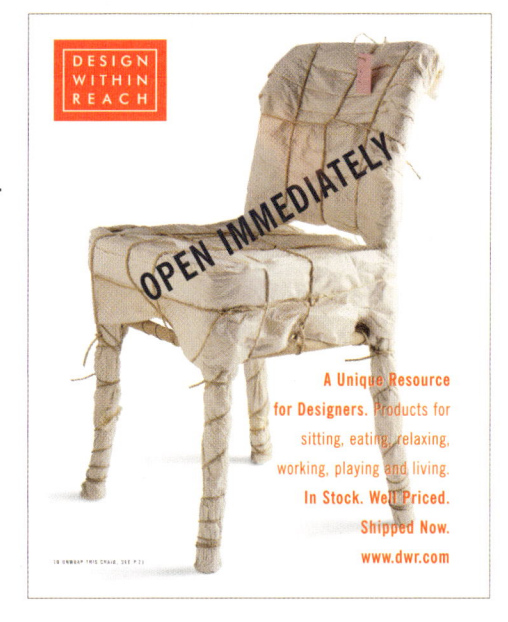

Design Within Reach, modern design's first successful effort at catalogue retailing for modernism's prestigious designs, launched its first mailer in 1999, and opened its first Studio Store in Jackson Square, San Francisco.

The D/R Legacy 179

D/R Graduates

Out of the core D/R stores emerged a cadre of experienced men and women trained in the visionary approach of Ben Thompson and loving the excitement of selling good-looking products to enthusiastic customers. A number of them shared Ben's entrepreneurial spirit and founded their own shops. Others branched into design-related businesses taking a variety of personal directions. Here we have gathered stories of some alumni who went on to make a design application the theme of their lives and later careers.

Retailers

Pauline Dora
Design Solutions, New Canaan, Connecticut
Nancy Hemenway
The Cottage, Tiverton, Rhode Island

After D/R closed, longtime employees Dora and Hemenway bought the U.S. rights to the Marimekko name and opened the first all-Marimekko shop in New York. Thompson designed the shop, which lasted from 1979 to 1992. Dora then led development of Sir Terence Conran's U.S. ventures, while Hemenway became an international retail consultant. Both eventually opened their own shops, selling select interior furnishings, housewares, and accessories. All told, each of them has been in independent retailing for forty years and still loves it.

Lu Wendel Lyndon and Maynard Hale Lyndon
Placewares, Gualala, California

The Lyndons met at D/R in 1971 and opened Placewares, in Concord, Massachusetts, two years later. Placewares extended the notion of good design to containers for beautiful objects. They ran Placewares successfully for thirty years in New England, closing it in 2004 to focus on their studio, LyndonDesign, on the West Coast. In 2006, Placewares reopened as a single outlet in Gualala, the Northern California town where Maynard's architect brother, Donlyn, and his partners at MLTW, designed the iconic Sea Ranch development. Both Lyndons felt the need for customer interaction to fuel their work as designers and to sell a strong assortment of modern home goods, including Marimekko products.

Julia McFarlane
Ad Hoc, New York City

Today, McFarlane works for Thomas O'Brien's Aero Studios, but for twenty years McFarlane sold her own vision of the home at Ad Hoc Softwares, the original Manhattan resource for useful and adaptable industrial products such as wire shelving, restaurant china, and scientific glassware reintroduced as home goods. Ad Hoc was eventually a victim of its own success; rents were raised, and the aesthetic went mainstream, diluting the clean and singular aesthetic McFarlane and partner Judy Auchincloss purveyed. They closed their Lexington Avenue store in 1986 and their SoHo store in 2002.

Astrid Vigeland
Folly 101, Portland, Maine

Vigeland, who worked at D/R Cambridge in the waning years, went to Crate & Barrel and then became an independent designer and stylist in New York. In Portland, Maine, she opened her own store, Folly 101, which follows in the D/R tradition in terms of its eclectic mixture of objects and furniture, its evolving displays, and its deeply personal vision.

Personal Design Careers

Sandra Smith Griswold
retail consulting

Griswold, manager of D/R West Coast, who launched many retail careers after 1966, went to Williams-Sonoma in 1974, then became a freelance food and prop stylist and art director, and was responsible for over forty cookbooks for Williams-Sonoma, among other clients. She recently reentered the world of retail as a consultant to the Carmel Bay Company, a thirty-five-year-old store in an Arts & Crafts building, creating its Web site, buying new products, and overseeing visual merchandising.

FAR LEFT: Placewares in Gualala.

NEAR LEFT: Arne Jacobsen fixtures sold by Kroin, Inc.

BELOW: The first U.S. Marimekko Concept Store opened on Huron Avenue in Cambridge in 2006.

Design Neighborhood

Huron Village, Cambridge

As Harvard Square slowly filled with national chains, it drained of the small-town quality that marked the early years of Design Research's presence. Other Cambridge neighborhoods have taken on the qualities of Brattle Street in the 1950s and 1960s, benefiting from the entrepreneurial talents stimulated in D/R staff members. Huron Village, a local main street with a rich mix of food, fashion, and service resources, is home to a remarkable group of D/R alumnae.

First on Huron Avenue came Pirjo Laine (a longtime D/R Cambridge display coordinator) who developed a business of custom mix-and-match cotton knit fashions in bright Finnish colors. (The shop closed when Laine died in 1994.) Across the street, Susi Cooper (D/R Cambridge toys, accessories) since 1989 has dedicated her Susi's shop to bright and fanciful clothes and toys for the modern child. On the corner, her sister, Libby (D/R children's buyer), opened Mobilia, a cutting-edge gallery of unique multimedia sculptures and art jewelry, with ever-changing exhibitions. East of Susi, Judy deMont (a former assistant to Pirjo) launched the fashion shop J. Miles and then in Fall 2006, with son, Jon, the first American Marimekko Concept Store on the corner. For Marimekko, it was more a homecoming than a radical departure, as the store united the neighborhood with a visible art and design identity and reunited many early D/R customers with their first love of modernism.

Larry Kroin
Kroin, Inc.

Kroin entered the old Cambridge store in 1968 as the low man (one of only a handful) on the totem pole, assembling furniture and carrying goods to customers' cars. In 1976 he started his own company in architectural imports, beginning with fixtures designed by Danish architect Arne Jacobsen. Kroin saw that kitchens and bathrooms had been overlooked in the design industry, which was a revolutionary idea at the time to focus on. Kroin, Inc.'s award-winning printed materials were designed by Massimo Vignelli, whose Max I melamine dinnerware was a D/R classic. Kroin closed the company in 2001 and continues as a design consultant.

Raymond Waites
fashion and interior design

In 1973 Waites was hired as creative vice president for D/R, and developed new products (including the Marimekko sheets), new stores (particularly Rittenhouse Square), and new graphics applied to bags, posters, and display. After D/R, Waites continued to work with Marimekko and with Ristomatti Ratia, eventually launching the soft luggage company Gear. By the 1980s, Waites changed his focus to home furnishings, developing lines that have moved from traditional to postmodern to baroque. He recently opened the New Vintage Gallery in High Point, N.C.

Sandy Reynolds-Wasco and David Wasco
set decoration, production design

The Wascos met at the Cambridge store in the mid-1970s. Today they are known for their collaborations with directors Wes Anderson and Quentin Tarantino. The Wascos' sets for *The Royal Tenenbaums* and *Kill Bill* indeed share with D/R the belief in décor as a revelation of character. Ben Thompson believed that decorating your own house was a form of self-exploration; for the on-screen alter egos of idiosyncratic directors, the Wascos, backstage, play the same interpretive role.

The D/R Legacy

Paul Goldberger "The most important development in American design in the last generation is not any single object that has been designed, but the democratization of design itself."

Afterword

By Paul Goldberger

The most important development in American design in the last generation is not any single object that has been designed, but the democratization of design itself. Design—modern design, that is—has moved from being the province of the elite to becoming a part, and sometimes even a central part, of mainstream taste. Now if you go to IKEA or Target or Williams-Sonoma or Crate & Barrel or Restoration Hardware, you see the extent to which American taste has shifted. Every one of these places represents a sea change in the ways in which the average person in this country now encounters design, and the way in which he or she perceives it. Suddenly, design is accessible to all. It has become embedded, a mass commodity. It is available everywhere and at a reasonable level of quality.

Not so many years ago that wasn't the case at all. There was no such thing as quality modern design at affordable prices, at least not in this country. The pioneer in this effort to bring modern design into American homes was Design Research, originally in Cambridge and later also on 57th Street in Manhattan and in San Francisco. As a retailer, D/R, as it was known, signaled the beginning of the movement to gain a broader, but more informed, audience. Bonniers on Madison Avenue was somewhat similar, and there was also the Museum of Modern Art store. But all of these were still fairly rarified places, even if they were retail stores. In the 1950s and '60s, quality modern design was by and large not a mass product. Even Design Research, for some, emitted an aura of design as religion. This was still a time when design was viewed as an elitist cult of uplift.

It's all very different now. I think we are now at a moment when a dream that has existed since the early part of the twentieth century is actually being fulfilled—the dream of seeing modern design accessible to the masses, even sought by them. This is the dream that energized the Bauhaus, that drove the creators of that institution whose name is synonymous with modern design to create what they did. For even though the work that emerged out of the Bauhaus was largely labor-intensive, much more craft-dependent than truly industrial and rarely available to or even sought by the great masses of people, the Bauhaus designers desperately wanted modern design to be a mass product: they dreamed of a moment when good modern design would be available to everyone at a decent price. They fooled themselves into believing that it could happen in their time. It couldn't, and it didn't. But it has happened now.

Bizarre as it sounds, the Bauhaus dream has been fulfilled, more than half a century later, in places like Target, or West Elm, or Muji. And we have seen a remarkable shift in the level of taste in general in this period, too, among the whole range of our consumer products. After all, when was the last time a contemporary furnishings store offered an avocado-colored refrigerator or a Naugahyde sofa? The design of computers and electronic equipment is likewise remarkably sophisticated, especially considering that these are all mass-market items. Apple is the most remarkable mass-market design company in the world right now, creating products that are better than IBM at its peak. Yet even non-Apple products are decent. A Nokia cell phone may not be as good a piece of design as an iPod or an iPhone, but it's pretty good.

There is a much higher level of visual literacy in our culture now. I think that the baby boom generation has grown up to be more visually sophisticated, by and large, than its parents were, and less comfortable with a certain kind of cheap fakery. That doesn't mean that it isn't quite happy to have expensive, serious fakery; thirtyish software zillionaires and fortyish investment bankers have been keeping certain architects in the money designing fake Shingle-Style villas and Georgian mansions for years now, and they will continue to. But we have come to associate a certain kind of design with cheapness, and the visual sophistication of this generation now in its prime is unwilling to tolerate it. Thus the design level and the visual sophistication of household appliances goes up, as do the computers and cell phones and PDAs and televisions and all of the other things that get put into that vast Georgian mansion. I have never seen a truly bad flat-screen TV, even though some are better than others, just as I've never seen a truly ugly laptop computer.

The democratization of design is not without its drawbacks. Along with democratization comes homogenization; along with the ubiquity of an IKEA comes sameness, a pushing of everything toward a common denominator. When Design Research was in its prime, everything seemed dazzlingly fresh. You hadn't seen it before, or you hadn't seen so much of it that your eyes glazed over. Everything in the store caught your eye. Now when you walk through Restoration Hardware, it's all too familiar. Today if you see Philippe Starck even that is familiar. The common denominator is a lot better than the average we saw twenty-five or thirty years ago, when Design Research could glisten beside, say, W & J Sloane or B. Altman. But in its relentless sameness, in the way in which all of this fine stuff is now mass-produced everywhere, we run the risk in design, as we do in so many other areas of our culture, of squeezing out surprise. No, you don't have to reinvent the wheel in design, and nothing is worse than design that tries too hard. But the power of our new mainstream market for design also means that eccentric design, individual design, and innovative design are harder things to establish in the marketplace, because the mass market rarely has patience for them. It is a paradox, actually, that the demand for modern design is higher than it has been at any time in our lifetimes, and yet it is tough for good, new, highly creative design to stand out. The mass market, the great consumer design machine, pushes us toward the center, toward what once was radical and now is commonplace. There is no free lunch, and this is the price we pay for our success—for the realization of the dream begun by the Bauhaus and pushed forward by Design Research.

Ben Thompson Chronology

1918 Born July 3, St. Paul, Minnesota

1937 Graduates Avon Old Farms School, after attending St. Paul Academy

1941 B.Arch, Yale School of Architecture

1941–45 Lieutenant, U.S. Navy, on *Destroyer Escort Courage* in North Atlantic and Pacific. Final duty in the Office of Strategic Services; provides design services at the United Nations founding conference, San Francisco

1946 Founder, The Architects Collaborative (TAC) with Walter Gropius and six other architect-partners

1953 First Design Research store opens at 57 Brattle Street in Cambridge

1959 D/R presents Marimekko in the exhibition "Finland's Designs": the American debut of the company's fabrics, fashion, and accessories

A second Design Research opens on Lexington Avenue in New York City

1963 A third Design Research opens on 57th Street in New York City

1963–67 Chairman, Department of Architecture, Harvard Graduate School of Design

1965 Design Research opens as the anchor store at Ghirardelli Square, San Francisco

1966 Benjamin Thompson and Associates (BTA) opens in Cambridge

1969 Opening of the new Design Research Headquarters at 48 Brattle Street. Loses control of D/R in a hostile takeover by a stockholder the following year

1969–74 BTA submits competition proposal for the restoration of Quincy Markets in Boston. The plan is selected, and Thompson brings in the Rouse Company as developer

1971 Design Research Headquarters receives the AIA National Honor Award

1975 Harvest Restaurant, co-owned by Ben and Jane Thompson and designed by BTA, opens at 48 Brattle Street

1976 Grand opening of Faneuil Hall Marketplace's Quincy Market, followed by the opening of South Market (1977) and North Market (1978)

1978 Opening of Landmark Inn (three restaurants) and Great Hall banquet facilities in Quincy Market, designed and operated by the Thompsons

1984 Opening of Ordway Music Theatre, St. Paul

1985 BTA receives Louis Sullivan Prize, International Union of Bricklayers and Allied Craftsmen

1986 BTA named AIA Architectural Firm of the Year

1988 Opening of revitalized Union Station, Washington, D.C.

1992 Receives AIA Gold Medal presented by First Lady Barbara Bush at the Kennedy Center, Washington, D.C.

1993 Retires from BTA

2000 In July, Ben and Jane Thompson are individually named by the President of Finland as Knights First Class of the Order of the Lion of Finland, the nation's highest recognition of civic and artistic contribution, in appreciation of their lifelong effort to communicate Finland's values, design, and way of life to America and the world

2002 Dies in Cambridge

2003 Design Research Headquarters receives AIA Twenty-five-Year Award for architecture of enduring significance

D/R Stores

The Backstory

(closed 1978–79, unless otherwise noted)

1953   Cambridge, Mass. (closed 1969)

1959   New York City, Lexington Avenue (closed 1964)

1960   Hyannis, Mass. (one summer only)

1963   New York City, East 57th Street

1965   Ghirardelli Square, San Francisco, Calif.

1969   D/R Headquarters, Cambridge, Mass.

1971   Easthampton, New York (closed 1973)

1971   Westport, Conn.

1971   Beverly Hills, Calif.

1972   South Shore Plaza, Braintree, Mass.

1973   Embarcadero Center, San Francisco, Calif.

1974   Chestnut Hill, Mass.

1975   Rittenhouse Square, Philadelphia, Penn.

Among postwar design stores, Design Research set a record for longevity—twenty-five years—by propelling a niche design business into a lifestyle industry. Under Thompson's seventeen-year leadership it did not fail, as commonly assumed, nor did Thompson sell out. At the time of refinancing in 1967, his property's success spurred an insider's hostile takeover, a term unknown at the time.

Ben Thompson ran D/R with inventive energy—he was an instinctive merchant without the rules taught in today's business schools. Yet virtually without capitalization in 1953 or after, and sustained with periodic loans from Ben's initial partner, Spencer Field, D/R had a rising sales curve. In fact, through 1965 Ben financed a three-store expansion, along with wholesale growth, by plowing back annual revenues into the business.

By 1967, seeking real capitalization, Ben met Peter Sprague, a young venture capitalist. Sprague agreed to buy out Field's half interest and each party agreed to a 50 percent cash investment; as CEO Ben would retain management and design control. On the November 1967 closing date, Thompson's funds were delivered but Sprague failed to appear to sign closing documents. Thereafter, in a series of preemptive moves, Sprague increased his stock ownership, disavowed Thompson's control, brought in a new president, and instructed Thompson to depart.

D/R's directors took legal action, starting with an injunction to keep Ben in control. A lawsuit proceeded even as the new D/R headquarters was under construction. In December, the 57 Brattle Street operation moved across the street for a festive Christmas grand opening at 48 Brattle—the last official celebration of the founder, staff, friends, customers, and neighbors.

In Summer 1970, Massachusetts Superior Court decreed that Thompson could not claim management control without the signed agreement. The Sprague group then preempted all business operations and assets. Ben and his investors, with only 49 percent stock holdings, had no power. The company continued for eight more years, with loyal staff members struggling to keep D/R's spirit and standards afloat, working under a succession of four presidents versed in conventional retailing but lacking D/R's design sensibility. Sprague's bankruptcy filing in 1978–79 closed the nine remaining D/R stores.

Sprague had assumed ownership of the new headquarters building in 1970, which he soon sold and leased back. In the mid-seventies, facing bankruptcy, Sprague persuaded realtor William Poorvu (who initially worked with Thompson to develop the site) to pay a cash sum to buy out D/R's lease, releasing Sprague from a major obligation. Poorvu became the owner of the award-winning building and for thirty years leased it to Crate & Barrel, an appropriate successor in lifestyle retailing.

Contributors

Paola Antonelli, curator, Department of Architecture and Design, Museum of Modern Art, New York.

Claud Bunyard, D/R Cambridge sales manager, furniture designer, interiors 1953–61; founder, Claud Bunyard Designs, died 2005.

Robert Campbell, architecture critic, *Boston Globe;* author, *Cityscapes of Boston;* coauthor, *Civic Builders;* Pulitzer Prize, 1996.

Ralph Caplan, design writer; author, *By Design; Cracking the Whip: Essays on Design and Its Side Effects.*

Susi Cooper, D/R Cambridge toys, accessories manager; D/R Chestnut Hill store manager, 1975–78; owner, Susi's, Cambridge, Mass.

Pauline Dora, D/R Cambridge accessories buyer, New York store manager, vice president for operations, 1968–77; owner, Design Solutions, New Canaan, Conn.

Lorna Dawson Elkus, D/R Cambridge and New York buyer, store manager, 1961–70; assistant to Ben Thompson, 1970–75.

Margaret Eskridge, TAC architectural renderer/presentation artist, 1956–57, 1958–63; Fulbright in Finland, 1957–58 and coordinated D/R's "Finland's Designs" exhibition, 1959; designed exhibition poster and graphics; architectural renderer.

Robert Eskridge, TAC intern, 1956–57; TAC staff 1958–63; with Margaret Eskridge, Fulbright in Finland, 1957–58 and coordinated D/R's "Finland's Designs" exhibition, 1959; architect.

Norman Fletcher, founding partner, The Architects Collaborative; died 2007.

Blase Gallo, D/R display, product development, 1971–78; restaurant designer, UNO Chicago Grill, private clients.

Dorothy Twining Globus, curator of exhibitions, Museum of Arts and Design; former director, Museum at the Fashion Institute of Technology, New York; former curator, Cooper-Hewitt, National Design Museum, New York.

Paul Goldberger, architecture critic, *The New Yorker;* Joseph Urban Professor of Design, The New School, New York; Pulitzer Prize, 1984; author, *Up from Zero: Politics, Architecture, and the Rebuilding of New York;* coauthor, *Yale in New Haven: Architecture and Urbanism.*

Tom Green, partner, Benjamin Thompson & Associates, 1966–80, 1988–2001; partner-in-charge, D/R headquarters.

Sandra Smith Griswold, D/R West Coast manager, three stores, 1966–74; interior designer, food and prop stylist, and retail consultant, Carmel Bay Company, Calif.

Sibyl Wahl Hanson, D/R Cambridge, New York, San Francisco management, 1962–66.

Chip Harkness, founding partner, The Architects Collaborative.

Alan Heller, furniture and housewares manufacturer; maker of new versions of Vignelli's best-selling stacking melamine dinnerware sold at D/R.

Nancy Hemenway, D/R Cambridge vice president for merchandising, Marimekko wholesale, 1968–76; owner, The Cottage, Tiverton, R.I.

Lorraine De Wet Howes, D/R Cambridge display, apparel designer, 1957–60; professor emerita and former chair, Apparel Design, Rhode Island School of Design, Providence.

Ati Gropius Johansen, graphic artist and teacher; daughter of architect Walter Gropius, founder of the Bauhaus, and TAC partner of Ben Thompson.

Alexander Julian, designer, fashion, textiles, home furnishings.

Agnete Larsen Kalckar, D/R Cambridge, coordinator, Scandinavian furniture, 1953–70; BTA Interiors, 1970–94; died 2007.

Kathy Keating, D/R Cambridge assistant, 1962–64, New York accessories, 1964–65; writer and poet, *Postcards from the Pearl; Sleeping Naked Under the Moon.*

Elizabeth Kendall, author, *Autobiography of a Wardrobe; Where She Danced; The Runaway Bride; American Daughter.*

Mary Brewster Kennedy, D/R Cambridge textiles, accessories, 1957–69; interior decorator and design consultant.

Larry Kroin, D/R Cambridge furniture sales, manager, buyer, 1968–75; founder, Kroin, Inc., importer of architectural fixtures.

Tizzie (Elizabeth) Lambert, D/R Cambridge accessories, 1962–64; international correspondent, *Architectural Digest.*

Jack Lenor Larsen, textile designer; D/R wholesale fabric supplier.

Paul R. Lawrence, professor emeritus, Harvard Business School; former chair, Organizational Behavior, MBA and AMP programs.

Emma-Gail Lombardi, D/R San Francisco display, 1965–78; artist.

Lu Wendel Lyndon, D/R San Francisco, accessories; Beverly Hills, Braintree display, store manager, 1965–73; cofounder, LyndonDesign and Placewares, Gualala, Calif.

Janet Malcolm, staff writer, *The New Yorker;* author, *Two Lives: Gertrude and Alice; Reading Chekhov: A Critical Journey.*

Elizabeth (Biffy) Malko, D/R New York display, 1966–68; former manager, Ad Hoc Workshop; former researcher, Fujisankei Communications International and "World Shopping Theater"; development, lifestyle television programs.

Christa Marcelli, D/R Cambridge accessories 1957–70; BTA Interiors 1970–94.

Cara McCarty, curatorial director, Cooper-Hewitt, National Design Museum, New York.

Sheila McCullough, consultant, Thompson Design Group; stepdaughter of Ben Thompson and lives in Northampton, Mass.

Julia McFarlane, D/R New York display, 1963–69; cofounder, Ad Hoc Softwares; sales associate, Aero Ltd.

Minkie West McKevitt, D/R Cambridge, New York Marimekko, 1961–64, 1968; sales, Marimekko New York, 1979, 1985–87; owner, Marimekko Beverly Hills, 1982–83.

Henriette Mladota, D/R administration, European buyer, 1955–70; baroness, Cerven Hradek (Red Castle), Czech Republic.

Russell Morash, director-producer of *The French Chef* (1963–73) and subsequent Julia Child programs, WGBH, Boston.

Sara Moulton, executive chef, *Gourmet* magazine; host, *Sara's Weeknight Meals,* PBS; food editor, *Good Morning America.*

Marian Parmenter (Wintersteen), D/R San Francisco furniture, 1972–77; cofounder, SFMOMA Artists Gallery at Fort Mason.

Chee Perlman, design writer and editor; former editor-in-chief, *I.D.* magazine.

Kathleen Parks Perry, D/R San Francisco accessories, furniture manager, 1975–77; president, Céladon Design Group, Sonoma, Calif.

Ristomatti Ratia, founder, Décembre Oy, 1970–74; Marimekko creative director, 1974–85; founder, Ratia Brand Co., Helsinki, Finland.

Sandy Reynolds-Wasco, D/R Cambridge accessories, fabric, toy manager, 1976–78; set decorator, *Redbelt, Collateral, Kill Bill,* and other films.

Nancy Gathercole Riaz, TAC assistant, summer 1953; D/R Cambridge, assistant to Ben Thompson, 1953–64.

William Roth, owner and developer, Ghirardelli Square; D/R board member, 1968–70; U.S. Trade Representative, 1967–69; former Regent, University of California.

Mildred F. Schmertz, FAIA; former editor in chief, *Architectural Record;* contributing writer, *Architectural Digest.*

Gordon Segal, cofounder and CEO, Crate & Barrel. Retired in 2008 after forty-six years, with over 160 stores in the United States.

Sandra Sheeline, assistant to Ben Thompson, The Architects Collaborative and BTA, 1960–65.

Margaret Turnbull Simon, D/R San Francisco display, West Coast display manager, 1969–75; head of interior design, Turnbull Griffin Haesloop Architects, San Francisco.

Colin Smith, architect BTA, 1966–69; partner, Architectural Resources Cambridge, 1969–present.

Anne Flynt Amory Solley, D/R Cambridge display, graphics, 1960–67; designer, BTA, 1967–81.

Anna Sui, fashion designer.

Patricia Moore Sullivan, longtime D/R Cambridge customer.

Astrid Vigeland, D/R Cambridge textiles, toy manager, 1974–76; owner, Folly 101, Portland, Me.

Massimo Vignelli, designer and cofounder Unimark and Vignelli Designs; creator of stacking melamine dinnerware sold at D/R.

Nancy Waites, D/R New York Marimekko, 1965–70; adjunct professor, Fashion Merchandising Management, Fashion Institute of Technology, New York.

Raymond Waites, D/R creative vice president, 1975–78; founder, Gear, Raymond Waites Design.

David Wasco, D/R San Francisco display; Beverly Hills, Cambridge display director, 1975–78; production designer, *Redbelt, Collateral, Kill Bill,* and other films.

Peter Wheeler, D/R Cambridge display, in-house designer, 1972–77; consultant, BTA, 1975–85; president and co-owner, Sara Campbell Ltd, Boston.

Elizabeth (Betsy) Cushman Whitman, TAC interior designer, 1952–53; D/R interior designer, D/R 1953–54, 1957–58.

Marianne Sundström Williams, D/R Cambridge kitchenwares, 1962–64; realtor, Belfast, Me.

About the Authors

Jane Thompson is an urbanist—designer and planner—who has spent her thirty-year career creating successful and well-loved places that contribute to the vitality and identity of cities worldwide, such as Dublin, Cardiff, Amsterdam, and Tokyo. Since 1994, she has been principal of Thompson Design Group in Boston, whose projects include Navy Pier in Chicago, the Grand Central District and Times Square Center in New York, the North Coast Harbor plan in Cleveland, and the Redevelopment Master Plan for Houston's Buffalo Bayou.

Jane graduated from Vassar College and pursued graduate studies at New York University's Institute of Fine Arts. She then worked for the Museum of Modern Art and became acting assistant curator in the Department of Architecture. This was followed by positions as architecture editor of *Interiors* magazine and founding editor of *Industrial Design* (now *I.D.*).

In the late 1960s Jane became co-owner of Design Research, Inc., founded by her late husband, architect Benjamin Thompson. With Thompson, she conceived and designed Boston's Faneuil Hall Marketplace and numerous waterfront restorations in the United States and abroad. She has been a board member of the International Design Conference in Aspen, the Institute for Urban Design, and the Waterfront Center in Washington, D.C. Jane chairs the Gropius House Advisory Committee in Lincoln, Massachusetts. She has received numerous awards for her work, including a lifetime achievement award from the Industrial Design Society of America and Institute Honors from the AIA. In 2000, Jane and Ben Thompson were each named Knight First Class, Order of the Lion of Finland.

Alexandra Lange is a journalist and architectural historian. She has written for the *Architect's Newspaper, Domino, I.D., Metropolis,* and the *New York Times,* and is a contributing editor at *New York* magazine. She has a B.A. in Architecture and Literature from Yale University and received a Ph.D. from the Institute of Fine Arts at New York University in 2005. Her essays and reviews have appeared in *Grey Room,* the *Journal of Design History,* and the *Journal of the Society of Architectural Historians.* She has contributed to the books *Eero Saarinen: Realizing American Utopia* (Yale University Press, 2006) and *New York Cool: Paintings and Sculptures from the NYU Collection* (Grey Art Gallery, NYU, 2008). She teaches architecture criticism in the Urban Design and Architecture Studies program at NYU and in the MFA in Design Criticism program at the School of Visual Arts. Alexandra Lange lives in Brooklyn with her husband, Mark Dixon, and son, Paul.

Acknowledgments

The authors would like to offer immense thanks to the many who assisted in the preparation of this book, without whom it truly could not have been written.

For interviews and personal histories: Jonathan Adler, Paola Antonelli, Mary Brewster Kennedy, Robert Campbell, Ralph Caplan, Libby and Susi Cooper, Judy and John deMont, Pauline Dora, Lorna Elkus, Blase Gallo, Tom Green, Sandra Griswold, Sybil Hansen and Sandra Sheeline, Alan Heller, Nancy Hemenway, Craig Hodgetts, Lorraine Howes, Lehr Jackson, Ati Gropius Johansen, Alexander Julian, Barbara Kapp and Paul Mitarachi, Kathy Keating, Larry Kroin, Tizzie Lambert, Jack Lenor Larsen, Marya Lianko, Phil Loheed, Emma-Gail Lombardi, Lu and Maynard Lyndon, Biffy Malko, Christa Marcelli, Julia McFarlane, Minkie McKevitt, Henriette Mladota, Russell Morash, Sara Moulton, Kathleen Parks Perry, Marian Parmenter, Chee Perlman, Barbara Plumb, Chris Pullman, Sandy Reynolds-Wasco and David Wasco, Nancy Gathercole Riaz, William Roth, Gordon Segal, Robert Segal, Margaret Turnbull Simon, Suzanne Slesin, Colin Smith, Anne Solley, Diane and Alan Spigelman, Anna Sui, Patricia Sullivan, Astrid Vigeland, Clara Wainwright, Nancy and Raymond Waites, Peter Wheeler, Betsy Whitman, Chuck Williams, and Marianne Sundström Williams.

For excerpts from published works: Geoffrey Hellman, Elizabeth Kendall, Janet Malcolm, and Herbert Muschamp.

For assistance in reconstructing history: Dorothy Globus; Peter McMahon; William J. Poorvu; Mildred F. Schmertz; Barbara Stauffacher Solomon; and Susan Ward, Museum of Fine Arts, Boston.

For wise words: Rob Forbes and Paul Goldberger.

For photography and special documentation: Marianne Aav and Merja Vulhunen, Design Museum, Helsinki; Jerry Bragstad; Elsa Dorfman; Joel Gardner; Design Collection, Museum of Modern Art, New York; Alex and Paul Herzan; Karen Philippi; Steve Rosenthal; Schlesinger Library, Harvard University; Erica Stoller, ESTO; Tony Vaccaro; Caroline Van Valkenburgh; and WGBH.

Special thanks: To the Cooper-Hewitt, National Design Museum, for access to their Design Research archives, and to curatorial director Cara McCarty for her advice on sources; and to Janet Parks, Avery Library, Columbia University, for expediting access to original D/R archival photos of George Cserna. And to Michael Beirut, Yve Ludwig, and Tamara McKenna at Pentagram, and to our editor Ruth Peltason, whom we enjoyed working with and learned a great deal from.

Alexandra Lange: I am grateful to my mother, Martha Scotford, and my husband, Mark Dixon, for allowing me to live in good taste.

Sheila McCullough: I wish to thank my husband, Peter Post, my daughters, Thea and Isabel, and my friends Lissa Rovetch, Peter Smith, and Kim Gordon for their support and great ideas. And of course, Ben.

Jane Thompson: Like so many others who have been part of the D/R story, I am thankful to have known Ben Thompson and to have shared the D/R adventure with him.

Credits

Every effort has been made by the authors to identify photo and text sources, as identified below. For generous assistance with historical and illustrative material illuminating D/R's lasting relationship with Finland's designers, craftsmen, and producers, the authors wish to acknowledge Marimekko Oy, iittala, Artek, and Fiskars.

Photography

AMAC Plastic Products Corporation: 133 (bottom right); **The Architects Collaborative (TAC):** 12 (top), 22 (top); **Artek:** 122 (top left), 136 (top right, middle right, bottom right); **Artemide:** 134 (top right); **BTA Archive:** 20 (bottom), 150; **Paul Child/Schlesinger Library, The Radcliffe Institute, Harvard University:** 64; **Paul Child/ WGBH Educational Foundation, © 2008, WGBH Boston:** 66, 67; **Conran:** 176; **Crate & Barrel:** 178; **George Cserna:** 4, 97, 103, 104 (bottom), 105, 107, 110, 113 (right); **De Padova:** 137 (bottom right); **Design Museum, Helsinki:** 129 (middle center); **Design Research:** 2, 18, 24, 35, 36–37, 38, 40–41, 43, 44, 46–47, 48, 49, 50, 51, 60, 61, 62, 65 (top), 75, 76 (top), 84, 85, 86, 87, 88, 89, 91, 98–99, 101 (right), 107 (bottom), 109, 111, 113 (left), 114, 117, 123 (top left, middle left, bottom right), 125 (bottom left, top right), 126 (top left, middle right), 130 (top right, bottom right), 132 (top right), 138 (top right), 139 (top right), 140–143, 148–149, 160, 161; **Design Within Reach:** 179; **Elsa Dorfman, © Elsa Dorfman 2007. All rights reserved. From** *It Wasn't Just a Dress,* **film produced by Caroline Van Valkenburgh:** 94, 95; **Erlau AG:** 137 (top center); **Peggy Eskridge:** 50 (bottom); **ESTO:** 32, 33, 39, 42, 68, 69, 131 (top), 145, 146, 151, 152–53, 155, 158–59, 162, 166–67, 170, 171; *Food & Wine* magazine: 21, 65 (bottom); **Joel Gardner:** 181 (bottom); **John Goell:** 22 (middle); **Ati Gropius:** 45; **Olga Gueft:** 168; **Harvard Graduate School of Design:** 25; **Heller, Inc.:** 134 (middle right); **iittala Group:** 129 (bottom left); **INDAV/ Timo Kauppila:** 128, 129; *Industrial Design* magazine: 28, 29, 52–59; **Knoll, Inc.:** 123 (bottom left), 136 (left), 137 (far right); **Kroin, Inc.:** 181 (top); **Jane Lidz:** 108; *Look* magazine: 23; **Luxo:** 133 (top center); **Maynard Hale Lyndon:** 173; **Elizabeth Malko:** 10, 101 (left), 112 (bottom), 126 (bottom right); **Marimekko Oy:** 74 (top), 85, 92, 93, 115; *Mobilia* magazine 1966 no. 134: 118; **Museo Kuva:** 71, 122 (top), 126 (bottom left), 127 (top right); **© Museum of Modern Art/ licensed by SCALA/Art Resource, New York:** Seth Joel, 122 (bottom left); Jacob Marczewski, 125 (top left); John Cross, Erica Stanton, 127 (bottom right); 132 (top left); Tom Giesel, 134 (bottom left, bottom right); **Karen Philippi:** 121, 122 (middle right), 123 (top right), 124 (left, bottom right), 125 (bottom right), 126 (top right), 127 (bottom left, middle right), 128 (bottom left, top right), 129 (top left, middle left, top right), 130 (top left, bottom left), 131 (bottom left, bottom right), 133 (top left, bottom left, top right), 136 (bottom left), 137 (top left, middle left, middle right, bottom left), 138 (top left), 139 (top middle, bottom right, bottom left); **Placewares/Hall Kelley:** 180; **Michael Proulx:** 156; **Jens Morits Sørrensen:** 136 (center row, top to bottom); *Sports Illustrated:* 76 (bottom); **Studio Joe Colombo/ Aldo Ballo:** 135 (top left); **Studio Joe Colombo/Ignazia Favata:** 127 (top left), 135 (top right, bottom right); **Ben Thompson:** 26, 27, 148–49; **Jane Thompson:** 19, 74 (bottom), 123 (middle right); **Rauno Träskelin:** 128 (top left, bottom right), 129 (middle right); **Tony Vaccaro:** 77–83; **Vitsoe:** 132 (bottom right); **Barbara Westman:** 164; **Bruce White/The Bard Center:** 125 (middle right), 126 (top right), 128 (left middle, center bottom), 129 (center bottom, bottom right); **Williams-Sonoma:** 177

Text

"Bright Spirit of Marimekko," *LIFE, Inc.*, June 24, 1966. Photos: Tony Vaccaro, © TIME Inc. All rights reserved. Reprinted with permission.

"Designs From Abroad, D/R's Long-Awaited Review of Finnish Design," *Industrial Design,* September 1959. © Whitney Publications.

"Finland's Forest Glade, Report on 1958 Brussels Worlds Fair," *Industrial Design*, August 1958. © Whitney Publications.

Geoffrey Hellman, "Talk of the Town: New Store," *The New Yorker*, December 28, 1963. © 2008 Condé Nast Publications. All rights reserved. Reprinted by permission.

Elizabeth Kendall, "A Backward Glance at the Dress that Changed Her Life," *Vogue*, April 2008. Text by Elizabeth Kendall, Courtesy of *Vogue*. © Condé Nast 2008, Condé Nast Publications. All rights reserved. Reprinted by permission.

Janet Malcolm, "On the Avenue: About the House," *The New Yorker*, November 7, 1970. Reprinted by permission of the author.

Herbert Muschamp, "In Search of Lost Research—Berlin-New York," *Like and Unlike*, by Josef P. Kleihues, Rizzoli, 1993. Reprinted by permission.

"U.S. Retailer Looks at Foreign Design," *Industrial Design*, September 1957. © Whitney Publications.

Barbara Westman, "Design Research Makes Your Heart Happy . . .," *The Beard and the Braid*, Barre Publishers, 1970. Reprinted by permission of the artist.

Excerpts from unpublished interviews of Claud Bunyard (2004), Robert and Peggy Eskridge (2007), and Betsy Whitman (2008) courtesy Susan Ward. Used by permission.

Text copyright © 2010 by Jane Thompson and Alexandra Lange.
Foreword copyright © 2010 by Rob Forbes.
Afterword copyright © 2010 by Paul Goldberger

All rights reserved. No part of this book may be reproduced in any form without written permission from the publisher.

Library of Congress Cataloging-in-Publication Data available.

ISBN: 978-0-8118-6818-1

Manufactured in China

Editor: Ruth A. Peltason, Bespoke Books
Designers: Michael Bierut, Yve Ludwig, Pentagram

10 9 8 7 6 5 4 3 2 1

Chronicle Books LLC
680 Second Street
San Francisco, California 94107

www.chroniclebooks.com